RENEWING CITIES

RENEWING CITIES

Ross J. Gittell

HT
175
.G56
1992

PRINCETON UNIVERSITY PRESS   PRINCETON, NEW JERSEY

JPL

Library of Congress Cataloging-in-Publication Data
Gittell, Ross J., 1957–
Renewing cities / Ross J. Gittell.
p.   cm.
Includes bibliographical references and index.
ISBN 0-691-04293-4
1. Urban renewal—United States—Case studies.   2. Urban renewal—
Economic aspects—United States—Case studies.   3. Community
development, Urban—United States—Case studies.   I. Title.
HT175.G56   1992
307.3'416'0973—dc20   92-10020

This book has been composed in Linotron Palatino

Printed in the United States of America

10 9 8 7 6 5 4 3 2 1

Contents

Figures and Tables

Figures

Tables

Acknowledgments ─────────────────────

IN A PROJECT as ambitious and as long in gestation as this, an author accumulates many debts. While it is impossible to credit every source of support and inspiration I received, a few people were so helpful that they must be singled out.

The book took shape in the lively intellectual settings of the Kennedy School of Government at Harvard University and the New School for Social Research. The substantive core of the book evolved from my 1989 doctoral thesis and profited significantly from the instruction of three dissertation advisors, Alan Altshuler, John T. Dunlop and John R. Meyer. Altshuler helped me recognize the usefulness of systematic comparative analysis. He also guided me on how to extract useful policy lessons from detailed case studies. Meyer helped clarify the practical value of different theories of urban growth and change, and together we conceived of the dynamic cycle theory outlined in chapter three, which provided a theoretical framework for linking local development acts and city economic performance. Finally, I was most fortunate to work under Professor Dunlop, who increased my sensitivity to the importance of local institutions and labor and management relations in urban development.

The idea for this book came from work on the Community Revitalization Project at the Center for Business and Government at Harvard from 1985 to 1989. I undertook much of the initial field work, interviews and data collection while a research fellow and then project director for the Community Revitalization Project. This research benefited significantly from my contact and intellectual exchange with Nancy Kelley, who was co-director of the project from June 1985 to June 1988, and Winthrop Knowlton, the Center's director at the time the project began. The contributions of research assistants at the Center for Business and Government—Adam Blumenthal, Sung Bae Kim, Martha Lester, Charles Ross, and Karl Schlacter—to the city development studies in Chapters four through seven must also be acknowledged, as well as the contributions of hundreds of individuals in the four cities whom we interviewed during various phases of the research.

At Harvard I benefited greatly from contact with faculty and students at the Kennedy School of Government and the Economics Department. Throughout my research for the Community Revitalization Project and thesis work, Peter Doeringer, Michael Barzelay and Ronald Ferguson provided helpful comments and guidance. I also benefited from the instruction of John Kain and interaction with other participants in the weekly Urban Economics seminar. In addition, several fellow students at the Kennedy School and the Economics Department—Sarmila Bose, Tom Kane, Paul Kerin and Glen Tobin—provided much valued encouragement and friendship.

I finished the book while at the Graduate School of Management and Urban Policy at the New School for Social Research. At the New School I profited greatly from my position at the Community Development Research Center (CDRC) and contact with faculty and students. Avis Vidal, the director of the CDRC, prodded me to explore in greater depth the role of community organization and community development corporations in city-wide economic development efforts and, along with faculty colleagues David Howell and Frank DeGiovanni, helped to provide the intellectual and moral support necessary for me to complete the book. In addition, at the New School, I benefited from the research assistance of William Gibbons and comments by students in my Community Development class.

Assistance from several institutions made this venture possible. My work at the Center for Business and Government was supported by a fellowship from the George S. Dively Foundation and funding from the Primerica Foundation. The Community Development Research Center provided generous support during the last year of work on the book. Jack Repcheck, the economics editor at Princeton University Press, and two reviewers, Thierry Noyelle and an anonymous reader, helped me through the difficult process of final preparation of the manuscript.

Throughout the work on this venture, my family provided tremendous support. My father and mother, Irwin and Marilyn Gittell, and sister and brother-in-law, Amy and Tom Gallagher, gave me constant encouragement. In addition, my mother provided invaluable guidance throughout the research and writing. She helped me engage in interdisciplinary inquiry and to probe critically, through the case studies, the relationship between city politics and local development policy. As with the members of the family into which I was born, the most special person in my life, Jody Hoffer, made contributions to this book and was most supportive during the critical final stages of the manuscript. I would like to dedicate this book to my family.

RENEWING CITIES

One

Renewing Industrial Cities

Introduction

Much of the literature on managing the economy focuses on the role of the federal government and, increasingly, on the role of state governments. However, the macroeconomic policies of the federal government and the specific development initiatives of state governments are not the whole story of economic management.[1] Throughout the country, city government officials, together with business and citizen groups, are actively engaged in local economic development. In some cases, local intervention in the economy seems to promote success; in other cases it fails.

There is inadequate understanding of the nature of successful local development efforts. This is unfortunate, particularly given the priorities of Federal administrators in the 1980s and early 1990s, changing relations between the private and public sectors, and the increase in community-based development activities. The "new" New Federalism of the Reagan and Bush administrations (which moved policy-making responsibility from the federal to the state and local levels)— together with the proliferation of public and private development partnerships and community development corporations (CDCs) in cities throughout the nation—strongly suggest the relevance of local development practice and policy.[2]

This study involves an interdisciplinary examination of the effect of public, private, and community-based local economic development initiatives on local economic performance, with a particular focus on how local development processes influence city capacity for economic regeneration. It includes assessment of the influence of local civic and corporate organization on aggregate output and productivity in four medium-sized (populations of approximately 25,000 to 110,000), declining industrial cities in the northeast United States—Lowell and New Bedford, Massachusetts, Jamestown, New York, and McKeesport, Pennsylvania.

Inductive theory building is pursued. This is in contrast to hypothesis testing, which is the method employed in much of the analysis of local development. Detailed "case studies" describe and compare local development practice in the four study cities in an effort to uncover what is going on, what works, and what does not work. Hypotheses are developed regarding the influence of various agents in local economic development and tested against the data and observations from the case studies. Discussion of the "standard" quantifiable determinants of local growth—such as industry mix, national and regional employment change, and local business costs—is supplemented with discussion of less tangible local factors, including corporate civic involvement, labor and management relations, political leadership, and local citizen participation.

Perhaps the principal contribution of this study is to suggest a shift in policy attention in local economic development from what has been described as the "zero-sum game" of attracting jobs from elsewhere, towards the goal of converting underutilized local resources to higher value uses through alternative forms of social, political, and economic organization. The analysis of economic revitalization efforts in the four industrial cities indicates that local economic intervention matters. It is suggested that under certain conditions city leaders and institutions can facilitate beneficial adjustment to changing economic circumstances through "reshuffling" and reorganization of local resources.

The analysis indicates that it is important to understand more than markets and factor prices to make sense of and usefully guide local economic development practice. The roles of various motivating, diagnostic and organizing agents are highlighted, including development strategies, local leadership and public, private, and community group cooperation. It is suggested that the benefits from effective, locally based development initiatives can include increased inputs, investment, and effort by local individuals and institutions; greater and more efficient cooperation among different development interests; and improvement in city economic positioning relative to the regional economy and local development cycles.

Methodology

The inquiry is divided into three main parts—theoretical review, detailed empirical study and conclusions. Chapter 2 reviews economic and political theories relevant to analysis in subsequent chapters. Chapter 3 provides a statistical baseline for the case study analyses of development efforts in the four cities, which follow in chapters 4 through 7. Chapter 8 synthesizes and further considers the hypotheses from the case studies. The final chapter, Chapter 9, suggests strategic and managerial guidelines for local development efforts.

The theoretical review in Chapter 2 suggests the value of interdisciplinary inquiry and offers a conceptual framework for consideration of the influence of local initiatives in economic development. The first part of Chapter 2 summarizes various economic theories of urban and regional change and the location of economic activity. Shift-share, factor price equalization and location theories are reviewed and their value in informing local economic development practice is examined. Three dynamic theories of regional change—product, process, and factor price life cycle—are suggested as most relevant to understanding the linkage between local development acts and local economic performance.

The second part of Chapter 2 examines political and public choice theories of local development practice and collective action. Paul Peterson's city limits theory is compared and contrasted with growth, regime politics, and dependent city theories of urban growth and decline. Theories of collective action and cooperation by Mancur Olson, Robert Axelrod, and Jane Mansbridge are also presented and related to concerted local development efforts.

Chapter 3 provides a statistical baseline for the case studies (i.e., city development analyses). The economic development histories of Lowell and New Bedford and Jamestown and McKeesport are compared and contrasted. The intent is to isolate the points in time when local efforts may have had a particularly significant effect, either positive or negative, on economic development in the four cities. The study cities are "paired-up" to control for cost and other regional factors that may influence local economic development. Shift-share analysis is employed to identify the effects of national and regional industrial trends.

Differences in local economic performance, as measured by employment change, in the paired cities are identified even after controlling for the effect of base period industry mix and other standard regional development factors. Lowell, compared to New Bedford, achieved significant employment growth in the late 1970s and early 1980s. Similarly, Jamestown, when compared to McKeesport, experienced significant economic vitality in the 1970s that cannot be fully explained by standard theories alone. These findings suggest that the late 1970s and early 1980s in Lowell and New Bedford and the 1970s in Jamestown and McKeesport might be appropriate times to look beyond shift-share and other traditional regional development factors and focus on the potential role of city-based development activities.

The focus of the analysis in Chapter 3 is on changes in total and manufacturing employment. Employment trends are a common and useful measure of city well-being. Manufacturing employment is particularly relevant to cities, such as the four study cities, whose development is closely linked to changes in manufacturing employment. However, employment trends are a limited indicator of development success. The discussion of employment (in Chapter 3 and in the city development analyses) will be supplemented by consideration of "other" measures that indicate city vitality and development success—including population change, median family income, levels of educational attainment, and unemployment rates.

In Chapters 4 through 7, detailed comparative study of development efforts are undertaken, focusing on the time periods and industrial sectors suggested by the analysis in Chapter 3. The different political and economic theories introduced in Chapter 2 are applied in the city development analyses to help explain changes in the economies of the four study cities. The case analyses attempt to illuminate and evaluate local efforts in economic development—quantifying, whenever feasible, their net local effects. The comparative studies make an effort to assess the influence of local development initiatives in a comprehensive manner. They explore not only direct economic impacts of local development efforts but also indirect effects, including (1) how organized local development activities affect individual and organizational psychology and behavior and community attitudes regarding development and (2) how changes in these may influence city economic positioning and the timing of local economic change and growth.

Each city development analysis documents selected locally based development initiatives and assesses their effect on a variety of factors: the local institutional, financial, social, physical, and intellectual capacity; the attitudes (psychology) and behavior of individuals and organizations in the community; and city positioning in product, process, and factor price cycles. The city studies consider the influence of local initiatives against a "base case"—what might have happened in the absence of city-based development activities. The city development analyses are not meant to test the relative merits of different political and economic theories, but to gain insight to how local initiatives influence local economic performance.

The city development analyses suggest that the organization and management of local development activities can make a difference. Lowell and Jamestown, compared to New Bedford and McKeesport, appear to have undertaken local development initiatives that have had positive economic influence in these cities. In Lowell, key local development factors appear to include local political leadership, the creation of a pooled fund among local banks for financing development projects, and the formation of a public-private partnership to guide and support development and promote the city. In James-town, the key local development initiative appears to have been the formation of a city-wide labor-management committee to foster co-operation between labor and management, facilitate improvements in worker productivity, and support city-wide training and industrial development opportunities.

Chapter 8 summarizes and evaluates the hypotheses generated from the case studies. First the findings from the city studies are reviewed. Then the key conclusions are considered in light of recent pronounced change in one of the study cities, Lowell. Finally, the development hypotheses are considered with regard to theories of local market failure to suggest a framework for generalizing the findings from the city development analyses. It is suggested that (1) local market and government failures can restrict the potential for private market activities alone to stimulate the revitalization of depressed cities and (2) that benefits may be derived from selective organization of city development activities outside of the market and local government.

The concluding chapter, Chapter 9, summarizes the discussion of the previous chapters and proposes strategies and management guidelines for local economic development. It highlights the role of various motivating, diagnostic, and organizing agents in local economic development, including city development strategies, local leadership, institutional innovation, and cooperation among public and private sectors and community groups.

The analysis concurs with much of the conventional wisdom—that the context in which local economic development efforts take place is in large part determined by outside influences, including international, national, and regional industrial, economic, and political factors. It is argued, however, that a city's development is not determined by outside forces alone. It appears that local organization and management of development activities can effect local economic outputs. The key benefits that can be derived from effective organization and management of locally based development efforts appear to be improvement in city economic positioning, increased effort by local individuals and institutions, and greater and more efficient cooperation among different development interests.

An Introduction to the Case Study Cities

There are a great variety of experiences with local development efforts. The cities selected for detailed study, Lowell and New Bedford, Massachusetts, Jamestown, New York and McKeesport, Pennsylvania, were purposely selected.[3] They are of similar size, with populations ranging from approximately 25,000 to 110,000. All emerged as manufacturing centers isolated from larger metropolitan areas during the nineteenth and early twentieth century, and they all endured periods of growth and decline yet remained primarily industrial cities (with employment concentration in manufacturing 50 percent greater than the United States average), in spite of historical concentration in employment in declining U.S. industries.[4] Each of the study cities has recently confronted, with varying degrees of success, "turnaround" situations in which attempts have been made to recover from an extended period of economic decline and significant loss of base industry employment.

To date, there has been relatively little discussion of economic development in smaller cities, such as the ones selected for detailed empirical inquiry here.[5] Much of the detailed analysis of local development efforts has considered efforts in larger cities and metropolitan areas.[6] Smaller jurisdictions are valuable to study not only because a significant portion of the population resides in areas of this type (approximately 15 percent of the U.S. population in 1980 lived in cities with populations between 25,000 and 100,000), but also because development cycles tend to be highly visible and pronounced in these jurisdictions. The influence of local development efforts on local economic performance and, particularly, on the nature and timing of local development cycles may be more easily observed and analyzed in smaller industrial cities than in larger metropolitan areas, which have more diversified economies and more complex networks of development factors to account for.[7]

An advantage of "honing in" on the development problems of a limited number of medium-sized cities is that the analysis can more easily extend beyond tangible factors and quantifiable effects of local development initiatives. Many studies of development in larger cities and metropolitan areas are highly dependent on aggregated economic data and have great difficulty considering how intangibles—such as local culture, political organization, and public and private institutional capacities—might influence economic change. Case study of development in four smaller cities can explore in detail how subtle factors in local development efforts may affect community psychology, as well as the attitudes and behavior of individuals and organizations, and how changes in these may affect city economic positioning.

Although the study focuses on turnaround situations in medium-sized industrial cities, some of its findings may be relevant to economic development in other areas, including larger metropolitan

FIGURE 1.1
Population 1860–1980

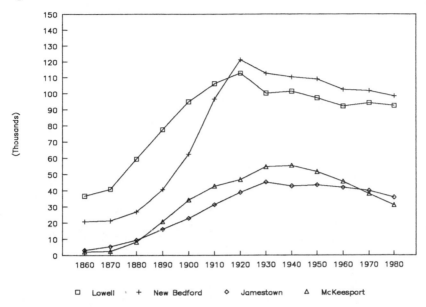

Source: *U.S. Census Bureau, Population and Housing.*

areas and inner city neighborhoods. Similar to larger cities and neighborhoods in inner cities, industrial cities have suffered not only from employment decline but also from social, political, and cultural upheaval involving the dislocation of individuals, the separation of families, and the loss of a sense of community.

As suggested by Figures 1.1 and 1.2, Lowell's development, decline, and revitalization have preceded that of the other cities. Lowell emerged in the latter half of the nineteenth century as the second planned industrial city in the United States after Paterson, New Jersey, and as a center for textile manufacturing in New England. At the turn of the century, Lowell had a population of nearly 100,000 and was the fortieth largest city in the United States.[8] In 1914, manufacturing employment in Lowell reached 30,000.[9] By 1937, however, Lowell's manufacturing employment had fallen by 45 percent to just over 16,000—the beginning of a long-term decline that lasted through the mid-1970s before a dramatic turnaround in the late 1970s and early 1980s.

Compared to Lowell, New Bedford emerged later as a manufactur-

FIGURE 1.2
Manufacturing Employment 1914–1982

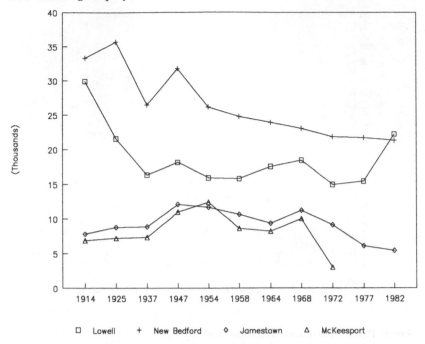

Source: *U.S. Census Bureau, Census of Manufacturing.*

ing center and its manufacturing employment was concentrated in finer, more specialized, and higher value-added textile and apparel products. As Lowell lost employment to lower cost Southern manufacturers of cotton cloth and other course textile products in the early part of the twentieth century, New Bedford was able to retain and increase its manufacturing employment base. By 1911, New Bedford emerged as the leading textile and apparel manufacturing city in the nation. New Bedford's manufacturing employment peaked in 1925 at just under 36,000.

New Bedford's economy was devastated by the Great Depression, and its manufacturing employment dropped by over 20 percent. After a brief postdepression rebound, New Bedford's manufacturing employment continued on a slow but steady decline that has continued up to the present. Unlike Lowell, New Bedford suffered a decline in manufacturing employment up through the 1980s and experienced no turnaround.

Smaller than Lowell and New Bedford, Jamestown and McKeesport are both located on the perimeter of the industrial triangle between Buffalo, Cleveland, and Pittsburgh that is commonly referred to as the "rust belt." Jamestown and McKeesport's growth and decline, like that of many North Atlantic cities, lagged behind that of Lowell and other New England industrial cities.

Jamestown's most rapid growth period occurred between the Great Depression and World War II and was principally spurred by increases in furniture production and fine wood product manufacturing. Manufacturing employment in Jamestown peaked in the late 1940s at over 12,000. After the Vietnam war, however, Jamestown experienced a pronounced decline in manufacturing employment. In the mid-1970s Jamestown—unlike many cities in the rust belt, including McKeesport—was able to arrest the decline in manufacturing employment and stabilize it.

McKeesport's development follows a similar pattern to Jamestown's until the mid-1970s. While metal tube and pipe manufacturing facilities were first located in McKeesport in 1851, the city's period of most rapid growth was during the first half of the twentieth century. Employment in McKeesport was heavily concentrated in metals manufacturing. Manufacturing employment in McKeesport peaked in 1954 at 12,000. Since the mid-1950s, however, manufacturing employment in McKeesport has declined, except for a brief increase during the Vietnam War years. In contrast to Jamestown, McKeesport has been unable to arrest employment decline. There are few indicators of turnaround in McKeesport.

Thus, of the four cities, Lowell experienced the most dramatic turnaround in the 1980s, when it was referred to as the "model city" for revitalization in Massachusetts and elsewhere in the Northeast in the *Wall Street Journal, New York Times* and other national publications.[10] Lowell went from having the highest unemployment rate of any city of its size in the nation in the late 1960s to having the lowest unemployment of any city in Massachusetts during most of the 1980s—including a period in which the state had the lowest unemployment rate of any industrialized state.

Lowell offers unique insight into the influence of local development acts on local economic performance. Since 1987 there have been significant changes in Lowell's economic prospects due to a declining regional economy, extensive problems at a major employer, Wang Laboratories Inc., and a fiscally constrained and less activist state government. In Chapter 8 in an "update" to the Lowell case study, consideration is given to whether the same local factors that contributed to superior economic performance during periods of regional growth also helped to reduce the negative influence of regional decline.

Jamestown follows Lowell in terms of apparent ability to engineer economic recovery. The Jamestown economy and industrial base have stabilized. Through the 1980s, Jamestown has maintained its level of manufacturing employment, and unemployment there has remained near the New York State average.

Although New Bedford is in the same state as Lowell, its recent economic experience is markedly different. Although it has many of the economic development attributes (including a favorable location, a relatively low-cost labor supply, and industrial facilities) that regional economic theory suggests would encourage revitalization, New Bedford has yet to recover from the loss of industrial jobs following the Depression and World War II. During the 1980s, as will be documented in Chapters 3 and 5, the city lagged behind Lowell and Massachusetts in terms of employment growth and suffered from significantly higher unemployment.

Like New Bedford, McKeesport has yet to experience economic revitalization. McKeesport has lost more than 50 percent of its manufacturing employment base in the past twenty years, and total employment and population have continued to decline throughout the 1980s. Economic change and growth in McKeesport are not apparent.

Study Cities Compared to Reference Cities

The economic changes in the four study cities over the past three decades appear to be typical of medium-sized industrial cities in the Northeast, as suggested by a comparison to a reference group of cities. Two reference cities were selected from each state in which a study city was located, Massachusetts, New York, and Pennsylvania. In addition, two cities each were selected from neighboring states, New Jersey and Rhode Island. The reference cities include the following: Lawrence and Fall River, Massachusetts; Johnstown and Reading, Pennsylvania; Rome and Amsterdam, New York; Paterson and Camden, New Jersey; and Woonsocket and Pawtucket, Rhode Island. The cities are presented in Tables 1.1 through 1.4 in pairs of cities from the same state.

The ten reference cities were selected, based on similar population and employment composition, as the four study cities in 1950. Reference city base year (1950) population averaged approximately 83,500

TABLE 1.1
Population 1950 to 1990—Study and Reference Cities

	Population			Percent Change	
	1950	1980	1990	1950–1980	1980–1990
Lowell	97,249	92,418	103,439	(5.0)	11.9
New Bedford	109,189	98,478	99,922	(9.8)	1.5
Jamestown	43,354	35,775	34,681	(17.5)	(3.1)
McKeesport	51,502	31,012	26,016	(39.8)	(16.1)
Lawrence	80,536	63,175	70,207	(21.6)	11.1
Fall River	111,963	90,420	92,703	(19.2)	2.5
Rome	41,682	43,826	44,350	5.1	1.2
Amsterdam	32,240	21,872	20,714	(32.2)	(5.3)
Johnstown	63,232	35,496	28,134	(43.9)	(20.7)
Reading	109,320	78,686	78,380	(28.0)	(0.4)
Camden	124,555	84,910	87,492	(31.8)	3.0
Paterson	139,336	144,830	140,891	3.9	(2.7)
Pawtucket	81,436	71,204	72,644	(12.6)	2.0
Woonsocket	50,211	45,914	43,877	(8.6)	(4.4)
Averages					
Study City	75,324	64,421	66,015	(14.5)	2.5
Reference City	83,451	68,033	67,939	(18.5)	(0.1)
United States				50.0	9.6

Source: *U.S. Census Bureau, Population and Housing.*

(compared to 75,300 for the study cities) and ranged from 139,000 in Paterson, New Jersey, to 32,000 in Amsterdam, New York (compared to the range of the study cities from 109,000 in New Bedford to 51,500 in McKeesport) (see Table 1.1). All the reference and study cities had over 50 percent greater employment concentration in manufacturing than the U.S. average in 1950, and both groups of cities (study and reference) averaged approximately double the employment concentration in manufacturing as the U.S. average (see Table 1.2). The study cities ranged in percent of 1950 employment in manufacturing from New Bedford's 53 percent to Lowell's 47 percent, as compared to the U.S. average of 26 percent. The reference cities ranged from Woonsocket, Rhode Island, with 60 percent of total employment in manufacturing to Camden, New Jersey, with 43 percent of employment in manufacturing. The reference cities also had simi-

TABLE 1.2
Manufacturing Employment Concentration—Study and
Reference Cities

	Percent of Employment in Manufacturing	
	1950	1980
Lowell	0.46	0.42
New Bedford	0.53	0.45
Jamestown	0.48	0.33
McKeesport	0.49	0.33
Lawrence	0.58	0.41
Fall River	0.55	0.46
Rome	0.44	0.23
Amsterdam	0.60	0.19
Johnstown	0.44	0.61
Reading	0.48	0.35
Camden	0.43	0.43
Paterson	0.47	0.33
Pawtucket	0.54	0.40
Woonsocket	0.60	0.22
Averages		
Study City	0.49	0.38
Reference City	0.51	0.36
United States	0.26	0.22

Source: U.S. Census Bureau, Population and Housing.

lar levels of employment as the study cities. The study cities' total
employment in 1950 averaged approximately 31,000—ranging from
46,400 in New Bedford to 19,000 in Jamestown. The reference city
average was 35,300 and ranged from 62,200 in Paterson to 13,250 in
Rome.

During the post–World War II period (1950 to 1980), the study and
reference cities experienced similar decline. All of the study cities
and eight of the ten reference cities lost population, while the U.S.
population increased by 50 percent. Population decline among the
study cities ranged from Lowell, which lost 5 percent of its population in the thirty-year period after the war, to McKeesport, which
lost nearly 40 percent of its population. Among the reference cities,

TABLE 1.3

Total and Manufacturing Employment—Study and Reference Cities

	Total Employment 1950	1980	% Change 1950–1980	Manufacturing Employment 1950	1980	% Change 1950–1980
Lowell	38,325	41,621	8.6	17,814	17,321	(2.8)
New Bedford	46,421	40,440	(12.9)	24,810	18,264	(26.4)
Jamestown	18,846	14,599	(22.5)	9,051	4,824	(46.7)
McKeesport	19,543	10,892	(44.3)	9,609	3,617	(62.4)
Lawrence	35,511	25,782	(27.4)	20,563	10,500	(48.9)
Fall River	47,169	38,608	(18.1)	25,916	17,900	(30.9)
Rome	13,255	14,664	10.6	5,812	3,400	(41.5)
Amsterdam	15,255	17,743	16.3	9,218	3,403	(63.1)
Johnstown	23,043	11,653	(49.4)	10,094	7,100	(29.7)
Reading	51,205	33,354	(34.9)	24,326	11,730	(51.8)
Camden	49,281	23,609	(52.1)	21,239	10,200	(52.0)
Paterson	62,218	52,753	(15.2)	29,419	17,300	(41.2)
Pawtucket	35,056	33,233	(5.2)	18,863	13,300	(29.5)
Woonsocket	21,380	19,741	(7.7)	12,920	4,400	(65.9)
Averages						
Study City	30,784	26,888	(17.8)	15,321	11,007	(34.6)
Reference City	35,337	27,114	(18.3)	17,837	9,923	(45.4)
United States			73.0			49.2

Source: *U.S. Census Bureau, Population and Housing.*

population change ranged from a 44 percent decline in Johnstown, Pennsylvania, to a 5 percent increase in Rome, New York.

All fourteen cities experienced decline in manufacturing employment, while manufacturing employment in the United States was increasing approximately 50 percent (see Table 1.3). Three out of four of the study cities (Lowell being the exception) and eight of the ten reference cities also experienced decline in total employment. All of the cities remained industrial, and in only one city did the employment concentration in manufacturing fall below the national average. The four study cities, in spite of an average 35 percent decline in manufacturing employment in the thirty-year period, retained 70 percent greater employment concentration in manufacturing than the U.S. average (see Table 1.2). Comparable figures for the reference cities were a 45 percent decline in manufacturing employment and an employment concentration in manufacturing that was 62 percent greater than the U.S. average.

The four study cities were better (on average) at retaining manufacturing employment and at keeping their cities industrial than were the reference cities. There was, however, significant variation among study cities. McKeesport and Jamestown were less successful than Lowell and New Bedford in retaining manufacturing employment. Manufacturing employment declined in Lowell and New Bedford by 3 and 27 percent respectively, compared to 47 and 63 percent in Jamestown and McKeesport. Both Lowell and New Bedford retained employment concentration in manufacturing above 40 percent, while employment concentration in manufacturing declined in both Jamestown and McKeesport from approximately one-half to one-third. The relative strength in manufacturing in Lowell and New Bedford reflects in part the superior performance of Massachusetts in manufacturing employment retention in the post–World War II period, particularly in the 1970s—see further discussion in Chapter 3. However, Lawrence, Massachusetts (a neighboring city to Lowell), was significantly less successful at retaining manufacturing employment than was Lowell and New Bedford. It lost nearly 50 percent of its manufacturing employment between 1950 and 1980 and experienced a decline in concentration of employment in manufacturing from 58 percent (above the figure for both New Bedford and Lowell) to 41 percent (below the levels in New Bedford and Lowell). In Fall River, the other reference city from Massachusetts (and a neighbor of New Bedford), manufacturing employment retention and change in concentration were similar to that in New Bedford.

Significantly, the reference and study cities, while remaining industrial, went from having income levels and employment opportunities greater than the U.S. average to having ones significantly below the U.S. average. These cities were historically a magnet for working class and immigrant groups and were the site for social and economic upward mobility. This is increasingly less so. Table 1.4 (together with the other tables) indicates a strong relation between declines in manufacturing employment and population and socioeconomic conditions in the study and reference cities. When manufacturing employment declined in all four of the study cities and eight of the ten reference cities, the unemployment rate increased in all of the cities (and increased relative to the U.S. average in three of the four study cities and eight of the ten reference cities), and median family income relative to the U.S. average declined in all of the study and reference cities.

TABLE 1.4
Unemployment and Median Family Income—Study and
Reference Cities

	Income Median Family		Unemployment Rate *	
	1950	1980	1970	1980
Lowell	3,063	17,942	4.4%	4.8%
New Bedford	2,947	14,930	2.9%	9.0%
Jamestown	3,463	15,973	4.5%	7.5%
McKeesport	3,187	17,129	5.5%	12.0%
Lawrence	3,048	15,457	4.5%	7.0%
Fall River	2,943	14,810	5.2%	7.6%
Rome	3,324	16,961	6.5%	9.9%
Amsterdam	3,684	12,511	5.2%	9.6%
Johnstown	3,118	15,439	5.2%	14.9%
Reading	3,397	16,262	3.3%	7.4%
Camden	3,241	10,607	6.2%	17.9%
Paterson	3,402	14,323	6.6%	10.6%
Pawtucket	3,296	17,407	4.2%	7.0%
Woonsocket	3,051	16,453	4.4%	6.6%
Averages				
Study City	3,165	16,494	4.3%	8.3%
Reference City	3,250	16,692	5.1%	9.9%
United States	3,073	21,017	4.4%	6.5%

Source: U.S. Census Bureau, Population and Housing.
* Unemployment data for 1950 was not available for all of the cities.

The most recent data suggests that many of the industrial (study
and reference) cities continue to experience decline. Between 1980
and 1990, half of the study and reference cities continued to lose population (see Table 1.1). All of the cities except for Lowell and Lawrence, Massachusetts, had population increases below the national
average.

Comparison of the study and reference cities suggests that Lowell,
New Bedford, Jamestown, and McKeesport are representative of a
larger group of cities—medium-sized industrial cities in the Northeast. Lowell outperformed the reference cities across the various

measures. McKeesport's economic and social decline was more pronounced than that of the reference cities. New Bedford and Jamestown's economic development during the post–World War II period
appeared to be most typical of medium-sized industrial cities in the
Northeast. This suggests that detailed comparative inquiry of development activities in the four study cities will be relevant to a large
number of declining industrial cities and, as will be indicated elsewhere, add insight to development issues in other cities.

Two

Theories of Local Development

Introduction

There is much discussion among political scientists and economists regarding when and whether public and other forms of intervention matter in local economic development. Various political and economic theories relevant to local development practice will be reviewed with illustrative reference to the development experiences in the four study cities. This will provide the theoretical foundation for subsequent chapters. The different economic and political theories will be applied in the city development analyses to gain insight into how local initiatives influence local economic performance.

Economists and political scientists have much to contribute to our understanding of local economic development, and together they suggest fruitful lines of interdisciplinary inquiry. Each of the disciplines focuses on particular aspects of local economic development. Political scientists are most concerned with how local development policies are made, who has the power to make decisions, and how the benefits from development are distributed. Economists focus on the economic effects of local development efforts and the limits thereof, including the influence of national and regional economic and industrial changes on local growth, the effect of local development initiatives on business location, and the aggregate (macroeconomic) effect of initiatives by individual cities to improve their economies.[1]

Economic Theories of Local Development

A variety of static and dynamic economic theories of urban and regional growth and change have been applied in analysis of local development. Static models are particularly useful at identifying the influence on local economies of national, regional, and industry changes and competition among localities. Dynamic models provide insights into the internal dynamics of local economies, help explain turning points in local economies, and suggest why local economies diverge from national, regional, and industry trends.

Static Urban Economic Theories

Commonly applied static economic models of regional change relevant to local economic development include shift-share, factor price equalization, location, and structural models. Shift-share models (see more detailed discussion in Chapter 3) highlight the influence of national and regional industry growth on local economies. Shift-share models provide an easy method to decompose period-to-period changes in employment into industry mix and residual components. The industry mix component represents the change in local employment if all industry sectors in a locality grow at their national and regional rates. The differential shift, or residual, component is simply calculated as the difference between actual growth and expected growth as determined by the base period local industry mix and industry growth rates. A positive (negative) period-to-period differential shift would suggest that the local economy grew at a rate greater (less) than expected if the employment base in the city grew at the national and regional rate.

Shift-share models suggest that cities with concentrated employment in industries in which U.S. and regional manufacturers are competitive and are producing for faster growing markets will tend to grow faster, all other things being equal. Conversely, cities with employment concentration in U.S. and regional industries that are not competitive and are producing for declining markets will tend to experience decline.

The residual remaining after accounting for the influence of industry mix on local employment is commonly attributed to differentials among localities in factor costs. Through changes in relative factor costs, cities experience shifts in their share of national and regional industry that can strongly influence their employment growth.[2]

Factor price equalization theory embodies a more theoretical approach to explaining regional economic growth than the shift-share model.[3] Factor price equalization theory is based on interregional trade theory and assumes that capital and labor are mobile and will move to areas with the highest returns until factor returns are equalized. It suggests that cities where factor returns are low will experience economic decline and that economic recovery can occur with declines in local factor costs and increases in local productivity.

While strong in theoretical foundation and useful in suggesting tendencies in local economic development, the factor price equalization model has its limitations, particularly with regard to its assumptions. As will be highlighted in the development analyses, labor is not perfectly mobile, capital (particularly investment in heavy plant and equipment, utilities and infrastructure) is imperfectly mobile and wages for a variety of institutional, cultural, and social reasons tend to be downwardly rigid. In each of the four study cities, the migration of labor and capital did not occur to the extent suggested by the factor price equalization model, local factor costs did not adjust as expected, and unemployment persisted at higher levels and for longer periods than predicted.[4]

The main distinguishing feature of location models is their attention to the significance of distance and the cost of overcoming it. In these models, transportation costs are the key factor determining the location of economic activities. Among the more well known locational models are von Thunen's model on the location of agricultural production, Christaller's and Losch's central-place approach, and Weber's least-cost theory.[5]

Least cost models, such as Weber's, are helpful in examining the locational tendencies of economic activities characterized by the processing of heavy or bulky materials. For example, the historical development of the Monongahela Valley as a steel manufacturing center can be explained in large part by its locational advantages in the early part of the twentieth century, see Chapter 7. With technological advancements in communications and transportation, however, location has become a somewhat less significant factor in industry location decisions, particularly for industries with low natural resource and bulk material requirements, such as light manufacturing and service industries.

Dynamic Cycle Theory

The static theories highlight equilibrium states and movements towards equilibrium; however, local economies tend not to be in equilibrium because of dynamism in the larger international, national and regional economies, rigidities in factor prices, and immobile local factors, including land, labor, plant, and equipment.[6] Three disequilibrium theories of regional change, product, process and factor price life cycle appear to be particularly relevant to local economic development.

The presentation here of a three cycle theory of local economic growth and change is somewhat analogous to business cycle theory, which often decomposes national economic cycles into three related cycles of different periodicity: inventory cycles, industry cycles, and long-term (approximately forty-year) secular cycles. There are other local cycles that operate, including demographic and labor market cycles, but product, process, and factor price life cycles tend to dominate.

The cycles suggest that local product demand, technological process advantages, and factor prices tend to follow distinct patterns. Positioning in product, process, and factor price life cycles, however, may be manipulated, suggesting a link between local development acts, city positioning in product, process and factor price cycles, and local economic performance.

Product life cycle theory proposes three distinct stages of development: rapid growth, maturation and decline.[7] Cities with employment concentration in new or innovating products will tend to exhibit rapid growth.[8] Examples of areas experiencing rapid growth with local industry product innovation are the steel towns in the Monongahela (Mon) Valley southeast of Pittsburgh, Pennsylvania, at the turn of the twentieth century (including McKeesport) and the cities surrounding Route 128 ("America's High Technology Highway") outside of Boston that emerged as international leaders in computer and electrical machinery manufacturing in the 1970s including Lowell.

As industries mature, competition increases with product standardization, growth slows down, production cost becomes critical, and industry tends to migrate to areas with the lowest production costs. This can result in significant economic decline in areas with employment concentrations in mature industries.

Product life cycle theory suggests that cities can sustain growth by nurturing or attracting innovating industry. This could involve existing industries innovating with new products; industries redefining product lines, concentrating on specialized niches within existing product categories that are at more advantageous stages in their product life cycle; or cities attracting entirely new industries that manufacture products at the growth stage in product life cycle.

Process life cycle theory, like product life cycle theory, suggests that cities can sustain growth by nurturing or attracting innovating industry. Process life cycle theory, however, suggests more sporadic and less predictable growth patterns and cyclical patterns potentially applicable to several industries in a region, even if the cyclical pattern itself is largely generated in the region's dominant industry.[9] That is, process life cycles need not be limited to one product or industrial sector.

As production processes mature and become more standardized, competition increases and factor costs become more important, just as it does with product maturation. However, process maturation tends not to be as smooth as product maturation.[10] New technologies can suddenly make mature technologies uncompetitive.

Lowell in the early nineteenth century offers an example of a city emerging as a leading process innovator, employing water power in textile manufacturing and saw mill operations (see Chapter 4). Japan in the second half of the twentieth century offers several examples of process innovations in mature industries. The Japanese have relied on process innovations in steel, automobile, and precision machinery manufacturing to bolster their economy during the post–World War II period.[11]

Lowell's development history also illustrates how the introduction of new production technologies can suddenly make old production processes uncompetitive and result in substantial decline in local employment. In Lowell, textile and saw mill industries lost their competitiveness in the early twentieth century, when electricity replaced water power as the most efficient and lowest cost energy source.

The unpredictable nature of process life cycles and their distinction from product life cycles are perhaps best illustrated by recent changes in the international steel industry, most notably the renewed competitiveness of the United States steel industry with the emergence of mini-mills. Mini-mill competitive advantages (not only in steel production but also in the production of other metal products such as aluminum) are based on the energy-efficient direct reduction of scrap materials and proximity to end-use markets. In comparison to basic oxygen and open hearth mills, mini-mills are dispersed across the country, in Houston, Texas, Portland, Oregon, Charleston, South Carolina and Bridgeport, Connecticut, and achieve scale economies at a modest scale (e.g., approximately 500,000 tons per year compared with at least 5 million tons per year for an integrated basic oxygen process mill). Mini-mills have generated additional market share for United States steel products, while worldwide steel product demand is declining due to the substitution of other materials (e.g., plastics and ceramics) for steel products.[12]

Local factor price life cycles will tend to follow product and process life cycles and be of longer periodicity. As cities experience growth, factor demand often rises faster than available supply and factor prices rise; as cities experience decline, factor demand falls faster than available supply and factor prices fall. Similar to process life cycle theory but unlike product life cycle theory, factor price cycles can apply to several industries and products simultaneously.

The favorable conditions that may initially attract industry to a city; such as low production costs and the availability of labor and land, tend to recede with economic growth. As factor prices rise with rapid growth, an area can lose its attractiveness. With increasing factor prices, local industry may lose market share, reduce output and employment, and consider relocating to lower cost sites. Often it is only after a certain level of economic decline and decline in factor prices that an area will regain its relative attractiveness and experience growth.

Factor price life cycle theory allows for consideration of a variety of production costs, including, wages, land, energy, transportation and taxes and other factors that directly or indirectly impact production costs (e.g., productivity and skill level of the local work force, local zoning and land use regulations, public subsidies to business establishments, and public services).

Factor price life cycle theory suggests that depressed cities can stimulate growth through initiatives that reduce production costs and accelerate adjustment to changes in factor supply and demand conditions. Initiatives that may attract new industry and help existing industry become more competitive include lowering taxes; increasing worker productivity through training and education and improved labor-management relations; subsidizing industry through specific financial inducements (e.g., industrial revenue bonds [IRBs]); adopting land-use regulations (e.g., changes in zoning) that work toward reducing production costs; and encouraging a group of firms with production linkages that can realize agglomeration economies to locate in a city.

Factor price life cycle theory highlights tendencies in local development and, perhaps most importantly for our purposes here, suggests how local development initiatives may influence local development by accelerating or inhibiting adjustment to local factor supply and demand conditions. Factor price life cycle theory can help explain why some cities stay depressed for long periods of time while other localities experience rapid recovery by recognizing how different localities adjust to changes in factor demand and supply conditions.

As will be highlighted in Chapters 6 and 7, the contrasting experiences in Jamestown and McKeesport during the 1970s reflects, in large part, differential local responses at different stages in development cycles. In Jamestown, labor and management cooperation favorably altered the city's positioning in the factor price life cycle before local product demand peaked. In contrast, in the Mon Valley, national union control of wages and work practices inhibited local factor price adjustment to the dramatic decline in local product demand.

Application of Dynamic Cycle Theory

Using the framework suggested by the dynamic cycle theories, we can gain insight into the development histories in the four study cities. Lowell's decline at the turn of the century can be attributed in large part to a combination of a cyclical rise in factor prices (primarily wages), a technological process change (introduction of electricity), and product (cotton cloth) maturation, while its recovery in the late 1970s can be attributed to employment concentration in innovating products (mini-computers) and factor price advantages. New Bedford's decline after World War II reflected a rise in cyclical factor prices, most notably wages, and concentration in mature segments of machine tool and apparel manufacturing. Jamestown's decline in the 1960s can be attributed to a cyclical rise in factor prices and declines in worker productivity, while its recovery in the early 1970s can be attributed to a decline in production costs and an increase in productivity instigated by changes in labor and management practices. The dramatic decline in the Mon Valley in the late 1960s and through the 1970s can be attributed to the compounding effects of employment concentration in mature product (steel) manufacturing, uncompetitive production process (open hearth steel production), and a cyclical rise in factor prices (primarily wages).

The cycle theories highlight tendencies in local development. However, the introduction to the city development analyses will suggest that city positioning in product, process, and factor price life cycles can be altered and that local development initiatives that influence city positioning in cycles can affect local economic performance.

Politics, Collective Action, and Local Economic Development

There is general agreement among economists that local actions that alter business costs, such as tax and regulatory policies, can influence the location of industry and, therefore, local economic development. Many economists, however, devalue local development efforts because of their projected net effect. The consensus seems to be that, in the aggregate, local development initiatives result in the redistribution of industrial capacity and economic resources and do not contribute to national economic growth.

Economists tend to take a narrow view of local development efforts, often equating local development initiatives with incentive

26   CHAPTER TWO

packages to relocating industry and assessing short term benefits and costs. In addition, there has been limited consideration of the indirect effects of local development efforts and how they influence the attitudes and behavior of individuals and local institutions, local development strategies, and the long-term economic positioning of cities.

There is greater controversy among political scientists regarding local development practices than there is among economists concerning their net value. There are four main areas of controversy: the importance in local development of economic forces external to the city compared to political forces within the city; the relevance of consensus politics and common interest in development policy making; the influence and efficacy of ordinary citizens compared to local economic and political elites; and the role of economic and other interests in explaining coalition building and citizen mobilization.

Politics and Local Development

Among political scientists, Paul Peterson has been most influential. In *City Limits*, Peterson suggests that cities' development policies are shaped by the permeability of their boundaries and the mobility of industry and residents.[13] Peterson contends that there is a common city interest in development (growth) policies that improve cities' competitive position and their overall economic well-being.[14] Consensus-generating growth policies are those that attract exporting industries, private investment, and federal and state dollars into cities and that increase the benefit/tax ratio for the average taxpayer (i.e., policies for which the marginal benefits exceed the marginal costs to the average taxpayer). We observe what appears to be a consensus-generating growth policy most prominently in Lowell—in citywide efforts in the late 1970s and early 1980s to attract a major international corporation, Wang Laboratories Inc., and secure federal funds for an urban national park.

With regard to the politics of development, Peterson suggests that the interests of business and political elites are coincident with the city's interests. That is why development policies tend to emerge in consensus fashion. Peterson suggests that economic factors shape politics. There will be a economically determined consensus as to what constitutes beneficial development policy in cities. For Peterson, development policies are distinct from allocative and redistributive policies, which are inherently conflictual.

As an analytic tool, Peterson's "city limits" framework is quite useful. Its major strengths are its parsimony and theoretical foundation. The underlying framework is posited on the pursuit of rational economic self-interest by individual residents and businesses. It provides a deductive framework that explains how the rational pursuit of economic interest affects policy making in cities, why cities tend to favor growth over redistributive policies, and why citizens tend to limit, or direct elsewhere, redistributive demands.[15] However, as will be highlighted in the "case studies," its value is limited in explaining how development policies are formulated, why and when particular types of development policies are pursued, and why cities pursue significantly different types of development strategies. In addition, Peterson ignores the redistributive effects of development policies. Even if almost everyone in a city benefits from a particular development initiative, it is hard to imagine a situation in which all will benefit equally.

Paul Kantor focuses, as Peterson does, on the limits of cities and the restricted role of politics in development policy making.[16] While Peterson emphasizes a common city interest in pursuing growth policies, Kantor and other critical urban theorists stress the dependency of cities on the larger political economy: "Placed within a larger politico-economic order, city governments are captives of many forces that shape and limit community choices."[17]

Kantor's "dependency theory" and neo-Marxist perspective emanate from the prominence he assigns to the influence of mobile and promiscuous capital on cities. Kantor notes that, with the emergence of multi-locational corporations, cities are increasingly forced to compete to induce industry to locate in their territory: "From the perspective of corporate managers, cities are usually interchangeable: from the perspective of those who live in the cities, they are economically dependent."[18]

While both Kantor's and Peterson's view of the urban political economy articulate the dominance of economic factors, Kantor (unlike Peterson) considers the influence of political conflict on development policy making. According to Kantor, it is the contemporaneous development of both declining economic conditions in the cities and increasing demands for popular control that creates tension for local policy makers and makes economic development policy making problematic and perhaps just as contentious as policy making on issues that are more obviously redistributive in nature.

Although Peterson cites the existence of independent development authorities—such as the Lowell Plan and the economic development task force in New Bedford (to be discussed in Chapters 4 and 5)—as evidence of consensus local politics, Kantor sees those same agencies as mechanisms used by economic elites to insulate policy making from popular control.

Peterson's and Kantor's economically deterministic views of the local political economy can be contrasted with those of Logan and Molotch and Clarke and Moss. The "growth politics" theorists suggest that the economic interests of the city can be countervailed by the political strategies of elected officials. They illustrate how city political leaders can manipulate the local political process and economic development policy making toward their own political self-interest.[19] The involvement of Mayor Stan Lundine in Jamestown and Senator Paul Tsongas in Lowell suggests an element of political opportunism in local development policy making, but also seems to reflect concern with broader economic interests in their respective cities. The "growth politics" authors propose that, under certain circumstances, local political leaders dominate local development policies and enact policies that may not serve corporate and economic interests or the collective city interest.[20] This description seems to apply more to the local political leaders and their role in development in New Bedford and the Mon Valley than to Lundine and Tsongas in Jamestown and Lowell.

Clarence Stone's view of the politics of local development, which combines elements of the political and economic determinists, might be most suggestive of the experiences across the four case cities.[21] In *Regime Politics*, a study of politics and development policy making in Atlanta, Stone identifies the dynamic interaction between politics and development policy making. "(P)olicy and politics are circular, each at various points causing and being caused by the other."[22] As observed by Stone, politicians do not determine development policy, as might be suggested by the "growth politics" authors, but neither does the nature of development policy uniquely shape politics, as is suggested by Peterson and Kantor.

Atlanta over the past two decades has seen the evolution of "regime politics"—a network of mutual interaction and cooperation among downtown real estate owners, metropolitan area corporate interests, and black middle class politicians and businessmen. The Central Atlanta Progress (CAP), comprising Atlanta's economic elite, appears to determine which projects are pursued. However, the political structure, which is strongly influenced by the Afro-American middle class, extracts concessions that affect the distribution of benefits from development projects.

According to Stone, the success of development projects in Atlanta of the type and on the scale of such projects as Hartsfield International Airport, the Metropolitan Atlanta Rapid Transportation Authority (MARTA) subway system, Underground Atlanta, and most recently the 1996 Olympics required the generation of collective and selective benefits: collective benefits to the city as a whole and selective benefits to minority business and middle class supporters of Afro-American politicians, primarily in the form of "set-aside" contracts on development projects. While middle class Afro-Americans benefited substantially, Stone suggests that community groups and white and Afro-American lower and working class interests were left out of development policy making and benefited only marginally from development policies in Atlanta.

The "growth politics" theorists and Stone have different views than Peterson and Kantor regarding the relative importance of economic and political factors in development policy making, but they come to similar conclusions regarding the limited influence of citizen groups and community organization. The "growth politics" view and Stone's analysis of Atlanta indicate that city political leaders tend to manipulate citizen and community groups to serve their own ends. Peterson and Kantor suggest that the influence of pluralistic politics and community groups in local development is severely restricted by cities' position in the larger political economy. In the "city limits" view, citizen and community groups tend to pursue redistributive policies that are not in the collective city interest and are politically problematic to undertake. In the dependent city framework of Kantor, cities' policy choices are limited because businesses do not invest in cities that pursue policies that benefit interests other than their own.

John Mollenkopf, in *The Contested City*, presents a modified growth politics view which suggests some influence of citizen organization and a pluralistic dimension in local development policy making.[23] He identifies community and neighborhood groups that, through strategic mobilization and reconciliation of conflicting interests with dominant urban economic institutions, affect local development policy. According to Mollenkopf, in San Francisco and Boston (the two cities he focuses on) "(n)eighborhood activism ended large scale clearance projects, drastically revised traditional planning practices by creating citizen review and participation procedures, and created a new policy emphasis on preservation and rehabilitation."[24] We observe two examples of citizen groups affecting local development policy in the city development analyses, the grass-roots organized Coalition for a Better Acre (CBA) in Lowell and community development corporations in the Mon Valley (organized by a team of community organizing professionals). The groups in Lowell and the Mon Valley employed very different approaches to gain similar ends. The CBA engaged in more "traditional" conflictual community organizing against dominant economic institutions, while efforts in the Mon Valley involved a novel consensus-based approach in collaboration with dominant economic institutions in the metropolitan area.

While the experiences of community groups in Lowell and the Mon Valley, as well as San Francisco and Boston, suggest their influence, Mollenkopf and others are ambiguous with regard to their efficacy. Mollenkopf highlights the declining significance of community-based development activities and the dominance of development policy by "pro-growth" elite-dominated coalitions. Over time, Mollenkopf contends, neighborhood groups in San Francisco, Boston and elsewhere were co-opted with the increased funding by city and county government of neighborhood-based service delivery organizations.[25] Citizen groups became more service/program oriented, more competitive, less concerned with city-wide interests, and increasingly reluctant to alienate City Hall and established political actors who had a strong influence on program funding.

The Contested City concludes with a discussion of the (economic) structural and political limits of citizen participation and community organization. In this regard Mollenkopf is in agreement with Kantor and the critical urban theorists. According to Mollenkopf, "the inherently local nature of *the neighborhood movement* has prevented it from addressing the structural sources of conflict over urban development . . . [furthermore] the lack of a national political presence inherently undermines community organization as an alternative source of political rationalization."[26] This suggests that, without any national political or economic effect, there can be no significant local influence of community-based development activity. This appears to be in contradiction with Mollenkopf's own study of San Francisco and Boston and the analysis of Browning, Marshall, and Tabb and Swanstrom.

Browning, Marshall, and Tabb (BMT) in *Protest is Not Enough* identify dominant local coalitions apart from pro-growth coalitions. In their study of ten cities in northern California, they suggest that low income minority groups can be incorporated into influential local coalitions and retain an independent voice. Citizen groups can significantly affect city development policies if they are mobilized, represent a substantial proportion of the local population, and can generate majority group support.[27] While more optimistic of the influence of community groups, BMT—along with Mollenkopf and Stone—bemoan community groups' lack of power. The only city in which they identify minority and protest group incorporation into the dominant local coalition is Berkeley, which is renowned for its unique politics.[28] In other cities they studied, community groups were either co-opted, excluded, or failed to mobilize.

Distinct from BMT, some theorists take a cautious view of citizen participation and community organization. In his analysis of New York City during the fiscal crisis in the mid-1970s, Peterson suggests that community interests can conflict with the city interest and thus detract from city economic development.[29] Ira Katznelson also is cautionary about citizen groups, but takes an opposite view from Peterson. In *City Trenches*, Katznelson suggests that neighborhood and community-based efforts can divide groups in cities with common interests. In particular, Katznelson is concerned with community-based activities detracting from working and lower class mobilization against economic elites on critical citywide issues.[30]

Todd Swanstrom and Norton Long take a more positive and prescriptive view of local politics and organized citizen groups in local economic development. In his study of growth politics in Cleveland and the Kucinich administration, Swanstrom rejects the view of a corporate-elite dominated development process: "Decision making in community development [in Cleveland] was shared by many different groups, almost classical pluralist fashion."[31] Swanstrom suggests that, after elected governmental officials, activist citizen groups wielded the most influence in community development in Cleveland.

Swanstrom rejects both the structuralist Marxist view and Peterson's theory of city limits. In his "urban populist" view, as suggested by the experience of the CBA in Lowell, "the economic space exists . . . for redistributive programs designed to ameliorate the worst aspects of uneven development in cities."[32] He suggests that "to avoid succumbing to conservative growth policies the local public sector must engage itself in an authentic [pluralistic] bargaining process in which it recognizes that it has something to give [and take] from corporate interests."[33] In addition, neighborhood and activist groups must avoid getting locked into a zero sum game among themselves and with downtown business interests. According to Swanstrom, neighborhoods can benefit from each others' growth and they can all benefit from a strong downtown.

Long states more cogently than Swanstrom the efficacy of citizen organization. He argues that politics and citizen participation can inspire and shape development activities in cities. Long suggests that local development is a political as well as an economic process and that enhancing participation in city life will bring about development that is both more efficient and equitable.

Long is critical of local officials who equate development with attracting outside investment into cities. In contrast to the views of Peterson and Kantor, Long contends that the major task of local government is "not only to sustain the social and economic structure but to alter it."[34]

Long stresses the need for cities to look for ways to develop and enhance homegrown productive and social capacity, using the examples of the Amish and Black Muslims as groups that have successfully found their strength from within, via collective self-improvement and purposeful cooperation. According to Long, "people by the transformation of their behavior from individually and collectively self-destructive patterns and by the efficient uses of their limited resources can radically alter their lives for the better."[35] By extension Long argues that, although their strength has been eroded, cities could perform a similar role to Amish and Black Muslim communities through the engagement of citizens in local development. Long's views appear to be supported by the activities of the newly organized CDCs in the Mon Valley in the late 1980s.

Long and BMT's views are posited on their observation of groups with distinctive and particularly strong organization (social activists in Berkeley, the Black Muslims, and the Amish). While indicating the potential for citizen input and effect, their analysis also suggests its limitations. To be influential, citizen groups have to act with unified interest and effectively confront larger economic and political forces.

Collective Action and Local Economic Development

Public choice theories of collective action inform much of the discussion of politics and local economic development. Stone's differentiation of collective and selective ("set aside") benefits used to sustain the regime in Atlanta emanates from Mancur Olson's theory of collective action (see discussion below).[36] BMT highlight the selective rewards—both direct economic (minority contracting by city government) and status (appointments to boards and commissions)—from minority group incorporation into influential coalitions.[37] Peterson's model of consensus politics in development policy making is posited on the common interest in cities in promoting economic growth.[38]

Public choice theories of collective action focus on problems of cooperation among self-interested individuals. These theories provide insight into the propensity of different economic, political, and community actors to act collectively in city development activities. The most cited construct (in economic theories of cooperation) is the prisoners' dilemma.[39] The two person, single play prisoners' dilemma game illustrates that pursuit of individual economic self-interest can lead to outcomes that are inferior to results with cooperation.

Olson in *The Logic of Collective Action* extends the basic idea of the prisoners' dilemma game.[40] Olson's focus is groups and organizations and the more general question of when individuals are most likely to act collectively. According to Olson, individuals act collectively to further individual ends or produce benefits they could not accomplish on their own (at similar cost).[41] This suggests that groups and organizations have the fundamental purpose of serving the interests of their members. For example, according to Olson, states are first of all organizations that provide benefits to their members (citizens) while the priority of corporations is to serve the interests of individual shareholders.[42]

The costs associated with joining collective efforts (both in terms of committing time and contributing resources) and problems with imperfectly excludable goods, such as citywide economic growth, strongly influence the logic of collective action. Olson argues that individuals will not contribute to collective efforts if they can free ride, i.e., benefit from a group's effort without contributing.[43]

Olson suggests that selective benefits and small groups can be used to overcome the free rider problem. If there are particular benefits from joining collective efforts, the incentive to cooperate (and incur the costs of joining groups) will be increased. In some cases imaginative entrepreneurs, such as Stan Lundine the mayor of Jamestown during the 1970s and Senator Paul Tsongas in Lowell, can create selective incentives to support a stable coalition providing collective goods. As described by Mollenkopf, "political entrepreneurs can bring together widely different, competing and even conflicting political actors and interests by creating new governmental bases for exercising new powers which none of these actors and interests could otherwise have experienced on its own."[44] If the situation before the leader arises is not optimal, it follows that the leader, as suggested by the growth politics authors, can also get something for himself out of the gains he brought about by inducing collective effort.[45]

Mollenkopf highlights the role of political entrepreneurs in pro-

growth coalitions and the organization of governmental institutions
for exercising power. However, as will be identified in the city development analyses, all local development coalition builders do not
come from the public sector, all influential local coalitions are not
pro-growth, and every collective effort is not institutionalized in a
governmental agency. BMT highlight the biracial electoral alliance in
Berkeley of liberal working and middle class Afro-Americans and
middle class whites; Stone identifies the role of private sector leaders
and the Central Atlanta Progress in Atlanta; and the city development analyses describe the influence of multi-sector development
agencies, including the Jamestown Area Labor and Management
Committee and the Lowell Plan.

Olson contends that small groups can also facilitate cooperation.[46]
In smaller groups, Olson suggests, as indicated by the discussion of
the organization of community development corporation in 17 cities
in the Mon Valley, that shirking and free riding will be less feasible
since there will be a greater chance that "missing" contributions will
be noticed. In smaller groups, individual contributions will have a
more significant effect on group production and monitoring will be
more prevalent since the expected net benefit from monitoring will
be higher. Olson also argues that, in smaller groups, each group
member will have a greater incentive to see that the efforts of the
group do not fail, since there is a greater personal stake in group
activities.

Olson's logic applied to local development efforts suggests that
local actors (including political officials, private developers, local corporations, financial institutions, and community groups) will act co-
operatively only when it is in their best economic interest to do so. If
the benefits from development are nonexcludable and evenly distributed, Olson suggests (counter to Peterson's contention) that it will
be difficult to generate collective effort in local economic development, it will be in the interest of different groups to attempt to free
ride, and the end result will be a tendency towards inaction. This
appears to be the case in New Bedford throughout the 1970s and
1980s.

If there were common benefits from development but those benefits were highly concentrated, Olson's logic would suggest a local
effort led by those who would benefit the most. This line of reasoning supports the critical urban theorists' view that economic elites
dominate and benefit the most from local development efforts. However, Stone and BMT suggest that there is nothing inherent in the
local development process that requires the pursuit of development

policies that concentrate benefits only among the economic elite. *Regime Politics*, *Protest is Not Enough*, and the experiences of the Coalition for a Better Acre in Lowell and the community development corporations in the Mon Valley indicate that the type of development policies pursued and the distribution of benefits from development are at least, in part, politically determined. In Atlanta middle class Afro-Americans were included in the dominant coalition and were guaranteed benefits from development projects. In Berkeley, working and middle class Afro-Americans and liberal whites formed the dominant coalition and pursued development policies that furthered their economic and social interests. In Lowell and the Mon Valley, low income residents were organized to gain a share of development benefits.

Olson would predict collective city action under two different scenarios: when benefits from development are concentrated and selective and it is in the interest of a "small" coalition of beneficiaries to take the lead in development efforts, as appears to be the case in Atlanta and Berkeley; or where there is a broad distribution of benefits and a political (or other kind of) entrepreneur overcomes problems of free riders and motivates action by convincing different local parties that collective action is superior to inaction, as seems to be the case in Cleveland during the Kucinich administration and in Lowell and Jamestown during the late 1970s and early 1980s.

Axelrod provides an insightful extension to Olson's theory of collective action that adds insight to local development practice.[47] Axelrod suggests that repeated interactions permit individuals and groups to see the shortcomings of noncooperation and to learn norms of cooperation. As applied to local development practice and supported by Stone's description of the evolution of the political regime in Atlanta, Axelrod indicates that, when development involves repeated interaction between different parties (or it is perceived as such), there is greater likelihood of mutually beneficial cooperation. The discussion of emerging CDCs in the Mon Valley will indicate the value of these organizations in institutionalizing the repeated interactions and cooperative behavior that Axelrod suggests. In contrast, if development is viewed as involving a single interaction (for example an effort to attract a large industrial employer), there might be greater likelihood of noncooperative behavior among local development actors, as we will observe with Mon Valley development efforts in the early 1980s.[48]

Olson and Axelrod's predictions on the propensity for collective action in local development are predicated on the belief that the fundamental motivation is individual economic self-interest. This presupposition ignores other incentives that may be relevant.

Beyond Self-Interest

Political scientists outside the public choice school identify incentives for political and collective action apart from economic self-interest.[49] James Q. Wilson and Peter Clark distinguish among "material," "solidary," and "purposive" incentives.[50] The first motive they describe, material, is similar to the economic self-interest emphasized by Olson and public choice theorists. The second incentive suggests that individuals are not only economic actors but also social beings and seek social goals.[51] The third incentive identified by Wilson and Clark recognizes that individuals and groups of individuals also act collectively to promote causes that are not necessarily related to their economic self-interest, such as those with religious, philosophical, and moral purposes. Richard Fenno, in *Congressmen in Committees*, suggests another motive for political and collective action, "making good policy." He identified, counter to public choice postulates, that members of some congressional committees tried to get on those committees (simply) because they wanted to help make good public policy.[52]

The "alternative" incentives for individuals and groups of individuals to cooperate and act collectively are often suggested as being less significant than economic self-interest. Their value in explaining collective efforts in local economic development will be explored, along with the other theories of political and collection action, in the city development analyses.

Conclusion

The statistical analysis in the next chapter and the city development analyses in Chapters 4 through 7 will employ the economic and political theories introduced here. Theories will be used to interpret local development efforts and patterns in local economic development and to consider how local development acts might have influenced each city's positioning in product, process, and factor price life cycles and contributed to or inhibited local economic change and growth.

Three

Growth and Decline in Four Cities

Introduction

This chapter provides analyses of post–World War II employment changes in the four study cities and background for the "case studies" of local development initiatives. The economic development histories of Lowell and New Bedford and Jamestown and McKeesport are compared and contrasted. The objective is to assess differences in growth between the cities and to identify points in time and employment sectors in which differential growth between the *paired* cities cannot be explained by regional economic change, industry mix and factor costs alone.

The focus of the discussion is on changes in employment. Employment data from the *U.S. Census of Manufacturing* and *U.S. Census of Population and Housing* are presented, unless otherwise indicated. These data are comparable and reflect similar trends and changes over time. The *Census of Manufacturing* data is part of a periodic census of manufacturing establishments. The *Census of Population and Housing* employment data is from the decennial census of households in which employment is derived from a three part question on the types of businesses in which household members are employed. Some household members work in cities outside the cities in which they reside, so the *Census of Population and Housing* data will reflect employment opportunities not only in individual cities but also in the surrounding labor market areas.

The historical development of the four cities suggests their dependence on manufacturing employment for their growth, economic well-being, and general vitality and justifies the focus on employment data. Employment trends, however, are a limited indicator of development success. The discussion (of employment) in this chapter and in the city development analyses in subsequent chapters will be supplemented with consideration of other measures that indicate city vitality and development success—including unemployment rates, population change, median family income, and average educational attainment.

Lowell and New Bedford

Both Lowell and New Bedford developed as manufacturing industry centers during the nineteenth century. Lowell emerged in the latter half of the nineteenth century as a center for cotton cloth manufacturing, benefiting from favorable positioning in process and factor price cycles. Lowell attracted textiles manufacturing because of its cheap and abundant supply of water power (channeled from the Merrimack River into canal systems throughout the city), labor supply, and proximity to end-use markets.

Opportunities for gainful employment first attracted young single women to Lowell from farms throughout New England. Later the promise of employment attracted waves of immigrants. The Irish came, followed by the French Canadians, Italians, and Greeks. By 1920 Lowell's population peaked at just over 112,000.

From the late nineteenth century to 1920, employment in the textile industry accounted for over 40 percent of all employment in Lowell.[1] During the first decade of the twentieth century, however, Lowell's positioning in textile industry process and factor price cycles weakened with the introduction of electricity and increased competition from Southern manufacturers employing lower wage nonunion labor. The city started to lose textile employment and entered a long period of economic decline which persisted through the mid-1970s.

Reflecting its past as a single industry town, Lowell possessed no other industry which could lessen the blow of losing textile industry employment. After 1914, Lowell experienced continuous decline in manufacturing employment until 1975, except for brief increases during World War II and the Vietnam War. Over the sixty-year period, manufacturing employment fell nearly in half, from nearly 30,000 in 1914 to approximately 15,000 in 1975.[2]

In the 1970s the long-term decline in manufacturing employment in Lowell ended with the emergence of industry at the growth stage in the product life cycle. As suggested by Table 3.1, it was only when employment surged in machinery and equipment manufacturing (including computer manufacturing and other high technology industries) that the long decline in manufacturing in Lowell was reversed. Employment in machinery and equipment manufacturing in Lowell rose from just over 1,000 (or 3 percent of total employment) in 1950 to over 7,300 (18 percent of total employment) in 1980. As employment in machinery manufacturing rose dramatically, textile and apparel manufacturing continued to decline, falling to just 6 percent of total employment by 1980.

TABLE 3.1
Lowell Employment 1950 to 1980

	1950	1960	1970	1980	Percentage Changes 1950-1960	1960-1970	1970-1980	1950-1980
Total Employment	38,325	36,595	38,645	41,621	(4.5)	5.6	7.7	8.6
Manufacturing	17,812	15,982	15,080	17,321	(10.3)	(5.6)	14.9	(2.8)
Total NonDurable	15,619	9,983	7,878	6,358	(36.1)	(21.1)	(19.3)	(59.3)
Textile & Apparel	10,929	4,365	2,751	2,284	(60.1)	(37.0)	(17.0)	(79.1)
Total Durable	2,115	5,999	7,202	10,963	183.6	20.1	52.2	418.3
Machinery	1,071	2,975	4,069	7,361	177.8	36.8	80.9	587.3
Trans., Com. & Util.	2,669	1,762	1,810	2,125	(34.0)	2.7	17.4	(20.4)
Wholesale & Retail	6,641	5,135	6,908	6,592	(22.7)	34.5	(4.6)	(0.7)
F.I.R.E.	827	1,098	1,059	1,216	32.8	(3.6)	14.8	47.0
Services	6,141	6,128	9,209	10,077	(0.2)	50.3	9.4	64.1
Agriculture	165	134	126	134	(18.8)	(6.0)	6.3	(18.8)

	Percentage Breakdown 1950	1960	1970	1980
Total Employment	100.0	100.0	100.0	100.0
Manufacturing	46.5	43.7	39.0	41.6
Total NonDurable	40.8	27.3	20.4	15.3
Textile & Apparel	28.5	11.9	7.1	5.5
Total Durable	5.5	16.4	18.6	26.3
Machinery	2.8	8.1	10.5	17.7
Trans., Com. & Util.	7.0	4.8	4.7	5.1
Wholesale & Retail	17.3	14.0	17.9	15.8
F.I.R.E.	2.2	3.0	2.7	2.9
Services	16.0	16.7	23.8	24.2
Agriculture	0.4	0.4	0.3	0.3

Source: *U.S. Census Bureau, Population and Housing.*

New Bedford's manufacturing industry development lagged behind Lowell's. New Bedford initially developed as a whaling port during the sixteenth century and emerged as a whaling center in the eighteenth century. A product innovation, the discovery of petroleum in Pennsylvania in 1849, however, reduced whaling's profitability and resulted in the decline of the whaling industry in New Bedford and throughout North America.

With the decline of the whaling industry, local investors shifted their investment capital from whaling into the textiles and apparel industry. Textile and apparel manufacturing in New Bedford was concentrated in finer and higher value-added cotton goods. New Bedford was favorably positioned for fine textiles manufacturing because of its low energy costs (with use of electrical power), proximity to end-use markets in the Northeast, low transportation costs (with its location on the water and road access), and reliable, low-cost supply of immigrant labor.

New Bedford's concentration in finer textiles initially made the city less vulnerable to Southern competition than Lowell. New Bedford established itself as a leading textile and apparel manufacturing city, and manufacturing employment in the city peaked in 1925 at 35,696. Population peaked with manufacturing employment at just over 120,000 in the 1920s, as New Bedford attracted a large influx of immigrants from Portugal and other European coastal areas to work in the city's textile mills and fishing industry.

During the Depression years, however, manufacturing employment in New Bedford dropped dramatically, declining 26 percent between 1925 and 1937. Compounding and extending the depression-induced downturn in New Bedford's economy was local product maturation and increased competition. Many textile and apparel manufacturers in New Bedford moved their operations to lower cost sites in the South or lost market share to Southern manufacturers employing new production technologies and lower cost labor.

New Bedford never recovered from its decline during the Depression years. During World War II, manufacturing employment increased as New Bedford manufacturers expanded production to meet war time demand. After the end of World War II, however, manufacturing employment once again continued its steady decline, falling to 21,700 in 1977, 68 percent of its 1947 level. As indicated by Table 3.2, from 1950 to 1980, New Bedford lost over 26 percent of its manufacturing employment.

Despite a 43 percent decline in textiles and apparel manufacturing employment between 1950 and 1980, over 44 percent of New Bedford's manufacturing jobs remained in textiles and apparel in 1980. In contrast to Lowell and Massachusetts, New Bedford's employment did not shift to growing national industries, such as computer manufacturing and financial and other services in the 1970s and 1980s. New Bedford has been particularly unsuccessful in expanding employment in machinery and equipment manufacturing and wholesale and retail trade, with thirty-year declines in New Bedford of 35 and 17 percent respectively, while nationally these industries grew by 139 and 177 percent (see Table 3.3).

TABLE 3.2
New Bedford Employment 1950 to 1980

	1950	1960	1970	1980	1950–1960	Percentage Changes 1960–1970	1970–1980	1950–1980
Total Employment	46,416	41,771	41,090	40,440	(10.0)	(1.6)	(1.6)	(12.9)
Manufacturing	24,810	21,605	18,816	18,264	(12.9)	(12.9)	(2.9)	(26.4)
Total NonDurable	18,030	14,432	12,296	11,401	(20.0)	(14.8)	(7.3)	(36.8)
Textile & Apparel	14,198	9,920	7,748	8,109	(30.1)	(21.9)	4.7	(42.9)
Total Durable	6,780	7,173	6,520	6,863	5.8	(9.1)	5.3	1.2
Machinery	4,317	4,582	2,956	2,803	6.1	(35.5)	(5.2)	(35.1)
Trans., Com. & Util.	2,169	1,839	1,961	1,708	(15.2)	6.6	(12.9)	(21.3)
Wholesale & Retail	7,896	6,103	7,471	6,579	(22.7)	22.4	(11.9)	(16.7)
F.I.R.E.	881	934	924	1,309	6.0	(1.1)	41.7	48.6
Services	5,945	5,679	7,035	8,186	(4.5)	23.9	16.4	37.7
Agriculture	1,085	724	667	968	(33.3)	(7.9)	45.1	(10.8)

Percentage Breakdown				
	1950	1960	1970	1980
Total Employment	100.0	100.0	100.0	100.0
Manufacturing	53.5	51.7	45.8	45.2
Total NonDurable	38.8	34.6	29.9	28.2
Textile & Apparel	30.6	23.7	18.9	20.1
Total Durable	14.6	17.2	15.9	17.0
Machinery	9.3	11.0	7.2	6.9
Trans., Com. & Util.	4.7	4.4	4.8	4.2
Wholesale & Retail	17.0	14.6	18.2	16.3
F.I.R.E.	1.9	2.2	2.2	3.2
Services	12.8	13.6	17.1	20.2
Agriculture	2.3	1.7	1.6	2.4

Source: U.S. Census Bureau, Population and Housing.

In Lowell and New Bedford, population decline, decline in family income, and increases in unemployment (relative to the U.S. average) were closely related to declines in total and manufacturing employment, as indicated in Table 3.4. The data for Lowell suggests a turnaround of sorts between 1970 and 1980, as unemployment dropped below the U.S. average for the first time in the post–World War II period. In New Bedford, however, unemployment remained above the U.S. average during the 1970s, and the city's median family income and the percentage of population with greater than high school education remained significantly below the U.S. average.

TABLE 3.3
United States Employment—Percentage Growth and Breakdown
1950 to 1980

	Percentage Changes			
	1950–1960	1960–1970	1970–1980	1950–1980
Total Employment	14.5	18.4	27.5	73.0
Manufacturing	19.3	13.4	10.3	49.2
Total NonDurable	11.0	4.0	5.6	21.9
Textile & Apparel	(7.8)	4.1	1.2	(2.9)
Total Durable	26.6	20.8	13.5	73.6
Furniture & Wood Products	(7.3)	(9.4)	17.7	(1.1)
Metal Industries	24.1	(5.9)	15.2	34.6
Machinery	45.5	28.5	27.5	138.5
Trans., Com. & Util.	0.2	33.0	19.5	59.3
Wholesale & Retail Trade	12.2	30.4	29.6	89.7
F.I.R.E.	40.4	42.8	53.3	207.3
Services	34.3	47.1	40.4	177.2
Agriculture	(38.2)	(34.8)	2.7	(58.6)

	Percent Breakdown			
	1950	1960	1970	1980
Total Employment	100.0	100.0	100.0	100.0
Manufacturing	26.0	27.1	26.0	22.4
Total NonDurable	12.3	11.9	10.4	8.6
Textile & Apparel	4.1	3.3	2.9	2.3
Total Durable	13.8	15.2	15.5	13.8
Furniture & Wood Products	2.1	1.7	1.3	1.2
Metal Industries	3.6	3.9	3.1	2.8
Machinery	3.7	4.7	5.1	5.1
Trans., Com. & Util.	7.9	6.9	7.7	7.3
Wholesale & Retail Trade	18.6	18.2	20.1	20.4
F.I.R.E.	3.4	4.2	5.0	6.0
Services	17.9	21.0	26.0	28.7
Agriculture	12.5	6.7	3.7	3.0

Source: U.S. Census Bureau, Population and Housing.

TABLE 3.4
Lowell and New Bedford Profiles 1950 to 1980

Lowell	1950	1960	1970	1980	Index Relative to the United States			
					1950	1960	1970	1980
Population	97,249	92,107	94,239	92,418				
Total Employment	38,325	36,595	38,645	41,621				
Percent Manufacturing	46.5%	43.7%	39.0%	41.6%	178.8	161.3	150.0	185.7
Unemployment Rate	7.0%	5.2%	4.4%	4.8%	142.9	102.0	100.0	73.8
Median Family Income	$3,063	$5,679	$9,495	$17,942	99.7	101.0	96.2	85.3
Percent H.S. Graduate	29.9%	32.6%	45.0%	57.7%	85.4	79.3	86.0	86.8
Percent Over 65	10.5%	12.1%	12.1%	13.0%	129.6	131.5	122.2	115.0

New Bedford	1950	1960	1970	1980	Index Relative to the United States			
					1950	1960	1970	1980
Population	109,189	102,477	101,777	98,487				
Total Employment	46,416	41,771	41,090	40,440				
Percent Manufacturing	53.5%	51.7%	45.8%	45.2%	205.8	190.8	176.1	201.6
Unemployment Rate	8.6%	6.5%	5.4%	9.0%	175.5	127.5	122.7	138.9
Median Family Income	$2,947	$5,019	$8,230	$14,930	95.9	89.3	83.4	71.0
Percent H.S. Graduate	18.2%	23.4%	27.8%	38.0%	53.2	56.9	53.2	57.1
Percent Over 65	10.4%	13.6%	14.6%	16.1%	127.8	148.2	147.8	142.8

Source: U.S. Census Bureau, Population and Housing.

These data, along with the employment data, indicate that, during the 1970s, the general decline in Lowell was abating and showed some indication of reversing, while in New Bedford this was not the case.

Employment Composition and Trend Analysis

Employment growth in both Lowell and New Bedford has lagged significantly behind national employment growth in the post–World War II period. Over the thirty-year period, Lowell's total employment increased 9 percent and New Bedford's declined by 13 percent, while total United States employment grew by 73 percent. During the post–World War II period, Lowell and New Bedford and industrial cities throughout the Northeast and the Midwest were impacted profoundly by the shift of economic and industrial activity in the United States to the South and the West.[3] The primary factors generally cited as contributing to the shift of economic activity to the South and West include lower business costs (e.g., lower wages and energy costs, fewer land use regulations and lower state and local taxes), more attractive climate (hence the reference to the area of regional growth in the United States in the post–World War II period as the "sun belt"), development of natural resources (particularly oil and gas in the Southwest and West and coal and related energy products in the mountain states and West), and federal military and other expenditures that directed investment and population away from the Northeast to the South and West.

Economic Base

In spite of significant declines in manufacturing employment, Lowell and New Bedford have remained industrial cities, as both cities have retained approximately twice the national average concentration of employment in manufacturing. In 1950, 26 percent of all United States workers were employed in manufacturing, while the figures in Lowell and New Bedford were 47 percent and 54 percent respectively. By 1980, the United States share of employment in manufacturing had declined to 22 percent, yet manufacturing as a share of total employment remained above 40 percent in both Lowell and New Bedford.

Economic base analysis and the calculation of city location quotients are a simple, yet useful, way to summarize changes in the employment composition in an area—particularly as compared to national averages. Location quotients are calculated as the percentage of an area's total employment in a particular industrial sector divided by the percentage of the nation's employment in the same sector. Local employment sectors with location quotients above one and employment shares above the national average are considered exporting sectors (i.e., sectors in the local economy that produce goods and services beyond the needs of the local population and export the excess), while sectors with location quotients below one are considered importing sectors.

Lowell's employment base in 1950, even after nearly fifty years of decline in the textiles industry, was concentrated in nondurable manufacturing, with a location quotient of over 3.0 (see Table 3.5). Lowell was least concentrated in durable manufacturing (including

TABLE 3.5
Location Quotients Lowell, New Bedford, and Massachusetts

| | 1950 | | | 1980 | | |
	Lowell	N.B.	Mass.	Lowell	N.B.	Mass.
Manufacturing	1.8	2.1	1.4	1.9	2.0	1.2
NonDurable	3.3	3.2	1.7	1.8	3.3	1.1
Textiles and Apparel	7.0	7.5	2.2	2.4	8.7	1.2
Durable	0.4	1.1	1.1	1.9	1.2	1.2
Machinery	0.8	2.5	1.9	3.5	1.4	1.6
Wholesale & Retail Trade	0.9	0.9	1.0	0.8	0.8	0.9
Services	0.9	0.7	1.3	0.8	0.7	1.1

Source: U.S. Census Bureau, Population and Housing.

machinery and equipment manufacturing), business, professional and entertainment services, and wholesale and retail trade—all with location quotients below 1.0. By 1980, Lowell's manufacturing employment composition had shifted. It was less concentrated in nondurable manufacturing (with the location quotient falling below 2.0) and substantially more concentrated in durable goods manufacturing, particularly machinery and equipment manufacturing (with a location quotient of 3.5).

In 1950, New Bedford's employment was concentrated in textiles and apparel manufacturing (with a location quotient of 7.5). In contrast to Lowell in 1950, however, New Bedford also had significant employment concentration in machinery and equipment manufacturing (with a location quotient of 2.5—significantly above Lowell's location quotient of .8). Again, in sharp contrast to Lowell, between 1950 and 1980, New Bedford experienced an increase in its relative employment concentration in textiles and apparel and a decrease in its concentration in machinery and equipment. While employment in textile and apparel manufacturing declined, the city's decline was less pronounced than the nation's and thus its concentration in textiles and apparel increased relative to the nation. In comparison, machinery and equipment manufacturing in New Bedford declined relative to the nation (with the location quotient dropping to 1.4).

These data suggest that New Bedford was unable to take advantage of what appeared to be relatively favorable positioning entering the post–World War II period: concentrated employment in an industry, machinery and equipment manufacturing, that had significant national growth potential. However, as described in the development analysis in Chapter 5, New Bedford's machinery industry was vulnerable to decline. In 1950, machinery and equipment employment in New Bedford was concentrated in a relatively mature segment of the industry, machine tool manufacturing. In contrast, Lowell's machine and equipment industry during the post–World War II period was concentrated in a rapidly growing segment, computer manufacturing.

Shift-Share Analysis

Shift-share models provide an accounting framework to identify the effects of national and state industry trends on local employment.[4] Shift-share analysis can relate changes in local employment to national and state growth rates. Using shift-share analysis, the period-to-period change in an area's total employment can be broken down into three main components: (1) an *industry-mix component*, which includes the change expected if the employment sectors in the locality grew at their national rate; (2) a *regional differential component*, which reflects the difference in the rate of growth between the state (in which the area is located) and the nation; and (3) a *residual component*, commonly referred to as the *differential shift*, which is the change in local employment above or below that expected if the employment sectors in an area grew at their national rate, including adjustment for differences in state and national growth. The performance of individual sectors of a local economy can be decomposed in a similar manner. Different sectors of a local economy can be assessed by comparing actual growth with what growth would have been if that sector of the local economy had grown at the same rate as the industry nationally, with adjustment for the different rate of growth (in that sector) in the state compared to the nation (see Figure 3.1).

A positive (negative) period-to-period differential shift suggests that the sector of the local economy grew at a rate greater (less) than expected if it grew at the national rate, with adjustment for differential growth between the nation and the state.

Regional and urban economic theory suggests that a significant portion of the differential shift in a locale's employment may emanate from changes in relative production costs. Pairing-up the cities controls in part for cost considerations. Lowell and New Bedford are both part of the greater Boston area and larger New England regional

FIGURE 3.1
Shift-Share Analysis: Differential Shift Calculation

Differential =	Actual –	Base Period * National Growth	–	Base Period * (Regional – National)
Shift	Growth	Local Employ. Rate		Local Employ. Growth Rates

Differential Shift = Actual Growth – (National Industry Effect + Regional Differential)

Note: This method is equivalent to calculating differential shifts by subtracting state growth rates multiplied
by base period employment from actual growth. The advantage of the calculation specified above is to
distinguish between national and regional effects on local growth. In Tables 3.6, 3.7, 3.15 and 3.16
the "total" differential shifts are presented for the four cities. In the text the discussion indicates the
relative effect of national and regional industry growth rates.

economy. Lowell and New Bedford had similar wages, transportation and energy costs and similar population and employment levels
and composition during the period of particular concern here, the
post–World War II period from 1950 to 1980. Pairing-up Jamestown
and McKeesport also controls in part for factor cost differentials.
Jamestown and McKeesport, while in different states, are only 150
miles apart and both are part of a larger mid-Atlantic and "rust belt"
regional economy. Jamestown and McKeesport had similar wages,
transportation and energy costs, and similar levels of population
and employment and composition during the period from 1950 to
1980.

The differential shift statistics in Tables 3.6 and 3.7 indicate that
Lowell outperformed New Bedford's economy during the post–
World War II period.[5] There was a 43 percent difference between actual and "expected" employment over the thirty-year period in New
Bedford, while in Lowell the similar figure was 11 percent. The
11,824 negative shift in employment over the post–World War II period (see Table 3.6) and the base (1950) employment of 46,400 suggests that New Bedford's employment would have increased to over
58,000—instead of declining by approximately 6,000 to 40,440—if its
employment sectors had grown at their national rates, with adjustment for different growth rates between the nation and Massachusetts. In comparison, if Lowell's employment sectors had grown at
their national rates, with adjustment for differences in industrial
growth between Massachusetts and the nation, employment in Low-

TABLE 3.6
New Bedford Differential Shifts

	1950–1960	1960–1970	1970–1980	Total	Total Shift as Percent of 1950 Employment
Manufacturing	(4,165)	(728)	(2,095)	(6,987)	(28)
Total NonDurable	(1,649)	986	302	(360)	(2)
Textile & Apparel	726	407	1,726	2,859	20
Total Durable	(1,339)	(802)	(1,054)	(3,195)	(47)
Machinery	(1,284)	(1,911)	(731)	(3,926)	(91)
Trans., Com. & Util.	(133)	(36)	(870)	(1,038)	(48)
Wholesale & Retail	(1,654)	(292)	(2,056)	(4,002)	(51)
F.I.R.E.	(160)	(303)	68	(395)	(45)
Services	(147)	(1,307)	(1,707)	(3,160)	(53)
Agriculture	(5)	124	208	327	30
Total	(5,087)	(1,629)	(5,108)	(11,824)	(25)

Source: U.S. Census Bureau, Population and Housing.

TABLE 3.7
Lowell Differential Shifts

	1950–1960	1960–1970	1970–1980	Total	Total Shift As Percent of 1950 Employment
Manufacturing	(2,519)	623	1,005	(892)	(5)
Total NonDurable	(3,947)	55	(753)	(4,646)	(30)
Textile & Apparel	(2,712)	(479)	18	(3,173)	(29)
Total Durable	3,344	1,078	2,218	6,640	314
Machinery	1,520	909	2,496	4,925	460
Trans., Com. & Util.	(664)	(103)	(254)	(1,022)	(38)
Wholesale & Retail	(1,389)	377	(1,392)	(2,405)	(36)
F.I.R.E.	71	(383)	(206)	(518)	(63)
Services	110	208	(2,873)	(2,555)	(42)
Agriculture	23	26	(10)	39	24
Total	(2,453)	1,256	(3,270)	(4,467)	(12)

Source: U.S. Census Bureau, Population and Housing.

ell would have been approximately 4,500 larger than it was (see Table 3.7).

New Bedford between 1950 and 1980 experienced negative differential shifts in every employment category except agriculture and textiles and apparel employment.[6] The most substantial negative shifts in employment in New Bedford between 1950 and 1980 were in wholesale and retail trade, services, and machinery and equipment manufacturing. Weakness in Lowell's economy was most pronounced in textiles and apparel, services, and wholesale and retail trade, as reflected in the large negative differential shifts in each of these categories over the thirty-year period. Lowell's employment sector with the most significant positive differential shift was machinery and equipment manufacturing.

The most pronounced difference in the employment changes in the cities (and the most relevant one for our purposes) was within the manufacturing sector. While New Bedford experienced a significant positive differential shift in textile and apparel manufacturing, Lowell showed particular weakness in this industrial sector. In contrast, the data suggests that Lowell had particular strength in machinery and equipment manufacturing, while New Bedford experienced significant negative differential shift in this sector. New Bedford's relatively weak performance in machinery and equipment manufacturing reflected its concentration in machine tool production (as noted previously). In contrast, Lowell's strength in machinery and equipment manufacturing during the post–World War II period reflected, to a significant degree, its favorable location just outside Route 128 (referred to as "America's High Technology Highway"), which attracted large numbers of innovating computer manufacturers during the 1970s and 1980s. The failure of some neighboring cities, most notably Lawrence (see the discussion of reference cities in Chapter 1), to benefit from the "transom effects" of growth in the Route 128 corridor during the same period that Lowell experienced substantial growth suggests, however, that at least some of Lowell's growth may be attributable to local development factors aside from location and agglomeration economies.

The positive differential shift in textile and apparel manufacturing was most pronounced in New Bedford in the period from 1970 to 1980, the same decade that Lowell experienced the most significant positive differential growth in machinery and equipment manufacturing. This indicates that, entering the 1980s, the relative strength in the New Bedford economy was dampened decline in a manufacturing industry, textiles and apparel, that was declining nationally (and had relatively poor future prospects, given increased competition from low-cost developing nations), while the comparative strength in Lowell's economy was superior positioning in what was, in 1980, a significant growth industry. This had major implications for the economic performance in the two cities during the 1980s, as will be discussed.

Lowell and New Bedford Relative to Massachusetts 1975–1987

During the period from 1950 to 1980, the Massachusetts economy did not keep pace with the United States economy. Total employment in Massachusetts increased by 47 percent compared to 73 percent nationally (see Table 3.8). The most pronounced differential growth between the state and nation was in manufacturing employment. United States manufacturing employment grew by 49 percent, while manufacturing employment in Massachusetts grew by less than 2 percent between 1950 and 1980.[7]

In the 1970s, Massachusetts experienced a manufacturing industry revival of sorts. The state's manufacturing employment growth rate, however, remained below the United States' rate and nondurable manufacturing employment continued to decline. The manufacturing sector that increased the most during the 1970s in Massachusetts was machinery and equipment manufacturing, which grew by nearly 20 percent. This growth, while widely recognized (national attention was given to the growth of computer and related industries in the Route 128 area), was still below the United States average growth rate in machinery and equipment manufacturing of 28 percent.

From 1975 to 1986, employment in both the New Bedford and Lowell labor market areas (according to the Massachusetts' Department of Employment and Training) increased, reflecting reversals of long-term declines in both cities (see Table 3.9).[8] However, Lowell's employment growth was significantly greater than New Bedford's. Over the eleven-year period, New Bedford's private employment increased by 5 percent, while Lowell's grew by 43 percent.

Lowell's employment growth was concentrated in manufacturing and services, with growth rates of 49 percent and 60 percent respectively over the eleven-year period. Manufacturing in Lowell peaked in 1984 at 19,365 (representing an increase of 54 percent from 1975). A large portion of the increase in manufacturing in Lowell was in high technology manufacturing. Between 1975 and 1984, high technology manufacturing employment in the city increased by over 300 percent, from approximately 3,000 to 13,000. The increase in high

TABLE 3.8
Massachusetts Employment 1950 to 1980

	Percentage Changes			
	1950–1960	1960–1970	1970–1980	1950–1980
Total Employment	9.5	16.1	15.1	46.4
Manufacturing	3.9	(9.5)	8.2	1.7
Total NonDurable	(10.8)	(21.6)	(9.7)	(36.9)
Textile & Apparel	(35.2)	(26.0)	(17.6)	(60.5)
Total Durable	25.5	2.1	21.4	55.6
Machinery	35.9	6.2	19.6	72.6
Trans., Com. & Util.	(9.1)	8.6	31.5	29.8
Wholesale & Retail	(1.8)	27.2	15.6	44.4
F.I.R.E.	24.2	31.3	34.3	119.0
Services	(2.0)	46.9	40.6	102.4
Agriculture	(32.8)	(25.0)	13.9	(42.6)

	Percentage Breakdown			
	1950	1960	1970	1980
Total Employment	100.0	100.0	100.0	100.0
Manufacturing	37.4	35.5	27.6	26.0
Total NonDurable	21.3	17.4	11.7	9.2
Textile & Apparel	9.1	5.4	3.4	2.5
Total Durable	15.8	18.1	15.9	16.8
Machinery	7.1	8.8	8.1	8.4
Trans., Com. & Util.	7.0	5.8	5.4	6.2
Wholesale & Retail	19.3	17.3	19.0	19.0
F.I.R.E.	4.2	4.8	5.4	6.4
Services	23.3	20.8	26.3	32.2
Agriculture	2.1	1.3	0.8	0.8

Source: U.S. Census Bureau, Population and Housing.

technology employment in the city was approximately 50 percent larger than Lowell's total growth in manufacturing between 1975 and 1984.[9] Much of the growth in high-technology employment represented new employment at one firm, Wang Laboratories, Inc. (Wang).[10] Even disregarding Wang's impact on Lowell, we can spec-

TABLE 3.9
Lowell and New Bedford Employment 1975 to 1986

| | 1975 | | 1986 | | Percent Change | |
	Lowell	N.B.	Lowell	N.B.	Lowell	N.B.
Manufacturing	12,592	19,487	18,723	18,325	48.7	(6.0)
Wholesale & Retail	6,114	12,174	7,495	7,914	22.6	(35.0)
Services	5,770	5,806	9,218	8,131	59.8	40.0
Total Private	28,304	38,370	40,435	40,376	42.9	5.2

Source: Mass. Department of Employment and Training.

ulate that Lowell would have experienced significant growth relative
to New Bedford. If Lowell's high technology industries had grown at
one-third their actual rate (as might have been the case if Lowell had
not attracted Wang but had still benefited from its location near
Route 128), Lowell's employment (assuming a rather conservative
one-to-one short-term multiplier effect from jobs in high technology
to other sectors of the economy) would have increased by 18 percent—still well above New Bedford's 5 percent rate of increase.

Employment in high technology industries grew significantly less
in New Bedford than in Lowell. High technology employment in
New Bedford increased at one-tenth the level it increased in Lowell—1,100 during the nine-year period compared to an increase of
close to 10,000 in Lowell. New Bedford's employment gains over the
nine-year "growth period" were concentrated in durable goods manufacturing, which grew by 36 percent, and services, which increased
by 29 percent.

Calculating differential employment shifts for the period from
1975 to 1987 (see Table 3.10), suggests that the period of most substantial differences in growth between Lowell and New Bedford
started in 1978 and ended in 1986. The difference in total differential
shift in employment between the two cities in that period was quite
large, representing approximately 40 percent of New Bedford's private employment in 1978. We have already speculated on some of
the factors that may have contributed to differential growth between
the two cities during this period, including location factors and advantageous positioning in product life cycle. In the development

TABLE 3.10
Differential Employment Shifts: Lowell and New Bedford Relative to Massachusetts

| | 1975 – 1978 | | 1978 – 1986 | | 1986 – 1987 | | 1975 – 1987 | |
	Lowell	N.B.	Lowell	N.B.	Lowell	N.B.	Lowell	N.B.
Agriculture	4	33	(26)	(545)	4	(78)	(18)	(517)
Construction	207	142	(155)	(149)	(86)	(1)	(34)	(45)
Manufacturing	(112)	2,039	6,201	(4,116)	71	(969)	6,160	(3,348)
Trans., Com. & Util.	(126)	(182)	(79)	(656)	(108)	168	(313)	(575)
Wholesale and Retail	409	(539)	(1,357)	(6,553)	(361)	710	(1,309)	(6,548)
F.I.R.E.	(71)	23	197	(375)	(10)	(37)	116	(361)
Services	121	(870)	(342)	956	(256)	(296)	(477)	278
Total	429	655	4,439	(12,232)	(747)	(502)	4,121	(12,014)

Source: Mass. Department of Employment and Training.

analyses of the two cities (Chapters 4 and 5), potential contributions of local development initiatives to the differentials in employment growth are considered, with particular attention to the time period and sectors of greatest differential growth. The city development analyses will focus on local efforts to stimulate employment in high technology, including the packaging of incentives to attract Wang to Lowell and efforts in New Bedford to retain machinery and equipment manufacturing employment during the late 1970s and early 1980s.

Jamestown and McKeesport

Jamestown and McKeesport, as do Lowell and New Bedford, have long and continuing industrial traditions. When James Prendergast first settled in Jamestown in 1806, he found a countryside covered with a thick forest of white pine, ash, and various hardwoods. The trees provided the foundation for the development of lumbering and furniture manufacturing in the city. Similarly when John McKee laid out the village of McKeesport in 1795 and solicited buyers for lots, he listed as the area's attractions the abundant supplies of coal and riverfront location. The supply of coal and riverfront location eventually attracted large-scale steel manufacturing into McKeesport.

Starting in the late 1800s, Swedish immigrants with woodcrafting expertise and Italian laborers were drawn to Jamestown for employment opportunities in the emerging furniture and wood product manufacturing industries. By 1940, Jamestown was widely recognized as one of the most prosperous furniture and wood manufacturing cities in the nation. Total manufacturing employment in Jamestown peaked in the late 1940s and early 1950s as demand for products manufactured in Jamestown surged right after World War II. Beginning in the early 1950s, however, total and manufacturing employment in Jamestown declined steadily (see Table 3.11). Employment decline in Jamestown was precipitated by product maturation. Declines in furniture manufacturing were brought on primarily by competition from lower cost nonunion furniture manufacturers in the South (concentrated in North and South Carolina) and overseas. By the late 1970s, manufacturing employment in Jamestown appeared to stabilize (see Chapter 6 for further discussion).

McKeesport and the Monongahela (Mon) Valley lie 150 miles south of Jamestown. Located to the immediate southeast of Pittsburgh, the Mon Valley stretches for 140 miles along the banks of the Monongahela and Youghiogheny Rivers and Turtle Creek. Primary and fabricated metals manufacturers first located in the Valley during the last half of the nineteenth century to take advantage of the raw materials, including coal and coke, river and rail transportation, access to supply and end-use markets and labor supply. By the turn of the century, the Monongahela Valley was considered the steelmaking capital of the world.[11]

McKeesport is the largest and central city in the Mon Valley and the site of two large U.S. Steel mills producing metal tubes and pipes. McKeesport residents took pride in their city's leadership of the Valley. For example, the city was big enough to support both its own brewery (Tube City Beer) and the largest daily newspaper in the region outside of Pittsburgh (the McKeesport Daily News).[12]

Employment trends in McKeesport, in terms of both absolute size and changes over time, are quite similar to Jamestown's. Manufacturing employment in McKeesport surged in the early part of the twentieth century. Manufacturing employment in McKeesport grew from under 7,000 in the 1910s to a peak of over 12,000 in the 1950s.[13] McKeesport's employment, however, has been significantly more concentrated in a single industry than Jamestown's. In 1950, 42 percent of McKeesport's employment was in metals manufacturing, compared to 17 percent in furniture and wood products manufacturing in Jamestown.

In the mid-1950s, after the immediate post–World War II boom, total and metals manufacturing industry employment in McKeesport plummeted. Between 1954 and 1958, manufacturing employment in McKeesport declined by over 30 percent.[14] Except for a brief increase

TABLE 3.11
Jamestown Employment 1950 to 1980

	1950	1960	1970	1980	Percentage Changes 1950–1960	1960–1970	1970–1980	1950–1980
Total Employment	18,846	16,550	15,253	14,599	(12.2)	(7.8)	(4.3)	(22.5)
Manufacturing	9,051	7,446	6,047	4,824	(17.7)	(18.8)	(20.2)	(46.7)
Total NonDurable	1,833	1,211	519	558	(33.9)	(57.1)	7.5	(69.6)
Total Durable	7,218	6,235	5,528	4,284	(13.6)	(11.3)	(22.5)	(40.6)
Furniture & Wood	3,112	2,684	1,422	1,167	(13.8)	(47.0)	(17.9)	(62.5)
Metal Industries	2,619	1,641	1,599	1,014	(37.3)	(2.6)	(36.6)	(61.3)
Machinery	1,161	1,528	1,795	1,318	31.6	17.5	(26.6)	13.5
Trans., Com. & Util.	823	561	651	677	(31.8)	16.0	4.0	(17.7)
Wholesale & Retail	3,932	3,212	3,186	3,219	(18.3)	(0.8)	1.0	(18.1)
F.I.R.E.	531	691	808	666	30.1	16.9	(17.6)	25.4
Services	3,107	3,283	3,525	3,960	5.7	7.4	12.3	27.5

	Percentage Breakdown 1950	1960	1970	1980
Total Employment	100.0	100.0	100.0	100.0
Manufacturing	48.0	45.0	39.6	33.0
Total NonDurable	9.7	7.3	3.4	3.8
Total Durable	38.3	37.7	36.2	29.3
Furniture & Wood	16.5	16.2	9.3	8.0
Metal Industries	13.9	9.9	10.5	6.9
Machinery	6.2	9.2	11.8	9.0
Trans., Com. & Util.	4.4	3.4	4.3	4.6
Wholesale & Retail	20.9	19.4	20.9	22.0
F.I.R.E.	2.8	4.2	5.3	4.6
Services	16.5	19.8	23.1	27.1

Source: U.S. Census Bureau, Population and Housing.

in employment during the Vietnam War, McKeesport's employment has continued to decline. As depicted in Table 3.12, metals manufacturing employment in McKeesport had fallen to 2,500 by 1980. Even though more updated *U.S. Census of Manufacturing* data is unavailable, all recent indicators (as documented in Chapter 7) are that metals industry employment continued to decline in McKeesport through the 1980s.[15]

As in Lowell and New Bedford, changes in employment, particularly manufacturing employment, have been indicative of general

TABLE 3.12
McKeesport Employment 1950 to 1980

	1950	1960	1970	1980	Percentage Changes 1950–1960	1960–1970	1970–1980	1950–1980
Total Employment	19,543	15,538	13,309	10,892	(20.5)	(14.3)	(18.2)	(44.3)
Manufacturing	9,609	6,804	5,801	3,617	(29.2)	(14.7)	(37.6)	(62.4)
Total NonDurable	605	598	465	333	(1.2)	(22.2)	(28.4)	(45.0)
Total Durable	9,004	6,206	4,616	3,284	(31.1)	(25.6)	(28.9)	(63.5)
Furniture & Wood	15	86	77	47	473.3	(10.5)	(39.0)	213.3
Metal Industries	8,183	5,055	3,375	2,537	(38.2)	(33.2)	(24.8)	(69.0)
Machinery	452	589	518	372	30.3	(12.1)	(28.2)	(17.7)
Trans., Com. & Util.	1,269	789	682	732	(37.8)	(13.6)	7.3	(42.3)
Wholesale & Retail	4,195	3,049	2,881	2,539	(27.3)	(5.5)	(11.9)	(39.5)
F.I.R.E.	424	513	512	437	21.0	(0.2)	(14.6)	3.1
Services	2,488	2,594	3,038	2,815	4.3	17.1	(7.3)	13.1

	Percentage Breakdown 1950	1960	1970	1980
Total Employment	100.0	100.0	100.0	100.0
Manufacturing	49.2	43.8	43.6	33.2
Total NonDurable	3.1	3.8	3.5	3.1
Total Durable	46.1	39.9	34.7	30.2
Furniture & Wood	0.1	0.6	0.6	0.4
Metal Industries	41.9	32.5	25.4	23.3
Machinery	2.3	3.8	3.9	3.4
Trans., Com. & Util.	6.5	5.1	5.1	6.7
Wholesale & Retail	21.5	19.6	21.6	23.3
F.I.R.E.	2.2	3.3	3.8	4.0
Services	12.7	16.7	22.8	25.8

Source: U.S. Census Bureau, Population and Housing.

economic and social conditions in Jamestown and McKeesport. Population changed with employment in both cities. For seven consecutive decades, from 1880 to 1930, Jamestown's population grew with employment. In 1930, Jamestown's population peaked at 45,000. By 1980, Jamestown's population had declined to approximately 36,000, less than 80 percent of the 1930 peak. McKeesport's population, like Jamestown's, surged in the last part of the nineteenth century and the early twentieth century with the rapid growth of industry. Between 1870 and 1890, when the number of residents soared from

TABLE 3.13
Jamestown and McKeesport Profiles 1950 to 1980

| Jamestown | 1950 | 1960 | 1970 | 1980 | Index Relative to the United States | | | |
					1950	1960	1970	1980
Population	43,354	41,818	39,795	35,775				
Total Employment	18,846	16,550	15,253	14,599				
Percent Manufacturing	48.0%	45.0%	39.6%	33.2%	184.6	166.1	152.3	148.2
Unemployment Rate	5.2%	6.9%	4.5%	7.5%	106.1	135.3	102.3	115.4
Median Family Income	$3,463	$5,607	$8,624	$15,973	112.7	99.8	87.4	78.9
Percent H.S. Graduate	20.7%	22.9%	32.5%	37.3%	60.5	55.7	62.1	56.1
Percent Over 65	12.0%	14.5%	15.9%	18.0%	148.1	157.6	160.6	159.3

| McKeesport | 1950 | 1960 | 1970 | 1980 | Index Relative to the United States | | | |
					1950	1960	1970	1980
Population	51,502	45,489	37,977	31,012				
Total Employment	19,543	15,538	13,309	10,892				
Percent Manufacturing	49.2%	43.8%	43.6%	33.2%	189.2	161.6	167.7	148.2
Unemployment Rate	6.5%	9.2%	5.5%	12.0%	132.7	180.4	125.0	184.6
Median Family Income	$3,186	$5,309	$8,566	$17,129	103.7	94.5	86.8	81.5
Percent H.S. Graduate	20.4%	22.9%	31.0%	40.8%	59.6	55.7	59.3	61.4
Percent Over 65	8.4%	12.0%	14.5%	18.0%	103.7	130.4	146.5	159.3

Source: *U.S. Census Bureau, Population and Housing.*

2,500 to 20,751, McKeesport was reported to be the fastest growing city in the nation.[16] As in Jamestown, population decline in Mc-Keesport slightly preceded employment decline. After peaking in 1940, McKeesport's population declined by over 44 percent to 31,000 in 1980. The most dramatic population decline in McKeesport occurred between 1960 and 1980. Other measures of city vitality and development success declined in the two cities with decline in manufacturing employment (see Table 3.13). For example, median family income in McKeesport dropped from above the United States average in 1950 to approximately 20 percent below the United States average in 1980. In Jamestown, over the same period, median family income declined from 112 percent to 79 percent of the United States average.

Employment Composition and Trend Analysis

Jamestown and McKeesport have both experienced significant employment decline in the thirty-year post–World War II period. However, employment has declined twice as much in McKeesport as in Jamestown. From 1950 to 1980, McKeesport lost almost half of its employment, close to 9,000 jobs, while Jamestown lost 4,400 jobs, one-quarter of its employment base.

It appears that Jamestown's employment decline has been less dramatic than McKeesport's for a multitude of reasons, including greater diversification of industrial employment, employment concentration in industries at a more favorable stage in product life cycle, and its success (relative to McKeesport) in replacing job loss in its industry of historical concentration with other manufacturing jobs.

Economic Base

In 1950, both Jamestown and McKeesport had approximately twice the national concentration of employment in manufacturing, as indicated in Table 3.14. However, while Jamestown's employment was heavily concentrated in furniture, lumber and wood products (with a location quotient of 7.9), its employment was less concentrated in a single industry than McKeesport's (which had a location quotient in metal's manufacturing of 11.5 in 1950). Also unlike McKeesport, Jamestown in 1950 had significant employment concentrations in other manufacturing industries, including primary and fabricated metal products and nonelectrical machinery (with location quotients of 3.9 and 2.5 respectively).

As furniture and related manufacturing employment fell in Jamestown, from over 3,000 in 1950 to under 1,200 in 1980, Jamestown was able to retain employment in a growing manufacturing industrial sector—nonelectrical machinery and equipment. By 1980, Jamestown's location quotient in furniture, lumber and wood products had dropped to 6.7, but Jamestown was able to retain more than twice the national average share of employment in nonelectrical machinery and primary and fabricated metals.

McKeesport's second manufacturing sector of concentration in 1950 (after metals manufacturing) was electrical machinery and equipment, in which its concentration of employment was not much greater than the national average (as indicated by the location quo-

TABLE 3.14

Location Quotients Jamestown, McKeesport, and Pennsylvania

	1950			1980		
	J'town	McK	Penn.	J'town	McK	Penn.
Manufacturing	1.9	1.9	1.4	1.5	1.5	1.3
NonDurable	0.8	0.3	1.3	0.4	0.4	1.3
Durable	2.8	3.4	1.5	2.1	2.2	1.3
Furniture & Wood	7.9	0.1	0.5	6.7	0.3	0.8
Metals	3.9	11.5	2.6	2.5	8.3	2.3
Machinery	2.5	0.3	1.0	2.8	0.7	1.1
Wholesale & Retail Trade	1.1	1.1	0.9	1.1	1.1	1.0
Services	0.9	0.7	0.9	0.9	0.9	1.0

Source: U.S. Census Bureau, Population and Housing.

tient of 1.2). By 1980, of all manufacturing industry categories, only primary and fabricated metals had a location quotient above one. That finding suggests that McKeesport did not replace lost jobs from the steel industry with other manufacturing jobs. This reflects the failure of local factor prices—most notably wages—to adjust to changing conditions and diseconomies associated with steel manufacturing (see Chapter 7 for detailed discussion).[17] It appears that McKeesport's concentration in metals manufacturing adversely affected its ability to diversify its economy and left it extremely vulnerable to decline in the United States' steel industry.

Even within its industry of historical concentration, McKeesport has suffered relative to the nation. Metal industry employment has declined more rapidly in McKeesport than in the nation as a whole, as indicated by the decline in the location quotient. By 1980 the location quotient for the metals industry in McKeesport had fallen to 8.3.

Both Jamestown and McKeesport retained their employment concentration in manufacturing (with manufacturing location quotients of 1.5, indicating employment concentration in manufacturing 50 percent greater than the nation's) even though they entered the post–World War II period heavily concentrated in declining United States industries.[18] The reasons why they remained industrial cities, however, were quite different. It appears that Jamestown remained an industrial city by further diversifying its mix of industrial employment. In contrast, McKeesport retained its concentration in manu-

facturing employment with population and employment declines
that nearly kept pace with the dramatic decline in metals manufacturing employment.

Shift-Share Analysis

Comparing Tables 3.15 and 3.16 suggests that over the thirty-year
post–World War II period, Jamestown's economic performance was
superior to McKeesport's except in the period from 1960 to 1970.
Using Pennsylvania as the "reference state" for both cities over the
entire period (see discussion below), the differences between Mc-
Keesport's actual and expected employment was over 75 percent of
its base period (1950) employment, while the comparable figure in
Jamestown was 61 percent. If McKeesport's industries had grown at
their national rate with adjustment for regional differentials, total
employment would have increased by approximately 6,000 between
1950 and 1980 instead of declining by 9,000. If Jamestown's industries had grown at their national rate with adjustment for regional

TABLE 3.15
Jamestown Differential Shifts

	1950–1960	1960–1970	1970–1980	Total	Total Shift as Percent of 1950 Employment
Manufacturing	(2,244)	(1,624)	(725)	(4,593)	(51)
Total NonDurable	(853)	(325)	100	(1,078)	(59)
Total Durable	(1,067)	(3,796)	(931)	(5,793)	(80)
Furniture & Wood	(195)	(1,684)	(308)	(2,187)	(70)
Metal Industries	(1,140)	71	(386)	(1,455)	(56)
Machinery	63	43	(449)	(343)	(30)
Trans., Com. & Util.	(152)	7	(1)	(147)	(18)
Wholesale & Retail	(871)	(691)	(408)	(1,970)	(50)
F.I.R.E.	22	(94)	(420)	(492)	(93)
Services	(538)	(537)	(1,093)	(2,168)	(70)
Total	(3,437)	(5,452)	(2,672)	(11,560)	(61)

Source: U.S. Census Bureau, Population and Housing.

growth differentials, the city's employment would have increased by 11,600 instead of declining by over 4,000. McKeesport's loss of employment was concentrated in metals manufacturing. Its job loss was approximately 5,000 greater than it would have been if the city's employment in that sector had declined at the expected rate. The other significant sectors of underperformance were wholesale and retail trade and services. Jamestown's underperformance in manufacturing was concentrated in the furniture and metals industries, with employment declines that were approximately 2,200 and 1,500 greater than expected. Jamestown also suffered from poor performance in services and wholesale and retail trade. Its employment growth was significantly less than it would have been if those sectors had grown at their national rates with adjustment for regional growth differentials.

Of particular note is Jamestown's superior performance in the 1970s. The difference in differential shift between the two cities during the decade was 995, or approximately 8 percent of McKeesport's total employment in 1970. During the 1970s, Jamestown was significantly more successful in retaining industrial employment than McKeesport, as suggested by the total manufacturing employment dif-

TABLE 3.16
McKeesport Differential Shifts

	1950–1960	1960–1970	1970–1980	Total	Total Shift as Percent of 1950 Employment
Manufacturing	(3,483)	(1,209)	(1,706)	(6,398)	(67)
Total NonDurable	(83)	48	(78)	(113)	(19)
Total Durable	(2,903)	(4,664)	(1,070)	(8,637)	(96)
Furniture & Wood	72	(23)	(33)	17	111
Metal Industries	(3,633)	(1,330)	(418)	(5,382)	(66)
Machinery	19	(157)	(138)	(277)	(61)
Trans., Com. & Util.	(311)	(224)	21	(513)	(40)
Wholesale & Retail	(1,307)	(799)	(741)	(2,847)	(68)
F.I.R.E.	(21)	(157)	(251)	(430)	(101)
Services	(466)	(172)	(1,540)	(2,177)	(88)
Total	(5,084)	(5,957)	(3,677)	(14,718)	(75)

Source: U.S. Census Bureau, Population and Housing.

ferential shifts for 1970 to 1980: –725 in Jamestown compared to
–1,706 in McKeesport. Nondurable manufacturing employment from
1970 to 1980 actually grew faster in Jamestown than expected, as
indicated by the positive differential shift. McKeesport's economy,
unlike Jamestown's, continued in a tailspin from 1970 to 1980. All
employment sectors in McKeesport except that of transportation,
communications, and utilities experienced negative differential
shifts.

This suggests that the 1970s would be a particularly useful period
for comparative analysis of local development efforts in Jamestown
and McKeesport. In particular, local development initiatives in
Jamestown and McKeesport that might have contributed to or inhibited manufacturing employment retention and diversification will be
assessed.

In comparing Jamestown and McKeesport, Pennsylvania is used
as the reference state to calculate regional differentials. Although
Jamestown is in New York State, it is less than twenty miles from the
Pennsylvania border. In terms of historical development, Jamestown
is quite similar to McKeesport and other medium-sized industrial
cities in Pennsylvania (see discussion of Johnstown and Reading—
reference cities—in Chapter 1).[19] Pennsylvania (as did Massachusetts) suffered from the post–World War II shift of manufacturing
from the Northeast and Midwest to the South and West. Over the
thirty-year period, manufacturing as a share of total employment in
Pennsylvania declined from 36 percent to 29 percent (see Table 3.17).
While manufacturing employment in Pennsylvania remained flat,
the composition of manufacturing in Pennsylvania changed substantially. Manufacturing employment in Pennsylvania shifted from
metals and textile mill production to machinery and equipment manufacturing. Both Jamestown and McKeesport underperformed the
Pennsylvania economy. Most significantly, neither city was able to
retain manufacturing employment or increase service and wholesale
and retail trade employment, as did Pennsylvania.

Pennsylvania and New York do not collect comparable annual employment data for McKeesport and Jamestown, as Massachusetts
does for Lowell and New Bedford. Therefore, more recent (i.e.,
post–1980) annual employment data could not be used in the comparative analysis of economic development in Jamestown and Mc-
Keesport. However, the key purpose of the analysis in this chapter
is to identify time periods when differential growth between the
paired cities is not explained by standard theories—it is not to analyze the most recent development activities.

TABLE 3.17
Pennsylvania Employment 1950 to 1980

	1950	1960	1970	1980	Percentage Changes 1950-1960	1960-1970	1970-1980	1950-1980
Total Employment	3,930,655	4,127,208	4,536,903	4,961,501	5.0	9.9	9.4	26.2
Manufacturing	1,403,810	1,502,885	1,548,300	1,420,837	7.1	3.0	(8.2)	1.2
Total NonDurable	780,620	879,041	612,349	540,872	12.6	(30.3)	(11.7)	(30.7)
Total Durable	613,153	620,289	927,570	874,980	1.2	49.5	(5.7)	42.7
Furniture & Wood	41,287	38,190	44,196	45,848	(7.5)	15.7	3.7	11.0
Metal Industries	364,304	386,805	360,058	315,298	6.2	(6.9)	(12.4)	(13.5)
Machinery	203,374	256,562	294,231	289,713	26.2	14.7	(1.5)	42.5
Trans., Com. & Util.	334,868	290,157	333,210	347,197	(13.4)	14.8	4.2	3.7
Wholesale & Retail	681,657	707,896	854,462	972,676	3.8	20.7	13.8	42.7
F.I.R.E.	116,108	146,318	190,927	256,725	26.0	30.5	34.5	121.1
Services	623,444	766,661	948,590	1,359,848	23.0	23.7	43.4	118.1

	Percentage Breakdown 1950	1960	1970	1980
Total Employment	100.0	100.0	100.0	100.0
Manufacturing	35.7	36.4	34.1	28.6
Total NonDurable	19.9	21.3	13.5	10.9
Total Durable	15.6	15.0	20.4	17.6
Furniture & Wood	1.1	0.9	1.0	0.9
Metal Industries	9.3	9.4	7.9	6.4
Machinery	5.2	6.2	6.5	5.8
Trans., Com. & Util.	8.5	7.0	7.3	7.0
Wholesale & Retail	17.3	17.2	18.8	19.6
F.I.R.E.	3.0	3.5	4.2	5.2
Services	15.9	18.6	20.9	27.4

Source: *U.S. Census Bureau, Population and Housing.*

Summary

It appears that the differences in economic performance between Lowell and New Bedford and Jamestown and McKeesport cannot be fully explained by standard theories of economic growth and change. Lowell, compared to New Bedford, achieved significant growth in the late 1970s and early 1980s, even after considering industry mix, production costs, and other factors. Similarly, Jamestown, compared to McKeesport, experienced economic and industrial vitality in the 1970s that cannot be fully explained by regional economic change, industry mix, and factor costs. These findings suggest that the late 1970s and early 1980s in Lowell and New Bedford and the 1970s in Jamestown and McKeesport might be particularly useful time periods to look beyond shift-share and other traditional regional development factors and to focus on the potential role of local development initiatives in these cities.

Four

Lowell: Successful Revitalization

Introduction to City Development Analyses

Chapter 3 suggests that the explanation for the differential growth between Lowell and New Bedford and Jamestown and McKeesport cannot be made by industry mix and national and regional industry growth alone. Standard economic theories are weakest at explaining turning points and persistent intraregional differences in economic growth. They do not fully explain Lowell's dramatic growth in the late 1970s and early 1980s after 50 years of economic decline; Jamestown's economic recovery in the 1970s after its weak performance in the 1960s; and the growth differences between Lowell and New Bedford and Jamestown and McKeesport in the 1970s and 1980s.

Doeringer, Terkla and Topakian (DTT) offer an alternative explanation of local economic change. They suggest that corporate practices and strategies can contribute to local economic growth and decline.[1] DTT argue for the importance of not easily quantified (what they term invisible) factors that can favorably alter individual firm and, thus, city positioning in product, process, and factor price cycles. These factors include creating a cooperative labor and management environment for improved worker productivity, training for a flexible workforce, the development of entrepreneurial skills, the deployment of product niche strategies, and taking advantage of local agglomeration economies. In contrast to DTT's approach, much analysis of local development has tended to discount, or simply ignore, the role of individual managers, entrepreneurs, and corporations and has focused instead on more aggregated and easily quantified factors in local economic development, most notably factor costs and industry mix.

While DTT's notion of invisible factors is insightful, their analysis is limited. DTT do not explore "invisible" local development factors beyond individual corporate actions. The city development analyses, presented in Chapters 4 through 7, will expand on DTT's method and notion of invisible factors in local economic development to consider the influence of local leaders, city government, community groups, and collective efforts in local economic development. One of the key observations of the city development analyses is that local development efforts, while not easy to quantify, are often highly visible and can influence, either positively or negatively, local development.

The city analyses draw from individual case studies prepared by the Community Revitalization Project (CRP) at the Kennedy School of Government at Harvard University. The Community Revitalization Project was a research project at the University's Center for Business and Government from 1985 to 1989. Ross Gittell served as project director. Nancy Kelley was co-director of the project from June 1985 to June 1988. The project directors, center director Winthrop Knowlton, and research fellows Adam Blumenthal, Sung Bae Kim, Charles Ross, and Karl Schlacter all contributed to the case studies.

The city development analyses focus on organized local development efforts in sectors of the economy and points in time with significant unexplained (by traditional theories) differential growth between the two paired communities (Lowell-New Bedford; Jamestown-McKeesport), as identified in the economic base and shift-share analysis in Chapter 3. They begin with socioeconomic profiles, which include descriptions of the historical, sociological, cultural, institutional, and political context in which economic development takes place. The introductory context-setting sections also include, where relevant, a discussion of earlier development efforts that appear to have had a strong influence on the local development environment. The city development analyses document selected local development efforts and assess their direct and indirect effects. The analyses will consider the effect of local development initiatives on several factors: (1) the attitudes (psychology) and behavior of individuals and organizations in the city; (2) city institutional, political, social and intellectual capacity; (3) employment and economic opportunities in the city; (4) city positioning in product, process, and factor price cycles; and (5) city long-term economic potential. Comparative analysis within and at the conclusion of the individual city analyses will compare and contrast the economic development dynamics in the four cities.[2]

The primary purpose of the city analyses and the comparative study is to shed some light on issues related to the importance of local initiatives and to develop hypotheses on how local initiatives affect city economic development. The city development analyses, along with the comparative case study, will allow for more extensive and intensive assessment of local circumstances, the political environment, decision processes, and special program experiences and provide the kinds of insight necessary for a fuller explanation of what seem to be anomalies. The individual and comparative studies allow for consideration of the influence of factors that are not easily quantified and enable the analysis to extend beyond first-order economic effects of local development initiatives.

Lowell Development Analysis

Of the four study cities, Lowell experienced the most dramatic turnaround during the period of observation. Lowell has been frequently cited as the model city for economic revitalization in the Northeast.[3] Lowell went from having the highest unemployment rate of any city of its size in the nation in the late 1960s to having the lowest unemployment of any city in Massachusetts through most of the 1980s, including a period in which the state had the lowest unemployment rate of any industrialized state.

The development experience in Lowell during the mid-1970s through the 1980s indicates a common city interest in economic growth, as suggested by Peterson. Lowell, particularly when compared to New Bedford, seems to have undertaken collective development acts that have had positive economic effects. Local leadership was key to development efforts in the city, as was the use of the history of the city as an economic development asset. The key local initiatives appears to have been the creation of a pooled fund among local banks for financing development projects, the formation of public-private partnerships to guide and support development, and organized effort by a community-based group to insure that development efforts benefited low income and minority residents in the city.

Lowell offers unique insight into the influence of local development acts and of motivating, diagnostic, and organizing agents on local economic performance. As will be described in an update to the Lowell analysis in Chapter 8, there have been significant changes in Lowell's economic prospects since 1986, such as a declining regional economy, extensive problems at a major employer, Wang Laboratories, and fiscally strained city and state government. The update will allow further consideration of the hypotheses identified in this chapter and the other city analyses.

Introduction to Lowell

The city of Lowell, Massachusetts is located twenty-eight miles northwest of Boston and forty miles south of Concord, New Hampshire, right outside the Route 128 high technology corridor. In 1986, with a population of 92,880, Lowell was the 207th largest city in the nation and the sixth largest in Massachusetts.[4]

Lowell was the second planned industrial city in the United States after Paterson, New Jersey. Lowell was founded on the vision of Francis Cabot Lowell, and its growth and development in the nineteenth century were tied to the industrialization of textile manufacturing. Textile mills were located in Lowell starting in the 1820s. The attractions of Lowell included its supply of water from the Merrimack River and the power canal system, which together provided the energy source for power looms, and its available labor force.

The textile mills incorporated the latest technology and spurred Lowell's transition from an agricultural community to an industrial city. Lowell's population grew rapidly with the introduction of industry, increasing from 2,500 in 1820 to just under 95,000 in 1900. By the turn of the century, Lowell had developed an international reputation as a textile manufacturing center.

Although gathering employment data for the nineteenth century is difficult, production statistics indicate a substantial growth of jobs in Lowell during the nineteenth century. For example, between 1835 and 1888, the number of textile mills in Lowell rose from 22 to 175, and the output of cotton cloth rose from approximately 750,000 to almost 5 million yards per week.

The promise of employment and early industrial success attracted migrants to Lowell. Originally young, single women from nearby family farms comprised most of the industrial workforce. Later waves of immigrants entered the city. By 1920, Lowell's population peaked at approximately 112,000, 41 percent of whom were foreign born (including a large concentration of Irish and French Canadian immigrants).

Starting at the turn of the century, adverse positioning in product, process, and factor price cycles had a profound influence on Lowell's development. Technological change, competitive shifts in the textile industry, and labor unrest prompted many mill owners in Lowell to move their operations to the South, where production costs were significantly lower. As steam power and electricity replaced water power as the lowest cost industrial energy source, the attractiveness of locating industry in Lowell diminished. In addition, poor working conditions in the mills sparked labor strikes in Lowell, starting in 1912 with demands for higher wages and better working conditions.

Lowell entered a period of slow and painful economic decline that was reflected in declining manufacturing employment. Manufacturing employment in the city fell nearly in half between 1914 and 1937, from just under 30,000 to approximately 16,000. Unlike other industrial areas, Lowell did not experience growth after the Great Depres-

TABLE 4.1
Lowell Profile

| Lowell | 1950 | 1960 | 1970 | 1980 | Index Relative to the United States | | | |
					1950	1960	1970	1980
Population	97,249	92,107	94,239	92,418				
Total Employment	38,325	36,595	38,645	41,621				
Percent Manufacturing	46.5%	43.7%	39.0%	41.6%	178.8	161.3	150.0	185.7
Unemployment Rate	7.0%	5.2%	4.4%	4.8%	142.9	102.0	100.0	73.8
Median Family Income	$3,063	$5,679	$9,495	$17,942	99.7	101.0	96.2	85.3
Percent H.S. Graduate	29.9%	32.6%	45.0%	57.7%	85.4	79.3	86.0	86.8
Percent Over 65	10.5%	12.1%	12.1%	13.0%	129.6	131.5	122.2	115.0

Source: U.S. Census Bureau, Population and Housing.

sion of the 1930s. Between the Depression and World War II, manufacturing employment remained flat. While the textile industry in Lowell experienced a dramatic decline, it continued to be the largest industrial employer. In 1940, 26 percent of total employment in Lowell remained in textile and apparel manufacturing.

Lowell did experience an increase in employment during World War II, when manufacturing employment increased by 11 percent. However, after the War (as indicated in Tables 4.1 and 4.2), Lowell's socioeconomic conditions continued their long term decline.[5] By 1970, Lowell's concentration of employment in manufacturing had fallen below 40 percent, and textile and apparel employment plummeted from nearly 11,000 in 1950 to below 3,000 in 1970 (only 7 percent of total employment). In 1970 median family income fell 4 percent below the national average.

The decline in manufacturing in Lowell was interrupted by the Korean and Vietnam War years (1958 to 1968), when manufacturing employment increased by 14 percent.[6] The World War II and Korean and Vietnam War year increases, however, were just brief interludes in a long-term decline in Lowell that lasted until the mid-1970s. In 1972, manufacturing employment, according to the *Census of Manufacturing* fell below 15,000 for the first time in over a century. During the nearly fifty years of decline (approximately 1920 to 1970), Lowell's unemployment rate exceeded the U.S. average and population declined (with only a small increase during the baby boom of the late 1950s and 1960s) as native Lowellians sought opportunities elsewhere. Between its peak in 1920 and its trough in 1960, Lowell lost nearly one-fifth of its population.

TABLE 4.2
Lowell Employment 1950 to 1980

	1950	1960	1970	1980	Percentage Changes 1950–1960	1960–1970	1970–1980	1950–1980
Total Employment	38,325	36,595	38,645	41,621	(4.5)	5.6	7.7	8.6
Manufacturing	17,812	15,982	15,080	17,321	(10.3)	(5.6)	14.9	(2.8)
Total NonDurable	15,619	9,983	7,878	6,358	(36.1)	(21.1)	(19.3)	(59.3)
Textile & Apparel	10,929	4,365	2,751	2,284	(60.1)	(37.0)	(17.0)	(79.1)
Total Durable	2,115	5,999	7,202	10,963	183.6	20.1	52.2	418.3
Machinery	1,071	2,975	4,069	7,361	177.8	36.8	80.9	587.3
Trans., Com. & Util.	2,669	1,762	1,810	2,125	(34.0)	2.7	17.4	(20.4)
Wholesale & Retail	6,641	5,135	6,908	6,592	(22.7)	34.5	(4.6)	(0.7)
F.I.R.E.	827	1,098	1,059	1,216	32.8	(3.6)	14.8	47.0
Services	6,141	6,128	9,209	10,077	(0.2)	50.3	9.4	64.1
Agriculture	165	134	126	134	(18.8)	(6.0)	6.3	(18.8)

	Percentage Breakdown 1950	1960	1970	1980
Total Employment	100.0	100.0	100.0	100.0
Manufacturing	46.5	43.7	39.0	41.6
Total NonDurable	40.8	27.3	20.4	15.3
Textile & Apparel	28.5	11.9	7.1	5.5
Total Durable	5.5	16.4	18.6	26.3
Machinery	2.8	8.1	10.5	17.7
Trans., Com. & Util.	7.0	4.8	4.7	5.1
Wholesale & Retail	17.3	14.0	17.9	15.8
F.I.R.E.	2.2	3.0	2.7	2.9
Services	16.0	16.7	23.8	24.2
Agriculture	0.4	0.4	0.3	0.3

Source: U.S. Census Bureau, Population and Housing.

Development Environment

Lowell's depressed state from the turn of the century to the mid-1970s can only be partially characterized by economic statistics. The physical and psychological city were in a state of decay. Lowell's textile mills, once the pride of the city, were largely empty, and many considered the canal system, once the critical source of energy to power the textile mills, a liability that occupied valuable space that could be used in other ways. For example, Lowell native Paul Tsongas, speaking as a city councilman in 1972, recommended filling the canals and paving them over.[7] The downtown was also deteriorating, experiencing high vacancy rates and abandonment.

In the face of economic decline, Lowell's residents were acquiescent.[8] They were paralyzed by hopelessness and a preoccupation with the way things always were. In 1970, many middle-aged Lowellians had never seen Lowell in any condition except decline and had little reason to believe that things would or could possibly change in the future. Many workers in the city could not imagine an economic future without the textile mills providing a large portion of employment, even though textile manufacturing had declined by 1970 to 7 percent of total employment in the city.

The greatest indication of the depressed nature of the city was what the people thought about themselves. The continual feeling of defeat brought on by half a century of economic decline created a mindset that had become self-perpetuating. Paul Tsongas remembers that very few of his classmates who went to college returned to Lowell to live and work after completing their education. According to Tsongas (the individual frequently cited as most responsible for Lowell's revitalization), "It was difficult to be proud of your hometown if you came from Lowell."[9] Pat Mogan who served as Superintendent of the Lowell Schools in the 1960s, described the attitude of the people of Lowell in the following way: "Too many people inside Lowell viewed the city in a negative frame of reference. This attitude permeated the schools, hampered the learning process, and prevented people from seeing beyond their immediate situation."[10] Lowell's economy deteriorated while political and city leaders found themselves immobilized by a general loss of confidence and direction throughout the city. There were no plans for the city's future.

A negative image of Lowell was also held by people outside the city. The chief economist for the Bank of Boston, James Howell, said of Lowell in 1975: "Lowell has no future, government officials should stop wasting their time trying to save the city—it has no hope."[11]

By 1970, Lowell had suffered over fifty years of decline in its base industry without any new industry emerging as a viable replacement. During the late 1960s, machinery and equipment manufacturing overtook textiles and apparel as the largest industrial employer. However, in 1970, machinery and equipment still represented less than 11 percent of total employment in Lowell and only 4,069 jobs (see Table 4.2).

It was only in the mid-1970s that machinery and equipment manufacturing employment increased dramatically and spurred Lowell's economic revival. Much of the growth in machinery and equipment manufacturing employment and turnaround of the local economy can be attributed to Lowell's favorable location right outside the Route 128 high technology corridor. However, the shift-share analysis (in the previous chapter) suggested that some of Lowell's growth, particularly during the period from 1977 to 1986, may have been attributed to factors beyond industry mix and production costs.

Examination of selected local development efforts in Lowell will concentrate on those that appear to have had the strongest influence on city positioning in product, process, and factor price cycles and the local economy during the period from 1977 to 1986. Development efforts to be examined include local planning and political strategizing for a national historical park, the formation of two public-private partnerships to promote long-term economic development of the city (the Central City Committee and the Lowell Plan), the creation of a pooled capital fund (the Lowell Development Financial Corporation), and an organized effort by a community group (the Coalition for a Better Acre) representing the interests of low income and minority residents in the city. The intention in reviewing these efforts is to suggest how city-based development efforts in Lowell may have contributed to economic revitalization, unlike local efforts in New Bedford during the same period. The analysis will suggest hypotheses regarding the role of local initiatives in city economic development.

Plans for a Historic Park in Lowell

Despite the problems in the city and comments by Howell and others, some people in Lowell were determined to create a new future for Lowell. School Superintendent Mogan, in commenting about the late 1960s and early 1970s recalled that, "the pieces of success were lying around unassembled. We needed a strategy for the revitalization of the city and that strategy had to come from Lowell's heritage. Until a city has a past, it has no future. We were sowing our own seeds of destruction by denying our own background."[12]

Lowell's assets at the time included the city's industrial heritage and the human story about immigrants and labor embodied in that heritage. Mogan believed it was possible to look to the past for a vision that could be used to unify and energize the city. His idea was to create an historic park that would tell the story of Lowell's people and industry and, at the same time, provide a theme around which the city could build a new future.[13]

The Model Cities Program provided an opportunity for Lowellians to reconsider their past and future. Lowell was one of the first Model Cities selected in 1968. Unlike many other Model Cities, such as New Bedford (as described in Chapter 5), the citizens of Lowell used the Model Cities Program to their advantage.[14] It gave a reason for a group of local leaders to work together and identify a novel path for Lowell's revitalization. The Model Cities Program did not provide a short-term panacea for Lowell, as indicated by continued high rates of unemployment and the decline in base industry employment through the 1960s (see Tables 4.1 and 4.2). However, Model Cities (which was discontinued in 1974) left Lowell in better shape in two crucial areas: first, the city had developed a group of active local individuals who were optimistic about the city's future; and second, the genesis of a vision for the future on which redevelopment efforts could be focused had been developed in the concept of a national urban park.

Pat Mogan, as School Superintendent, first acted on his vision for the city in 1969, when he recruited students and academic researchers from Harvard and M.I.T. to visit Lowell and write their masters and doctoral theses on the city, using Model Cities Program funds. The students provided a data base on the city and documented the city's resources. The research highlighted Lowell's rich history, including the significance of the canal system, the historical value of the mill buildings, the strengths of the local labor force, and the cultural diversity of the population. Documenting the past gave Lowellians insights into the future. A key benefit of documenting the past was to increase awareness of why industry was first attracted to Lowell and what it would take in the future to attract new industry to the city, including an available labor force, sound infrastructure, and local leaders promoting the city. The research undertaken under the Model Cities Program helped the city awaken to itself. In Mogan's words, "A positive sense of the future was formulated in the Model Cities days when we in Lowell were overwhelmed with a sense of depression and negativism."[15]

While Lowellians became more optimistic about their future, Mogan realized that his idea for a national urban park in Lowell would require substantial political support to become a reality. Federal program administrators and the Congress would have to accept the idea. To make plans for a national park more concrete and, therefore, more attractive to federal program officials, Mogan again drew on the resources provided by the Model Cities Program. He commissioned an M.I.T. student to research the National Park Service, a separate agency of the Department of Interior, to identify its structure, priorities, and agenda. The student identified themes that different National Park Service departments looked for when evaluating projects and allocating resources. The student's work provided the foundation for an architect to draw up a plan for a historical park. The architect tailored the plan to the themes the study had identified. Mogan then sent nine plans to Washington emphasizing different themes, one for each department of the National Park Service.

After the plan was documented and tailored to the requirements and preferences of the National Park Service, the idea of an urban historical park was transformed from the dream of a visionary to a part of the city's economic development plan that could be used to get funding from the federal and state government. In 1972, the city council voted to make the park concept central to the city's development efforts and was supported by its local congressman.[16] In March 1972, U.S. Representative F. Bradford Morse (R-Lowell) submitted to Congress the first of a series of Lowell urban park bills. Paul Tsongas assumed a leadership position in the push to create a national park in Lowell in 1974, when he was elected to the House seat vacated by Morse (who had become United Nations Undersecretary General). Tsongas's role became critical, especially after 1976, when a Democratic administration occupied the White House.

In April 1977, with 40 co-sponsors, Tsongas formally introduced a bill to create a national park in Lowell. Tsongas, with the assistance of other members of the Massachusetts congressional delegation, was able to gather support from representatives throughout the Northeast and Midwest and from many freshman representatives elected in the post-Watergate elections who were sympathetic to Lowell's circumstances and liked the precedent established by using historical preservation as a vehicle for urban economic development. Despite opposition from conservatives and representatives from Western states, the bill for creation of a national park in Lowell (P.L. 95-290) passed in both the House of Representatives and the Senate in May 1978. It then went to the White House, where it was signed by President Carter in June 1978.

The bill authorized a total of $40 million for the Lowell Historic Park and a Lowell Historical Preservation District.[17] The purpose of the federal appropriation of funds was to "preserve and interpret the nationally significant historical and cultural sites, and districts in Lowell, Massachusetts, for the benefit and inspiration of present and future generations."[18] As justification for the federal involvement, the bill stated that "without federal assistance, the early buildings and other structures in Lowell would be lost."[19]

The national urban park in Lowell provided diverse benefits to the city. The direct benefits included over $40 million of federal investment in the city and new employment opportunities at the national park and in industries complementing the urban park—primarily service and entertainment industry–related employment associated with increased tourism. The less visible benefits, which were nonetheless significant, included changing the mindset of local citizens to being proud of their heritage and city, building confidence and experience among local development leaders, putting Lowell in a positive light to outsiders, and increasing connections and points of contact between Lowell and the federal government.

Planning and Organizing Development Activities

Simultaneous with new enthusiasm in Lowell over the prospects for a national park was the formation of local organizations to address broader development matters and coordinate efforts among an emerging group of local individuals dedicated to Lowell's revitalization. The first of these organizations was the Central City Committee (CCC), which was created in 1972. The Committee's mission was ambitious yet simply stated: "To create in Lowell a beneficial environment for the economic, cultural, intellectual and social development of all its citizens."[20]

The goals of the Committee included (1) reducing unemployment in the city by removing structural rigidities (such as transportation and lack of worker skills) and diversifying of the economy and (2) broadening the tax base in order to stabilize the tax rate (to compare favorably with other cities in the area) and both improve the quality and increase the quantity of municipal services.

The Central City Committee was an offshoot of the New England Regional Commission. The Commission was a federally funded program consisting of the governors of the six New England states (Connecticut, Massachusetts, New Hampshire, Maine, Rhode Island, and Vermont) and a federal co-chairman appointed by the president. The Commission was charged with the broad mission of addressing the economic growth of the New England Region. William (Bill) Lipchitz, a member of the Central City Committee who had been involved in Model Cities Program administration, described how the CCC came into existence:

> In 1972 the New England Regional Commission had a lot of unspent funds. The Boston Globe did a critical expose and the Commission decided they had to get some of their money spent. So they picked nine cities in New England, cities that were troubled economically. They gave

Jim Sullivan (the Lowell city manager at the time) $750,000 and he appointed a local group to decide how the money should be spent. The group came to be known as the Central City Committee.[21]

The initial Committee membership was composed of persons nominated by the city manager. The first Chairman of the Committee was Robert B. Kennedy, who was later elected mayor of the city (in 1986). The other CCC members included Pat Mogan, Frank Keefe (from the City Planning and Development Department), and Bill Lipchitz.[22] The first quarterly report of the Committee in October 1972 formalized the membership criteria by providing that seven members be from the business community, six members be from low income organizations, and three members be municipal officials. In addition, three others—the director of the industrial development section of the city's development authority, a representative from the North Middlesex Area Commission (a state economic development agency), and a resident of the Model Cities target neighborhood—were to be on the Committee.

Under Keefe's careful guidance, the Committee undertook specific projects. For example, to further its goal of reducing the city's tax rate, the CCC was instrumental in getting the city to foreclose on tax delinquent property. In the early 1970s, there were $2.6 million in delinquent property taxes that the city had not collected, and over 800 properties were listed as delinquent.[23] The Committee proposed a tax title program that effectively reduced the rate of delinquency by foreclosing on delinquent properties and either selling the property or using the power of eminent domain to retain the property for the city's use, depending upon the nature of the property and its market value.

The Committee's major contribution, however, was to give insightful direction to long-term development efforts. The Committee provided funds to establish a data base of employment trends and conduct surveys of the industrial firms in Lowell. One of the major premises that the two studies attempted to verify was the idea that industries located in the old textile mills were marginal industries that created only temporary, and thus unstable, jobs and did not contribute to the long-term health of the city's economy.[24] The studies showed this premise to be incorrect. The surveys identified that some start-up high technology companies were locating in the low cost mill space and that Lowell seemed to be benefiting from its location right outside the rapidly developing Route 128 corridor. The evidence indicated that the firms located in mill space in Lowell compared favorably with respect to their growth in employment with firms in other types of facilities and with national growth rates. Furthermore, the firms located in the mills appeared to pay high wages. Since there was an estimated two to four million square feet of mill space available in 1972, these conclusions were very significant.

Eventually, the conclusions of the studies sponsored by the CCC were combined in an economic development strategy (EDS), which was completed in January 1975. The EDS recommended that Lowell concentrate its development efforts in retaining and attracting new innovating industry with significant growth potential. In essence, the EDS proposed that Lowell could improve its positioning in product and process life cycles by taking advantage of its favorable positioning (relative to other cities in the Route 128 corridor) in the local factor price cycle. The EDS also recommended that the urban national park be the centerpiece of the city's economic development program.

Through the efforts of the CCC, Lowell's potential for growth, as represented by the type of firms locating in the once vacant mills, was identified and the urban park came to be viewed as a local economic development tool. The CCC was successful in moving the city forward on matters that would prove to be critical for future development, including planning and analysis, increasing the tax base, and improving infrastructure and municipal services. The Committee also created an institutional vehicle (which was later replicated) for private, public, and community leaders in Lowell to come together to consider the city's economic future.

The CCC acted outside of formal governmental channels and was subject to criticism. Indicative of Kantor's view of independent development agencies and counter to Peterson's view, not everyone in Lowell was comfortable with the CCC's having such a strong influence in development policy making. In 1975, the city council voted to remove the Committee as an official advisory body. This, along with the loss of funding from the demise of the federal New England Regional Commission, caused the Committee to cease to function in any meaningful and substantive way in 1975.[25] The CCC became a *pro forma* organization. As a last gasp of sorts, the Committee contributed $50,000 to the Lowell Development and Financial Corporation (LDFC) (see discussion below), thus buying itself a seat on the new financial organization.[25] Lipchitz, the director of the Committee in 1975, was chosen to represent the CCC on the LDFC board and was chosen clerk of the LDFC, a position he still held 11 years later in 1986.

In retrospect, the actions of the CCC were beneficial to the city's economy. It appears that the CCC's authority was removed because of its threat to the city council's authority, rather than because its actions were inappropriate or not in the city's interest (as defined by Peterson). In spite of its loss of authority, the Committee did establish the precedent for independent development organizations in Lowell and laid the foundation for the work of two public-private partnership organizations that played a large role in the city's revitalization, the LDFC and the Lowell Plan.

The Lowell Development and Financial Corporation

The LDFC was a product of Paul Tsongas's decision to use the perceived political clout of his office to pressure locally based financial institutions to increase their investment levels in the city. The LDFC was envisioned as a counter of sorts to a Republican party official's development proposal of bringing an oil refinery to Lowell. According to Tsongas (commenting in 1986), the oil refinery proposal "sounds crazy now, but at the time the attitude was: anything is better than we now have."[27]

Tsongas' strategy was to threaten local bankers into increasing their investment in the city. He publicly accused local bankers in the local paper, *The Lowell Sun*, of not investing in Lowell and thereby contributing to the city's economic decline. Tsongas then asked the head of the Union National Bank in Lowell (the largest local bank at the time) to organize a meeting of the presidents of the city's nine largest banks.[28] At the meeting with the bank presidents, Tsongas proposed that the banks each contribute .05 percent of their deposits to a pool of money to fund the city's redevelopment efforts. Some of the bankers at the meeting thought the idea was ridiculous, while others thought, "What have we got to lose? We own most of the property in the downtown anyway (because of the high rates of loan defaults at the time)." To get the banks' commitment, Tsongas finally used the threat that he was on the banking committee of the U.S. Congress and would not listen to the bankers' requests if they did not contribute to the pooled fund for local redevelopment. More important than Tsongas's threat, however, was the fact that many of the bankers felt there was little risk. The consensus among the bankers was that the pooled money would never be used, because there would be no development projects in the downtown forthcoming.

The organization established to administer the pooled fund was the LDFC. The stockholders of the LDFC consisted of the nine local financial institutions plus, as discussed previously, a representative from the CCC. The largest single initial contribution was $50,000.

The board of directors for the LDFC consisted of forty members, representing banks, businesses, and government. The city manager and the president of the Greater Lowell Chamber of Commerce were directors by bylaw. The remaining directors were elected by the shareholders. A seven member executive committee of the board met at least every other month to review specific loan proposals and implement the policy direction set by the board.

The LDFC was established with a limited charter that confined its activities exclusively to the rehabilitation and restoration of the central business district (CBD).[29] The state statute authorizing the LDFC specified that the organization was to give priority to the (so called) Middle Street rehabilitation project in Lowell's downtown, with an emphasis consistent with the historical theme of the urban national park.

The LDFC enhanced Lowell's deal-making capacity, both among private firms and with the federal and state government. A key component of the authorizing legislation was that the LDFC was allowed to use local, state, and federal public funds in carrying out its purpose. Section 8 of the enabling statute provided that "the city of Lowell may raise and appropriate, or may borrow in aid of the corporation, such sums as may be necessary to make a loan or grant to the corporation."[30] The only real limitation upon its authority to use public funds was a provision that the LDFC not apply for governmental funds in competition with any department, agency, or instrumentality of the city of Lowell "without the written consent of the city manager."[31]

The initial purpose of the LDFC was twofold: to provide a source of unconventional financing for risky ventures that could not obtain financing through normal market sources and to provide below market rate funding for conventional projects that could contribute to downtown revitalization. For the first nine months of the LDFC's existence, however, the bankers premonition was correct—there was no demand for the organization's money. The first business to apply, Barney's Deli, was also the first to receive an LDFC loan. The deli did not meet the location criteria and did not fit the purpose of what was supposed to be funded. Nevertheless, the LDFC executive committee approved the loan. They felt that it was a start and would "get the ball moving." That it did.

While the LDFC's contribution to Lowell's recovery cannot be quantified fully, its levels of investment are impressive, particularly after a long period when local loan commitments were not forthcoming. From 1975 to 1986—the period in which the analysis in Chapter 3 suggests Lowell has experienced the largest positive differential growth relative to the state and New Bedford—the LDFC made 88 loan commitments, for a total outlay of $5,950,276, or approximately $.5 million ($5.25 per capita) per year. The LDFC's loan commitments were followed by significant increases in private loan commitments by shareholders in the LDFC and by Boston banks, which increased activity in Lowell after 1977.

The decision by Wang Laboratories, Inc. (Wang), a major international manufacturer of minicomputers, to locate in Lowell and the decision by Hilton, Inc. to build a hotel in downtown Lowell further suggest how the LDFC contributed to increased employment opportunities in the city. The key incentive the city used to convince Wang to locate in Lowell was LDFC-coordinated financing. The LDFC was a conduit for a $5 million loan at 4 percent interest (40 percent of the prime rate at the time), with the loan money coming from a federal Urban Development Action Grant (UDAG).[32] Since the loan was subordinated to other financiers in the project, it helped Wang secure additional, more traditional, financing.

Much of the growth from 1980 to 1984 in high technology employment—which nearly doubled from 7,000 to 13,000 (see discussion in Chapter 3)—can be attributed to Wang's decision to locate in Lowell. Questions critical to enhancing our understanding of the influence of local development efforts arise with regard to Wang's decision to locate in Lowell: What was the role of subsidized financing in enticing Wang to move its corporate headquarters from a neighboring city (Tewksbury) into Lowell? Would Lowell have experienced such impressive growth without Wang locating in the city? Did the proposed use of the UDAG as a loan rather than a grant influence the securing of federal funding? These are difficult questions. In Chapter 3, it was suggested that Lowell was in a good position to grow because of its location, relative low costs and available labor supply. However, we can be reasonably sure that Lowell would not have experienced such large increases in employment in such a short time period without attracting a firm of Wang's size and growth rates. However, interviews with the former city manager, William Taupier, and city planning and development department staff suggest that the decision of Wang to locate in Lowell was not just a fortuitous event. They suggest instead that Lowell would have attracted another large high technology employer even if Wang had located elsewhere. In fact, when the city first applied for the UDAG, it was thought that another large mini-computer manufacturer, not Wang Laboratories, would be the recipient of federally subsidized loan monies. Furthermore, if the negotiations with Wang had not been successful, the city planning department had identified other high technology companies who were interested in locating in Lowell and in receiving financial subsidies similar to those offered Wang.

Insights into whether UDAG subsidized financing was necessary to attract Wang to Lowell may be derived from comments by one of the most influential persons in getting the UDAG and in persuading Wang to locate in Lowell, city manager William Taupier. As Taupier explained the circumstances, "Wang kept growing. For awhile they wanted to expand into Burlington, Massachusetts. . . . Wang didn't need the UDAG. They could have put the building somewhere else. But when Dr. Wang saw the numbers, with a low interest subordinated loan for $5 million, those numbers were very persuasive."[33]

Additional insights may be inferred from the UDAG program regulations, which required certification that "the project would not proceed but for the UDAG, and that the UDAG was the least amount necessary to make the project feasible."[34] Both the comments of the city manager and inference from the UDAG regulations suggest that, if Lowell had not come up with the subsidized loan, Wang might have located elsewhere in the Route 128 corridor.

The role of the proposal to use UDAG funds as a loan and the LDFC in securing UDAG funds is less clear. Given the multiple criteria for UDAGs and the politics of program awards, we can only speculate as to how the proposed innovative use of the UDAG influenced HUD's approval of the Wang UDAG. We can be more certain that, without the LDFC, the city would not have been positioned to propose using UDAG funds as a loan rather than a grant and would not have been able to recycle $5 million in federal grant money to future development projects in the city.

Until the Wang deal, UDAGs had only been used as outright grants to promote urban development. In 1978, city manager William Taupier came up with the idea of using a UDAG as a loan rather than a grant. The idea was unprecedented, but the city worked through Senator Tsongas and Congressman James Shannon (D-Lowell) to get the idea approved by HUD officials in the Carter administration. This allowed Lowell, in effect, to leverage federal grant funds by recycling Wang loan repayments through the LDFC. This outcome has had a significant, positive long-term influence on the city's development, as will be suggested in the Lowell update. The recycling of development funds has enabled the city to draw on funds from a more prosperous era when it experienced difficult economic times in the late 1980s and early 1990s.

Another example of the role of the LDFC in Lowell's revitalization is the financing of the Lowell Hilton. Promoted as "the cornerstone of downtown development in Lowell" by the city's development leaders, the Hilton deal transpired between 1984 and 1985 and involved the LDFC. The LDFC served as a conduit for a $2 million UDAG loan to hotel developers as part of a $4 million second mortgage, on the condition that, similar to the Wang UDAG, the loan repayment would be recycled through the LDFC for future development loans.[35]

As with the Wang UDAG, the downtown Hilton project was an example of the increasing political shrewdness and determination of the leaders in Lowell. Initially, the developers of the project wanted to locate the hotel on the outskirts of town, on the interstate highway bypass of the city. City manager Joe Tully, however, was determined that the hotel be located downtown. State Senator Paul Sheehy, a former city manager, described the way the city leaders approached the project:

> There were all kinds of reasons why the Hilton Hotel shouldn't go downtown. The city administration—in particular Tully and Campbell (the assistant city manager)—just adopted an attitude of it's going to go downtown and we'er [sic] going to make sure that it is downtown and whatever it takes to get it down there, that's what we're going to do. So they started working on it and every obstacle they encountered they just looked for a plan to attack it, whether it required state funding or federal funding or assistance with the property owners or whatever. Their minds were made up, and they were going to do it, and they did it. And it really was as simple as that.[36]

In city negotiations with the hotel developers, it was determined that the hotel would not be profitable in the downtown unless Wang put its planned new international training center in downtown Lowell, not in the neighboring city of Burlington, as had been proposed. City leaders went to Dr. An Wang, the founder, chief executive officer, and chairman of the board of Wang, and convinced him to locate the company's training center in the downtown and furthermore to inform the Hilton developers that Wang would not use the hotel unless it was located downtown.[37]

Along with the National Park, the Hilton helped transform Lowell into a tourist attraction. In 1987, over 800,000 visitors came to Lowell. This helped bolster service employment. As documented previously, service industry employment increased nearly 300 percent between 1977 and 1987 to over 5,300.[38]

The LDFC combined the advantages of a private and public capital fund, as demonstrated by the two examples above. Like a private capital fund, it could approve financing without the need for city council approval and it could adapt to private industry and developer requests as they evolved, while subjecting loans to measures of credit worthiness deemed appropriate by stockholders. However, like a public fund, some of its resources came from public sources, its appropriations were influenced by political actors, and it considered the broader citywide effects of the development efforts it funded (not just the expected value of individual loan requests).

The LDFC appeared to improve the city's positioning with regard to factor prices by reducing the capital costs and financial risk of firms locating in Lowell and increasing the supply of funds available to local firms. Without the LDFC, Lowell's development leaders would have been considerably less effective deal makers. They would not have had a local institution to provide "creative" financing for the Wang, Hilton, and other deals and would not have been able to react as expediently to developer requests and the priorities of federal program officials.

The LDFC appears to have been particularly effective in the initial "momentum-building" deals, which were undertaken when the city was still economically stagnant and conventional loans were not forthcoming. Two years after the LDFC was organized, a ten-year period began in which, as suggested in the analysis in Chapter 3, Lowell experienced significant growth. Without the LDFC in place, local banks would not have had a vehicle to spread and share (with each other and the public sector) the risks and benefits associated with the Wang and other momentum-building deals and might have still been reluctant to invest in the city (see Chapter 8 for further discussion).

Over time, the LDFC has expanded its role. It now also provides secondary financing and loans for industrial and commercial development, low interest loans to encourage building owners to renovate their properties in harmony with the national park theme, and loans for affordable housing (see discussion in Lowell update). The LDFC has increasingly worked with other local agencies and organizations, including the city planning department, the Lowell Plan, and community groups (including the Coalition for a Better Acre) on innovative financing packages.

The Lowell Plan

After the Center City Committee was disbanded, there was no local organization that took a long-term interest in the economic development of the city and considered the city's positioning in product, process and factor price cycles. To fill this gap, the Lowell Plan, a private nonprofit organization supported by private membership contributions, was organized in 1980. The Lowell Plan, as suggested by its name, has concentrated on long term planning issues in the city. The large majority of its membership are business leaders. The board of the Lowell Plan consists of thirteen officers of major businesses in Lowell (mostly chief executive officers), the mayor, the city manager, the director of the planning department, the executive director of the LDFC, and the president of the University of Lowell.[39] The Lowell Plan accepts no public funds. Though its public members appear at meetings, they do not have voting rights.

The Lowell Plan was the brainchild of Senator Paul Tsongas and City Manager Joseph Tully. Tsongas's continued involvement in Lowell's development as a U.S. Senator was quite unusual. His involvement with the Lowell Plan was a reaction to the city council's choice of city manager in 1980. As Tsongas describes its birth:

> The Lowell Plan came out of a conversation with Tully when he was still a state senator. There was a rumor that he had enough votes on the city council to become city manager, and all my reformer friends came to me and said this is terrible, you have to do something about this. So I looked into it, and found out he had seven votes, and I figured I had better sit down with him. So I came to him with this idea for the Lowell Plan, and he agreed with it.[40]

Tully's description of how the meeting with Tsongas came about is much the same:

> I had the votes and he (Tsongas) sat down with me and said, "Now I've got some ideas, Joe. I know you've done a lot for the city in the state senate, but, you know, our philosophies are different. Let's talk. I have some ideas about public and private sector being in partnership," and I (Tully) said, "So do I," and we scribbled them off.[41]

Tsongas and Tully were opposites in many respects.[42] Tsongas's career had largely involved public service. Joseph (Joe) Tully, was a businessman turned politician, who had been involved in private business for most of his professional career before serving as a state senator, moving up quickly to a leadership position in the state senate, and becoming the city manager of Lowell.

Given their differences, many people, including Tsongas himself, were surprised that the two were able to work together. On the other hand, Tsongas and Tully also had much in common. They both were committed to the city and they both viewed the exercise of political power the same way—they believed that political leadership involved the ability to get things done. In a statement as revealing of Tsongas's role in Lowell as it is of Tully's, Tsongas stated in 1986, "As far as I'm concerned, Joe Tully is the best city manager in the state. I would propose something, and it would get carried out."[43]

One of the Lowell Plan's first and most worthwhile actions was to hire the American Cities Corporation to do a detailed study of the city and make recommendations on how the city could encourage investment. The result was an ambitious plan that called for $106 million in downtown projects. By 1986, over 75 percent of the projects identified by the American Cities Corporation study had been completed or were in progress. The Lowell Hilton opened its doors in April 1985. The Lowell Memorial Auditorium was completely renovated. A deteriorated mill building was converted into the Wannalancit Office and Technology Center. Three new garages and several access roads were built. Over 80 percent of the buildings in downtown were rehabilitated. Downtown retailer Jordan Marsh signed a new lease and renovated its storefront. The Lowell Plan was not responsible for the completion or start of any of these projects; however, it was involved in some way in their development through planning, gap financing, or political suasion. The organization set the tone for what might best be described as a "can do" atmosphere in the city by insisting on actions and results with development projects.

The most distinctive feature of the Lowell Plan is that it uses private dollars for public purposes and thus can frequently, as described by city manager Joseph Tully, "take the city off the hook by doing a financial end run around the city's normal bureaucratic processes." The Lowell Plan, as a private organization, can act in a manner different from an agency of city government. Whereas many public agencies have an agenda tied to the timing of local elections and require public hearings before they can provide funding and perform certain acts, the Lowell Plan takes a long-term interest in the city and can act at the discretion of its executive director, who is hired by the board.

The Lowell Plan helps to coordinate development activities among private sector actors and between the private and public sectors. It appears to some degree to be the institutional vehicle in Lowell that operationalizes Peterson's notion of the common city interest and consensus-based effort in local development. The Lowell Plan's greatest influence has been in encouraging local business and government leaders to take a collective and more strategic view of development and, together with the LDFC and the city's planning department, in enhancing Lowell's deal-making capacity. This suggests some correlation between the Lowell Plan's contributions and Lowell's success in economic development.

Of note is the fact that the period of exceptional growth began before the Lowell Plan was organized. An alternative hypothesis—indicative of the critical urban theorists' view of business-led and elite-dominated local development efforts—is that the Lowell Plan was organized to ensure that Lowell's growth was concentrated in the downtown business district and benefited private business interests. However, the Lowell Plan (reflecting its concern for citywide development rather than just the promotion of business development and employment) began expanding its activities in the mid-1980s into new areas, including cultural development and education.[44] For example, in 1984, the organization, in conjunction with the city, funded a study on how to improve Lowell's public schools.[45]

Leadership-Driven Development

The Lowell Plan and the LDFC, together with the city's planning department, both play an important role in development activities in Lowell. The Lowell Plan has a longer term and more strategic focus than the other organizations, while the Lowell Development and Financial Corporation provides a valuable source of funds for development activities. The city planning department serves as a technical staff to the Lowell Plan, the LDFC, the city council, and the city manager on all publicly supported development projects in the city.

Lowell's planning department has grown with development activity in the city and more than doubled in size, from under twenty in the early 1970s to over forty in the late 1980s. It has the technical expertise, including architects, planners and financial analysts, to carry through projects and development deals initiated by development leaders in the city. The city planning department is responsible for completing development deals (e.g., packaging development incentives, including local public, private, nonprofit, federal, and state resources) to attract investment to the city. It appears to have contributed to an improvement in the city's positioning in the factor price cycle by effectively lowering the costs of "doing development" in Lowell.

Each of Lowell's development organizations (the LDFC, Lowell Plan, and planning department) has a specific purpose, but their leadership and activities often overlap. For instance, the LDFC and

Lowell Plan have, since 1986, shared executive directors who, prior to serving these organizations, had directed the city's planning department. The organizational overlap provides for coordination of activities and ensures communication, both formal and informal, between the different organizations and between the public and private sectors. It has also enabled a small core of local leaders, including Tsongas, City Manager Tully (and later, City Manager Jim Campbell, who succeeded Tully in 1987), the director of the city planning department, and the executive directors of the Lowell Plan and the LDFC to strongly influence local development.

In a sense, the role of Tsongas and the others in the small group leading the revitalization efforts can be compared to a wheel, with the hub of the wheel representing the leadership group, the spokes representing the three core local development organizations, and the rim of the wheel representing the rest of the community.[45] The wheel analogy also applies to the vision of economic revitalization that the leadership group had for the city. The central idea was that, if you could make the "core" vibrant, it would spill out into the rest of the city.[46]

The interdependence of the three development organizations has allowed for a great deal of continuity in actors and has provided for smooth transitions and coordination within and between local development institutions. In the city planning department, for example, the director from 1978 to 1983 was Jim Milinazzo, a former Tsongas staffer in Congress. In 1983, Milinazzo left the planning department to become executive director of the LDFC. Then in 1986, he also became executive director of the Lowell Plan. After Milinazzo's departure from the city's planning department, Peter Aucella took over as director. When Aucella moved on to become executive director of the Lowell Historical Preservation Commission, James Cook, who was an assistant to both Milinazzo and Aucella, took over the directorship of the planning office. When Milinazzo left the LDFC and Lowell Plan to become a vice president at the Lowell Institution for Savings, Cook replaced him and Cook's assistant, Robert Malavich, became director of planning.

Tsongas himself is candid about the centralized and close-knit nature of the leadership of Lowell's revitalization: "The vast majority of what has happened here has been top down. . . . Eliminate a dozen people and none of it would have happened."[48] It could be argued that Tsongas is too modest. The discussion here suggests that Lowell's revitalization would not have been nearly as dramatic if one individual, Tsongas, had not been involved. As Tsongas himself suggested, "The bottom line is, economic conditions have to be favorable, and if they are, who goes up and how high they go is a question of leadership and the organization of local development activities."[49]

The Two Faces of Lowell

Not all groups in the city agreed with the centralized concept of leadership or the idea of concentrating redevelopment efforts in the downtown business district. Though the downtown and the general economy had improved between 1977 and 1986, the benefits of Lowell's well publicized revitalization had not been distributed evenly.

According to a study done for Community Teamwork Inc., a locally based community organization, the rise in the cost of housing in Lowell greatly exceeded the percentage increase in income in the city for the years between 1975 and 1985. The percentage of the average medium income in Lowell needed for rental housing had risen from 22 percent in 1975 to 40 percent in 1985. The 1985 figure was substantially higher than the average for the state. For Hispanics (the largest minority group in the city), the rise was from 29 percent to 54 percent. After factoring in other necessary living expenses, many employed people were worse off in 1985 than they had been ten years earlier, before Lowell's heralded revitalization.[50]

Another group, the Northern Middlesex Area Commission, also studied housing affordability issues in Lowell in 1986 and reported findings similar to those of the Community Teamwork study. The Middlesex Commission found that, while the medium income level in Lowell was up 50 percent between 1980 and 1985, the average housing price and rental rates in the Lowell area were up 125 percent for the same period. Regarding homeownership, 65 percent of Lowell's families could not afford the average price of a house in 1980. In 1981, that percentage was 81 percent, which was again significantly above the state average. The Commission noted that most home-owning families were already established in the housing market prior to the dramatic increases in cost and, for those families, the rising cost of buying a home did not create a major problem. However, the figures presented significant problems for newly formed households, families displaced with new development, and new arrivals to Lowell (which were significant, given the substantial migration of Vietnamese and Cambodian immigrants into the community during the 1980s).[51]

One of the sections of Lowell bypassed by revitalization was the Acre Triangle (Acre) neighborhood. The Acre adjoins the downtown and contains a large percentage of Lowell's minority population (mostly Hispanic and increasingly Asian). In the early 1980s, the Acre was suffering from deteriorating housing conditions, high crime rates, and low levels of community services.

Many residents of the Acre and community activists saw Lowell's revitalization effort as an exclusionary effort that was improving the downtown business district while hiding the less attractive "underside" of the city.

Opposition to business- and government-led development, however, did not emerge until redevelopment plans directly threatened the Acre neighborhood. Those plans were to clear the Acre and encourage new development as part of a longer term strategy to attract additional investment into the downtown and immediately surrounding areas. A key leader in the neighborhood resistance to the plans "to clear the Acre" was Charlie Gargiulo, a white Lowell native who had spent time in the Army before graduating from the University of Lowell. According to Gargiulo, the reason the Acre was in such bad shape was that all the services and resources of the city were going into the CBD. Moreover, Gargiulo believed that the Acre neighborhood would be a prime area for up-scale development, since the urban park and the CBD were being revitalized and there was no other place to build housing. Gargiulo's concern was that the housing would not be the type that minorities and other low income people could afford and, as a result, they would be forced out of the city and the neighborhood that was their home.

One of the biggest problems in organizing community resistance to the "razing" plan was the lack of political awareness and sophistication on the part of the neighborhood residents. Thus, a first step was to raise the consciousness of the people in the neighborhood and of the people outside of Lowell to the problems and the need for action. The vision that Gargiulo had for a community effort included more than just stopping the plans for clearance; he also wanted to develop a community organization that had the ability to undertake development efforts on its own and to represent the interests of those not represented by the Lowell Plan, the LDFC, and the city manager.

Gargiulo started the Coalition for a Better Acre (CBA), which drew from existing, mostly religious and cultural, community organizations scattered throughout ethnic neighborhoods in Lowell. The initial organizers and board members of CBA included representatives from seven community organizations in Lowell, including Lowell Fair Share (an organization focused on housing issues), the Oblate Missionary Center, UNITAS, St. Jean Baptiste Church, the Lowell

Ethnic Covenant, the Puerto Rican Festival Committee, and the Spanish Church of the Nazarene.[52] Gargiulo, as president, and other people from Fair Share who had experience in community organizing in other cities formed the leadership core of the new organization.

One of the first actions the CBA took was arranging publicity "to illuminate the other side of Lowell's development story, to demonstrate that the Lowell Miracle was not quite what local politicians and business leaders were making it out to be."[53] The CBA was able to get an article in the *Phoenix*, a Boston weekly newspaper, and then some publicity in an article that *Newsweek* magazine did on the city. The greatest publicity triumph, however, was when "Good Morning America," the ABC morning show, did an interview with the city leaders, including city manager Tully. Gargiulo was able to get on the show to discuss the problems in the city. According to Gargiulo, "This drove the city politicians absolutely nuts."[54]

The CBA was also engaged in organizing large numbers of residents. Initially, the CBA had a difficult time arousing people's interest because the plans to clear the neighborhood had not been made public. However, the CBA's difficulty in arousing neighborhood-wide interest was changed when city manager Tully attacked Gargiulo for the organization's negative publicity and their attempts to stop the city's development plan for the Acre. The CBA was able to make the attack an issue and, according to Gargiulo, Tully was so angered that he admitted that a plan existed to raze the neighborhood, even though the city had still not officially announced its plans. As a result of Tully's leak, the CBA's success in organizing community residents began to change. In Gargiulo's words:

> The Acre needed to be changed, we knew the resources were there, but their (the core development groups in the city) plan wasn't something we could go along with. City manager Joe Tully jumped the gun with it (i.e., by going public with the announcement of the city's plan) before he had the resources. We (the CBA) went out with that headline about the city's plans and went to everybody's house and we organized people with Tully's admission. Then we were able to get 100 people out to meetings to discuss it. We started saying, if there's going to be a plan, it has to involve everyone and there can't be displacement.[55]

It was clear to Gargiulo that, if the CBA hoped to do more than stop the city's clearance plan, more than publicity and community outrage was required. The CBA would have to initiate development efforts in the Acre to benefit residents. To do that, outside financial assistance would be necessary, as would formal organization as a nonprofit development corporation. The CBA turned to the Aetna Insurance Company for financial assistance. Aetna had established the National Association of Community Organizations (NACO) to increase investment in lower income communities, as required by federal regulation.[56] Aetna originally was to be the financial supporter of the city's plans for the Acre. The city manager wanted the NACO representative in Lowell to be the Acre Model Neighborhood Organization (AMNO). However, the CBA opposed AMNO because, in Gargiulo's words, AMNO was a "a puppet organization." According to another CBA board member, Jerry Rubin, AMNO's plans for the neighborhood were to build middle income condos, not affordable housing for low income families.

Due to the persistence of Gargiulo, Rubin, and other CBA members, the CBA became the community organization in Lowell that Aetna choose as the local conduit for its investments. Gargiulo went to Washington to a National People's Action Conference and managed to speak with Gail Cincotta, who was on the board of NACO. Cincotta put Gargiulo in touch with Jerry Altman, a consultant to NACO, whom Gargiulo invited to Lowell to hear the CBA's story and redevelopment plans. When Altman visited Lowell, he was impressed by the CBA, suggested that they incorporate, and requested a proposal for a development project in the Acre that Aetna could fund. Within four weeks the CBA had incorporated, gotten 501(c)(3) nonprofit corporation status, and put out its first proposal for the Acre. Aetna made a three-part commitment to support the CBA. As Jerry Altman describes Aetna's commitment, "Aetna was willing to stand behind CBA. We knew they were controversial, we chose them on purpose, we thought they were truly representative of the neighborhood's interest and that they had a lot of potential."[57]

First, Aetna provided an upfront commitment of mortgage financing for group-sponsored housing projects, giving the CBA more leverage in dealing with foundations and banks to arrange additional financing. Second, Aetna provided technical assistance for developing and promoting projects. Third, Aetna provided $30,000 per year for two years for the CBA to hire staff people, with the hope that CBA would retain staffers for future projects when Aetna was no longer involved. The commitment from Aetna was crucial—it legitimated the CBA, put it in the leadership position concerning development efforts in the Acre, and enabled the organization to go to other private companies, as well as the state and federal government, for additional funding.[58]

Aetna's support helped the CBA undertake an affordable housing development project in 1985. The project developed a vacant lot and abandoned buildings and provided thirty-six home ownership opportunities for residents of the Acre. The total project cost was $1.5 million. Financing for the project came from a combination of sources, including Aetna, a UDAG grant, the City, the LDFC, and the Massachusetts Land Bank. The cost for a single family home was $63,000. Home-owner financing included first mortgage Aetna financing of $37,000 at 10.75 percent for thirty years, second mortgage UDAG financing for $11,500 at zero percent for ten years, city of Lowell financing of $8,200 at zero percent for ten years, and an LDFC grant for $2,500 for total financing of $59,200.[59] No repayment on the UDAG and city loans was required if the owner did not sell the home for ten years.

Conclusion

The CBA was able to use community organizing, the influence of publicity, and leverage from outsiders—including Aetna, the state and federal government, and private foundations—to become an important participant in local development and meet the needs of a segment of the population that had been neglected by revitalization efforts in Lowell. The efforts of the CBA and Gargiulo suggest the efficacy of well organized and strategic community-based development efforts, since the CBA successfully confronted established development leaders and institutions. The efforts of the CBA with the Acre homeownership project and later with the North Canal Apartments (see discussion in Lowell update) also demonstrate the importance of organization and leadership for successful community-based development. The revitalization story of Lowell illustrates that the trickle down aspects of development cannot be assumed; it often requires an engaged citizenry to ensure that the benefits from development are more evenly distributed.

The story of "the other side of Lowell" suggests a dynamic and interactive element to the politics of local development, which is often undervalued by critical urban theorists. The efforts of the CBA appear to have sensitized business and political leaders in Lowell to the problems of the working class and the poor. Tsongas, in 1986, admitted that the major weakness of Lowell's revitalization was its exclusion of working class and neighborhood interests. The LDFC's and city council's increased concern for the needs of the working and lower class is reflected in their contributions to the Acre homeowner project and the LDFC's establishment of an affordable housing fund in 1989. In addition, the increased political involvement by Lowell's lower income and minority residents and the increased responsiveness of the city council to neighborhood groups are reflected in the council's choice of a city manager to replace Tully in 1987. New City Manager Jim Campbell's prior experience had been working with neighborhood groups as the assistant city manager. Since becoming city manager, Campbell has continued to reach out to residents of the Acre and other working class neighborhoods in Lowell. As indicated in the discussion in the Lowell update, the interests of working and lower class residents in Lowell are no longer ignored, as community groups stay politically active and maintain links with private corporations, foundations, and state government.

Five _____

New Bedford: Extended Decline

IN CONTRAST TO LOWELL, New Bedford has been unable to generate economic revitalization. New Bedford has suffered from a poor image, a resistance among residents to concerted development activities, a focus on saving jobs in declining industries, and political division. There have been attempts at increasing employment and economic opportunities—most notably a concerted effort to prevent a plant closing and an economic task force formed by the mayor in 1986—but these have largely failed.

Introduction

The city of New Bedford is the fourth largest city in Massachusetts, with a population of 96,450 in 1986.[1] New Bedford is approximately eighty miles southeast of Lowell, sixty miles south of Boston, thirty miles east of Providence, Rhode Island, and a ferry ride to Cape Cod. It is served by two highways, I-195, which provides easy access to Rhode Island, Connecticut, and New York, and Route 140, which connects it to the Boston metropolitan area and northern New England. Since New Bedford lies on the coast aligning Buzzard's Bay, it is an attractive site for tourism and recreational activities.

New Bedford has a rich history, a history at least as significant as Lowell's. New Bedford, however, has not been able to exploit its history to the degree that Lowell has. The city first developed as a whaling center in the seventeenth century. It surpassed Nantucket, Massachusetts, as the country's leading whaling port in 1830. During its whaling era, New Bedford boasted of having the country's and, by some reports, the world's highest per capita income. Its whaling industry peaked in 1857, with a 329-ship fleet valued at over $12 million.

The first Portuguese came to New Bedford in the early 1800s, when captains from New Bedford sailed to Europe in search of crews. The city through the nineteenth and twentieth centuries continued to attract large numbers of Portuguese immigrants, as reflected in the 1980 census, in which over 60 percent of the city's residents indicated they were of Portuguese descent.[2] Portuguese were attracted to New Bedford because of employment opportunities (initially in whaling and fishing and, later, in textile and apparel manufacturing) and because of the city's seaside location.

The discovery of crude oil in Pennsylvania in 1849 undercut demand for high priced whale oil as both a fuel and a lubricant. The 1880s marked the end of whaling as the dominant industry in New Bedford and a transformation to textile and apparel manufacturing. Local whaling investors reacted to product maturation and the downturn in the industry by shifting their investment capital to textile manufacturing.

As a relative latecomer to the textile industry, New Bedford had several advantages.[3] The city was able to adopt newer and lower cost technology and transportation. The almost exclusive use of steam power, accompanied by superior water-to-rail links, made New Bedford's fuel and transportation costs significantly lower than those of Lowell and other New England cities. For example, New Bedford's cost per ton of coal at the turn of the century was $4.07, significantly below that of Lowell ($5.37) and Manchester, New Hampshire ($5.52). New Bedford in the late nineteenth century also had an abundant supply of labor because of the decline in the local whaling industry. Maybe the most important factor in New Bedford's success in textile manufacturing was its concentration in a growing segment in which it could compete effectively with emerging Southern manufacturers. New Bedford was concentrated in the fine textile, higher value-added segment of the market, which included finished and specialized textile products, where proximity to end-use markets in the Northeast was a critical advantage. This positioning allowed New Bedford to become the nation's leading textile manufacturing city in 1911.

While the cotton cloth producing cities in New England, including Lowell, faced severe competition from the lower cost Southern producers by the turn of the century, New Bedford was able to expand textile and apparel industry employment until the Great Depression. Southern textile manufacturers first concentrated in coarse textiles (e.g. cotton cloth), achieving clear dominance over Lowell and other New England producers at the turn of the century. Southern manufacturers later moved into "the medium market," dominating that segment of the market by 1914, and finally moved into "the fine market," in which it surpassed the North in the 1930s.

In the late 1920s, New Bedford manufacturers started to experience pressure from Southern competition and demanded a 10 percent reduction in wages from mill workers. The owners' demands were met with a violent six-month strike, which received publicity nationwide and closed most of the mills in New Bedford. The textile worker strike was followed by the Depression. The combined effect of Southern competition, striking workers, and the (Depression-induced) reduction in demand devastated the local textile industry. There was a dramatic, 60 percent decline in the number of wage earners in textile manufacturing between 1927 and 1932. Although the industry recovered some jobs after the Depression, New Bedford's economy never fully recovered. Disturbed by continued labor unrest, unionization, and negative publicity, many New Bedford investors redirected their investment capital to the South, where lower wage nonunion workers were employed in newer and more efficient manufacturing operations.

New Bedford's population and manufacturing employment have never risen back to their pre-depression levels. However, in contrast to Lowell, New Bedford's economy never collapsed or reached a condition which was perceived as a crisis. Compared to Lowell, New Bedford had favorable positioning in the local product life cycle after World War II (see Chapter 3). Nonetheless, since World War II, New Bedford has experienced extended decline.

After the Depression, between 1937 and 1947, manufacturing employment in New Bedford increased by 20 percent. During World War II, New Bedford benefited from increased demand for its industrial products, including military garments and parachutes. Unemployment levels in New Bedford during the first half of the twentieth century never reached the levels they reached in Lowell and, even when unemployment was high, most families were able to have at least one worker employed at any given point in time.[4]

In 1950 the New Bedford Industrial Development Commission (NBIDC) was organized as an agency of the city government. Its purpose, as its name suggests, was to promote industrial development in the city. The NBIDC promoted the attractions of locating in New Bedford, including transportation links to New York City (and other major markets in the Northeast), hard working and relatively low wage immigrant laborers, industrial space in a new industrial park, and special public financial assistance. The NBIDC was moderately successful in attracting apparel manufacturers, particularly garment and shirt manufacturers from New York City (as suggested by New Bedford's stronger retention of textile and apparel employment compared to Lowell and Massachusetts, which is discussed in Chapter 3).[5] The NBIDC was not successful, however, at increasing employment in other manufacturing industries and expanding overall employment.

TABLE 5.1
New Bedford Profile

| New Bedford | 1950 | 1960 | 1970 | 1980 | Index Relative to the United States | | | |
					1950	1960	1970	1980
Population	109,189	102,477	101,777	98,487				
Total Employment	46,416	41,771	41,090	40,440				
Percent Manufacturing	53.5%	51.7%	45.8%	45.2%	205.8	190.8	176.1	201.6
Unemployment Rate	8.6%	6.5%	5.4%	9.0%	175.5	127.5	122.7	138.9
Median Family Income	$2,947	$5,019	$8,230	$14,930	95.9	89.3	83.4	71.0
Percent H.S. Graduate	18.2%	23.4%	27.8%	38.0%	53.2	56.9	53.2	57.1
Percent Over 65	10.4%	13.6%	14.6%	16.1%	127.8	148.2	147.8	142.8

Source: U.S. Census Bureau, Population and Housing.

Aside from recruiting apparel manufacturers, the NBIDC also attempted to expand waterfront businesses and the fishing industry. The waterfront has always been an important part of New Bedford's culture and history. Starting with the whaling era and continuing with the immigration of large number of immigrants from Portugal, New Bedfordites have prided themselves on their "working waterfront." Residents have resisted efforts to establish other activities on the waterfront, including restaurants, hotels, and retail establishments. The whaling and fishing industries have always been perceived as playing an important role in the local economy. This appears to be a misperception. Even with all the emphasis in New Bedford on its working waterfront, local employment in fishing and fish processing has never exceeded 2,000.[6] The industry has never accounted for more than 15 percent of total employment in the city (even after combining direct and multiplier effects).

In spite of the NBIDC's efforts, New Bedford during the post–World War II period (1950 to 1980) experienced an extended period of stagnation. Total employment declined by 13 percent (see Table 5.1). Employment decline was concentrated in manufacturing, which declined at greater than twice the rate of total employment (see Table 5.2). The malaise in the New Bedford economy after World War II, however, was widespread. It affected not only base manufacturing employment but also secondary sectors of the economy (as highlighted in the shift-share analysis in Chapter 3). For example, employment in wholesale and retail trade, transportation,

TABLE 5.2
New Bedford Employment 1950 to 1980

	1950	1960	1970	1980	Percentage Changes 1950–1960	1960–1970	1970–1980	1950–1980
Total Employment	46,416	41,771	41,090	40,440	(10.0)	(1.6)	(1.6)	(12.9)
Manufacturing	24,810	21,605	18,816	18,264	(12.9)	(12.9)	(2.9)	(26.4)
Total NonDurable	18,030	14,432	12,296	11,401	(20.0)	(14.8)	(7.3)	(36.8)
Textile & Apparel	14,198	9,920	7,748	8,109	(30.1)	(21.9)	4.7	(42.9)
Total Durable	6,780	7,173	6,520	6,863	5.8	(9.1)	5.3	1.2
Machinery	4,317	4,582	2,956	2,803	6.1	(35.5)	(5.2)	(35.1)
Trans., Com. & Util.	2,169	1,839	1,961	1,708	(15.2)	6.6	(12.9)	(21.3)
Wholesale & Retail	7,896	6,103	7,471	6,579	(22.7)	22.4	(11.9)	(16.7)
F.I.R.E.	881	934	924	1,309	6.0	(1.1)	41.7	48.6
Services	5,945	5,679	7,035	8,186	(4.5)	23.9	16.4	37.7
Agriculture	1,085	724	667	968	(33.3)	(7.9)	45.1	(10.8)

Percentage Breakdown	1950	1960	1970	1980
Total Employment	100.0	100.0	100.0	100.0
Manufacturing	53.5	51.7	45.8	45.2
Total NonDurable	38.8	34.6	29.9	28.2
Textile & Apparel	30.6	23.7	18.9	20.1
Total Durable	14.6	17.2	15.9	17.0
Machinery	9.3	11.0	7.2	6.9
Trans., Com. & Util.	4.7	4.4	4.8	4.2
Wholesale & Retail	17.0	14.6	18.2	16.3
F.I.R.E.	1.9	2.2	2.2	3.2
Services	12.8	13.6	17.1	20.2
Agriculture	2.3	1.7	1.6	2.4

Source: U.S. Census Bureau, Population and Housing.

communications, and utilities declined by 17 and 21 percent respectively (see Table 5.2). Through the post–World War II period, unemployment rates in New Bedford were consistently above the national average and median family income continued to decline relative to the national average, falling to nearly 30 percent below the national level in 1980 (see Table 5.1). As manufacturing employment declined in New Bedford, it appeared that the young and the educated left the city to seek better opportunities elsewhere (as they had in Lowell prior to the late 1970s). The percentage of city residents with high school degrees remained at approximately one-half the national average through 1980 and the percent of the city's residents over sixty-five was approximately one-half as great as the U.S. average. In 1980 New Bedford's economy demonstrated few signs of recovery, and the city's working class and poor residents appeared to be worse off than they were prior to World War II.

Problems in the New Bedford economy have persisted through the 1980s. This is suggested by the shift-share analysis in Chapter 3 and by additional revealing statistics. Between 1982 and 1987, according to the *Census of Manufacturing* the city lost 4,000 (18 percent) of its manufacturing jobs. In 1986 unemployment in New Bedford stood at 7.1 percent—nearly twice the state level (3.8 percent) and significantly higher than Lowell's unemployment rate (4.9 percent). In 1985, per capita income in New Bedford was $8,156, just 65 percent of the state average and nearly 20 percent lower than Lowell's level.[7]

Development Environment

New Bedford political leaders, citizens, and industrialists have not pursued collective development activities. Organized citywide development activities have been perceived as unnecessary and even as a threat. This appears to emanate from the lack of any sense of economic crisis, negative prior experience with organized development activities (most notably Urban Renewal and Model Cities), local political conflicts that perpetuate neighborhood and ethnic group divisions, and short-sighted development policy making. This has make it difficult to act consensually on development matters in the city and suggests that Peterson's notion of city interest in growth policies (which seemed to be apparent in Lowell) requires forces beyond city economic interest. To better comprehend the lack of a political consensus on development matters and how it has been an impediment to city economic revitalization it will be instructive to review the city's development environment and political culture.

New Bedford's high concentration of immigrant and working class residents appears to have influenced the city's attitude and approach to development. Through prosperous and depressed periods, New Bedford has attracted immigrants, since immigrants tend to migrate to communities that have residents from similar backgrounds. The percent of New Bedford's population in 1950 that was foreign born was 22 percent—three times the United States average. Even without the pull of a healthy economy, the percentage of New Bedford citizens that were foreign born increased to 24 percent in 1980, while the percentage of foreign born citizens nationwide declined to 6 percent.[8] Today Portuguese and other immigrants work mostly in low-skilled and low-wage jobs in manufacturing industries, in apparel shops, and in the fishing industry.

New Bedford's working class and immigrant residents have concentrated their energies in their work and in neighborhood-based activities. Most New Bedfordites live in single ethnic group concentrations.[9] Like the residents of the Acre in Lowell prior to the efforts of the CBA, New Bedford residents have not been active in city politics and on citywide economic development issues. Their reluctance to become engaged in these activities can be attributed to numerous factors, including language barriers, focus on ethnic group and neighborhood issues, and low income and education levels.[10] However, a key factor appears to be citizen perception of organized citywide development activities as a threat to their neighborhoods. This perception emanates from prior experience. During the 1960s and 1970s funding from the federal Urban Renewal and Model Cities programs was used to demolish several neighborhoods and displaced many residents.

Over $80 million was spent on urban renewal in New Bedford and $12 million was spent in supplemental Model Cities grants over a twelve-year period from 1962 to 1974.[11] The socioeconomic and economic statistics presented in Tables 5.1 and 5.2 and the shift-share analysis in Chapter 3 suggest that the Urban Renewal and Model Cities programs in New Bedford did not turn around, or significantly dampen, longer term trends.[12] As documented previously, throughout the post–World War II period (1950 to 1980), employment, population, and median family income declined (relative to the U.S. average).

Herbert Gans' assessment of the federal Urban Renewal program seems to apply to the experience in New Bedford: "The public interest to be served by Urban Renewal turned out to be a handful of special interests, with the poor who lived in the central cities conspicuously left out."[13] As happened in many other cities undergoing urban renewal, New Bedford's working class and poor suffered the greatest displacement and were not the primary beneficiaries of urban renewal programs.[14] The major beneficiaries of urban renewal in New Bedford appeared to be real estate developers (many of whom came from New York City and Boston and were involved in urban renewal projects throughout the Northeast), the local fishing industry (which had its facilities rebuilt and, maybe even more significantly, had its dominance of waterfront activity preserved with

federal money), those placed in new subsidized senior citizen housing, businesses located in facilities subsidized with federal, money
and those employed by the New Bedford Redevelopment Authority
(which was created in 1962 to administer the city's urban renewal
program).[15]

In part to atone for the sins of the urban renewal program, New
Bedford was designated a "model city" in 1969.[16] By the end of 1970,
the Model Cities' target area in New Bedford included 18,000 residents (close to 20 percent of the total New Bedford population).[17] At
its peak, the Model Cities agency in New Bedford city government
had an annual budget of over $2 million and employed 175 full-time
and 115 part-time workers.[18] As with the urban renewal program,
the Model Cities program in New Bedford never lived up to its expectations. In contrast to what occurred in Lowell, few innovative
efforts were undertaken and citizen participation was minimal.
There were no new plans developed for the city, there was little increase in community participation in development activities, and
there were no organized city-based efforts that evolved out of Model
Cities activities.

In contrast to the citizens of Lowell, many New Bedford residents
believed the town would have been better off if it had never been
designated a Model City. Instead of engaging local citizens, encouraging commitment to future development activities, and making city
residents feel more optimistic about their future, the Model Cities
program created feelings of unfilled expectation, apathy, and frustration among New Bedfordites. Model Cities brought high expectations that went unfulfilled and created tensions between the two
neighborhoods competing for Model Cities funds. Most Model Cities
target area residents were resentful. They were frustrated by federal
program standards that did not address local needs, and they felt
that their fate was in the hands of a few top administrators (none of
whom lived in the target areas), who were not terribly innovative
and seemed more concerned about their own position than with the
residents in the target neighborhoods.

The experience with urban renewal and Model Cities appears to
have made New Bedford citizens distrustful of public officials and
private developers and weary of organized development efforts between the public and private sector. Local residents have remained
critical of both the urban renewal and Model Cities programs.[19] They
have complained about projects funded by the two federal programs
and how development monies have been used to displace vibrant
inner-city neighborhoods.

In addition to a negative attitude toward development among its citizens, New Bedford has had to confront a reputation as a backward and aging industrial city. Dating back to the textile worker strikes in the 1920s, a number of events in the city have received significant national attention and contributed to New Bedford's negative image. Recent events that have hurt the city's image include a prolonged and often violent strike by local fisherman in 1986, the threat by the city government in 1985 to take over a local manufacturing company (Morse Cutting Tool) by eminent domain to prevent a plant closing, a gang rape at a local bar (Big Dan's) in 1984 that was made into a motion picture in 1988 ("The Accused"), and sexual misconduct by Congressman Gerry Studds (D-New Bedford) in 1984.

Adding to New Bedford's image problems, *The Places Rated Almanac* in 1985 ranked the city 303rd out of 329 on its list of attractive cities to live. New Bedford ranked particularly low on employment opportunities, crime, education, transportation, and environment.[20] New Bedford residents, already vulnerable because of their immigrant status and low education levels, developed a defensive posture about their city and themselves as they became inundated by economic problems and negative press reports. Consistent with their defensive posture and in contrast to Lowell residents during the late 1970s, New Bedford residents appeared to feel threatened by change, rather than perceiving change as necessary for improving their condition.

Private and public sector officials in New Bedford have yet to demonstrate the type of leadership and commitment that appeared critical in inspiring citywide support for revitalization efforts in Lowell. It seems that many industrial employers in New Bedford fear that wage increases will follow increased economic activity and therefore resist development initiatives, particularly those that may attract a major new employer to the city.[21] Representative of a dominant philosophy in the city are the comments made by the former (1982–1985) mayor, Brian Lawler, who stated that "the best thing the city government can do for the local economy is get out of the way of business and let them do their thing."[22] (Interestingly, Lawler violated his own credo when he threatened to have the city take over Morse Cutting Tool.)

Part of the reluctance of mayors in New Bedford to play a more active role in economic development is related to the contentious political environment and history of conflict between the mayor's office and the city council. Unlike Lowell, New Bedford has a strong mayoral form of government. Accordingly, the mayor of New Bedford is more visible than in Lowell and is held directly accountable for development policies. In addition, because of two-year terms of office, mayors in New Bedford have faced special pressures. Of particular note, development initiatives that require several years to show results represent risky political undertakings. Even if willing to take risks, the mayor faces a city council in which councillors are elected by ward and are focused on constituent neighborhood concerns rather than city-wide development issues.

As suggested by the shift-share analysis in Chapter 3, it might be fruitful to focus on development efforts in New Bedford during the period from 1975 to 1986 and contrast New Bedford's experience with Lowell's, as documented in the previous chapter. Three distinct local development efforts in New Bedford are significant during this period: one is the historical restoration in the downtown led by WHALE, a private nonprofit organization, because it is a rare example of a positively received development effort in New Bedford; the other two are a local union organized effort to prevent a local plant (Morse Cutting Tool) from closing down and the formation of an economic development task force by Mayor John Bullard, because they are typical of the development problems that New Bedford has experienced during the past decade and one-half. These local efforts are presented in chronological order, starting with a brief description of the efforts of WHALE and concluding with Mayor Bullard's efforts. Again, the purpose of this analysis, as with the other city analyses, is to generate hypotheses regarding the attributes of successful and failed city economic development initiatives. Here the hypotheses will largely emanate from comparing and contrasting the locally based development activities in New Bedford with those undertaken in Lowell during the same time period.

Historical Preservation Efforts

In the late 1970s and early 1980s, an area in the downtown bordering the waterfront underwent extensive restoration. A three-pronged (federal, private, and nonprofit sector) effort coordinated by a local organization and led by a competent and energetic individual was a critical factor in New Bedford's success in historic preservation. Also contributing to New Bedford's success in historical preservation was the relatively small scale of preservation efforts, especially when compared to urban renewal and Model Cities projects, and its benign objective of preserving the past.

The Waterfront Historic Area League (WHALE) was created in 1962, the same year that the New Bedford Redevelopment Authority was organized and urban renewal efforts began in the city. WHALE was organized by a small group of New Bedford residents interested in preserving historical structures, many of which dated back to New Bedford's whaling era and which were being threatened by urban renewal.

The early days of WHALE were devoted to (1) getting an area in the downtown designated as a historical district; (2) generating public interest in historical preservation; (3) coordinating activities among local property owners and various local historical societies; (4) creating an inventory of the city's historical assets; and (5) securing financial commitment. In 1966 the city designated a nineteen-acre area as a historic district. However, it was not until 1974 and the availability of federal Community Development Block Grant funds that historical preservation projects of any significance were undertaken in the city.

John Bullard directed WHALE's operations from 1974 to 1985, the period in which historical preservation activity in the city peaked. Bullard had family roots in New Bedford going back to the whaling era. He first became interested in historical preservation in 1969 while completing a graduate degree in urban planning and architecture at M.I.T. Bullard's master's thesis outlined a plan for preserving New Bedford's historical district that was adopted by WHALE. This meant that when the federal government launched the Community Development Block Grant (CDBG) program in 1974, WHALE had a proposal in hand (Bullard's thesis) for using the block grant money. As one observer stated, "Bullard (and WHALE) was the only one in New Bedford with a real plan for using CDBG money at the time." Not surprisingly, when New Bedford was given $10.1 million in Community Development Block Grant money in 1975, $1.3 million was allocated to WHALE for historical preservation projects.

With the CDBG money, WHALE hired its first full-time staff, which, in addition to planning and executing projects, began to solicit money from the private sector. By the mid-1980s, WHALE had successfully completed the restoration of thirty-three buildings in the historic district. With the momentum from its initial success, WHALE added a historic theater to its original objectives.[23] Many New Bedfordites cite the restoration work of WHALE as the most positive development activity in the city in the past twenty-five years. Standing in sharp contrast to the efforts of WHALE are the other development efforts undertaken in the city.

Local Efforts to Save Morse Cutting Tool Company

Morse Cutting Tool, a machine tool manufacturer, survived in New Bedford for more than 120 years. Throughout its existence Morse has been a highly desirable place for New Bedfordites to work and a symbol of New Bedford's industrial heritage.

Development efforts in New Bedford from 1982 to 1985 were concentrated on preventing Morse Cutting Tool from closing.[24] While union, local, and state government officials concentrated their resources and collective energy on saving Morse, New Bedford's economy continued to decline. The purpose of this discussion is to highlight issues regarding efforts to save Morse Cutting Tool, suggest why these efforts failed, and question why local development efforts were focused on trying to prevent a single plant from closing.

Morse Cutting Tool was started in 1864 as a family firm. Its founder, Stephen Morse, invented the modern twist drill. The Morse Cutting Tool plant in New Bedford was the first plant of its kind in the nation, producing bits used in household drills as well as standard and special cutting tools used in the automobile, steel, and other heavy manufacturing industries. Morse's best years were during World War II and the immediate post–World War II period, when it employed 2,400 workers in New Bedford.

Wages and benefits at Morse—and in the machine tool industry in general—were higher than in most other New Bedford industries. For example, in 1982, a typical Morse worker earned $8.00 an hour, while average wages at a textile mill were approximately $5.00 an hour. Workers were first unionized at Morse in 1940. Local 277 of the United Electrical, Radio, and Machine Workers of America represented Morse workers and had a reputation for settling its differences with management away from the picket line. Prior to 1982 there had been only one strike at Morse in over forty years.

In 1965 Gulf and Western (G&W), a large conglomerate headquartered in New York City, bought Morse Cutting Tools. G&W's purchase of Morse was part of a corporate diversification and expansion strategy. G&W wanted to position itself to take advantage of the anticipated increased demand for industrial goods in the late 1960s. The Morse buyout was also part of a trend in the machine tool industry. Until the late 1960s, firms in the machine tool industry were mostly separate enterprises; however, between 1965 and 1970, most were acquired by conglomerates. Much to G&W's disappointment, the Vietnam War years of increasing industrial product demand proved to be just a temporary uptick in a longer downward trend in the United States machine tool industry. Increased competition, along with the introduction of new materials and technologies, reduced demand for Morse's major products and resulted in declining profits.

As pressure on profits increased at Morse, so did management demands and threats to workers. G&W's corporate strategy was to relocate production to areas with lower cost labor and more efficient production. In January 1982, G&W approached the local (277) union with a demand that the workers meet four key productivity conditions in order to prevent transfer of machines and jobs to G&W's (Super Tool) plant in Michigan. Negotiations and counterproposals by the union failed to change the company's mind about moving the machines. In the end, the union agreed to the productivity changes, only to see management renege on its earlier pledge. Subsequently six machines were sent to Super Tool over the objections of local 277.

In March of 1982, G&W submitted new demands to the union and this time threatened to close all operations if demands were not met.[25] That was a significant threat. New Bedfordites could not easily accept the plant closing and the loss of approximately 500 jobs.[26] To many residents, Morse was one of the few remaining symbols of New Bedford's industrial past—a tradition that had been slowly deteriorating but one which residents wanted to preserve.

Local 277, frustrated in its negotiations with management, sought to generate citywide support for their cause. The union felt that this would improve their bargaining position in ongoing negotiations with G&W. The union decided to bring the issue of the potential plant closing and its problems with G&W before as large a city audience as possible and hosted a luncheon and press conference to present a study by the Industrial Cooperative Association (ICA).[27] The study reported that "G&W's strategy was to milk profits before closing the Morse plant in New Bedford." Over one hundred political and labor officials in the city attended the meeting. As a result of the press conference, a local citizen's committee to support Morse workers was formed. Membership on the committee included representatives from thirty-five unions in the city (including the Clothing and Textile Workers Union, the Bricklayers Unions, the International Brotherhood of Electrical Workers, the Fishlumpers Union, the International Women's Garment Workers Union, and the International Autoworkers Union), political leaders (including Congressman Studds, State Rep. MacLean and Mayor Brian Lawler), community groups, clergy, and small businessmen.

The city council got involved when local 277 went on strike and brought 150 of its members to the council chambers. The union suc-

cessfully lobbied the council for passage of a council resolution indicating a concern over the impact of disinvestment at Morse on the
New Bedford economy and calling on G&W to "state their plans for
future investment to make Morse competitive and keep it a viable
operation, and to assure jobs for our city." The council also made
arrangements for industrial revenue bond (IRB) financing to help
G&W modernize the Morse operation and requested a meeting with
G&W corporate management, the mayor, and union leaders. G&W
management rejected the council's offer of IRB financing and its request for a meeting, stating that "labor costs and productivity were
the important issues not plant modernization."

Despite rejecting the city council's proposals, G&W seemed to be
influenced by the council's actions. The company cancelled all wage
cuts initially proposed and pledged investment in modern equipment. The union agreed to the new proposal and ended its strike.
The resolution of the strike, however, did not end the problems at
Morse. Only 200 of 500 workers were called back to work after the
strike ended; others were placed on layoff subject to recall. Management made no further promises to keep Morse open or to "retool"
the plant.

One year after the strike, G&W announced its plans to divest itself
of all its manufacturing operations, including the Morse plant in
New Bedford. G&W Vice President Neil Feola promised local 277
that Morse would remain open and a buyer would be found who
would continue to operate the plant in New Bedford. After the union
went public with G&W's plans and its promise to the union, the
Massachusetts Executive Office of Labor and the New Bedford city
council pledged to provide assistance in finding and financing a
buyer.

Since G&W did not take the city or state up on their offers, saving
the New Bedford plant again became problematic. The process of
finding a buyer was conducted behind closed doors at G&W corporate headquarters. In October 1983, G&W disclosed the name of a
buyer, Carlisle Capital Corporation, and assured the union that Carlisle had agreed to abide by the terms of the union contract. Carlisle
Capital turned out to be a group of managers at G&W that were interested in a leveraged buyout of Morse. The proposed buyout included the provision that a significant majority of the funds to purchase the plant would be loaned by G&W and secured by the assets
of the plant.

The Carlisle Capital investors also wanted, as one of the conditions of the buyout, the right to change the labor contract negotiated
the previous year. Local 277 rejected concessions and Carlisle shortly

thereafter withdrew its offer to purchase Morse. Union leaders felt that if G&W had used state assistance they could have found a buyer who would not have immediately asked for wage concessions. The union was also concerned that, in a leveraged buyout, the new owner would not have any operating capital to invest in the new equipment and plant improvements needed to keep Morse competitive.

In the spring of 1984, the battle between the union and G&W corporate management intensified, with neither side willing to make concessions. G&W stymied state efforts to assist in locating a buyer and refused to disclose any information about sales negotiations, while continuing to be frustrated by the local union's refusals to grant concessions to its favored buyers. Frustration spurred G&W to issue an ultimatum to the union. In April 1984, Feola arrived in New Bedford and announced that G&W was determined to sever its ties with Morse at the end of the fiscal year and that, if the union continued to refuse concessions, G&W would consider selling to a buyer whose intent was to use Morse's name but liquidate the New Bedford facility.

G&W's threat to sell to a buyer who would close the New Bedford plant brought the coalition formed after the April 1982 luncheon back into action. Local 277 leaders also went directly to Mayor Brian Lawler for help. Lawler announced that the city intended to intensify its efforts to find a suitable buyer for Morse, a buyer who would keep it as an ongoing operation in New Bedford. The mayor threatened that, if a suitable buyer was found and was rejected by G&W, the city would seize the plant through rights of eminent domain.

The threat of a takeover by eminent domain, together with the coalition working to keep the Morse plant open, helped break the stalemate. It caused G&W to back off its end-of-fiscal-year liquidation deadline. It also brought new interest in the plant from buyers around the country who had become aware of the Morse situation through the national publicity given to the city's eminent domain threat.[28]

James Lambert, an industrialist from Troy, Michigan, felt that he could turn Morse around. His reasoning was that "conglomerates often do not understand how to run smaller, specialized companies, particularly old manufacturing companies. What is required is specialized knowledge about an industry and shop floor engineering; not just expertise in financial deal-making."[29] The union supported Lambert's purchase of Morse because of his good intentions, even though his $12 million purchase was highly leveraged.

After Lambert's purchase had been finalized in August 1984, politicians and union leaders wasted little time in taking credit for "saving Morse and saving the New Bedford economy." Mayor Lawler, anticipating a difficult re-election campaign in 1985, took credit for "getting tough with G&W and helping local workers win their fight." Governor Dukakis, who was up for re-election himself in 1986 and harbored higher political ambitions, described the fight at Morse as "another Massachusetts success story and part of an economic policy by his administration in which older industries are accorded as much attention as emerging, technology-based industries."[30] Labor leaders throughout the country pointed to Morse as an example of how concerted action by local unions could effectively prevent plant closings.

Despite new ownership and all the accolades, Morse continued to experience major difficulties. Lambert stated that he expected to break even in the Morse plant by 1987, but his expectations were never met. During the first fiscal year under Lambert, Morse lost $980,000.[31] In January 1986, twenty-two top and middle management executives were laid off. This triggered rumors that further layoffs were imminent. The union and the company flatly denied those rumors. Less then four months later, 275 of approximately 450 workers were laid off without pay. Just one day after the announcement of the layoffs, State Senator MacLean and other members of the city's legislative delegation lobbied to get Morse gap financing, including a $1.5 million state loan to help Morse continue operations. This money eventually came from the state's Economic Stabilization Trust, which was set-up "to aid viable companies in mature industries through difficult short-term adjustment periods." Of significant note, Lambert's initial loan request to the state was rejected, reportedly because the Industrial Services Program board (which oversees the Economic Stabilization Trust) feared the loan was too risky. Then, according to United Electrical Workers Union official Ronald Carver, he (Carver) went over the heads of the mid-level bureaucrats who had turned down the loan and asked for help from John Sasso, Dukakis's chief of staff, to get the loan to Lambert approved.[32]

In addition to getting gap financing from the state, both labor and management made concessions to help continue operations at Morse. Labor concessions included a cancelation of a scheduled 3 percent pay increase and a six-month moratorium on paid vacations. In return for these concessions, a plan was set up to qualify employees for stock ownership and profit sharing. Management, including Lambert, agreed to take pay cuts. The company and union also mutually agreed on productivity changes and cost saving measures. Productivity changes, combined with the other concessions, saved the company $1.3 million. In spite of the productivity improvements and labor concessions, Morse shut down the plant in January 1987 and filed for bankruptcy.

The efforts to save Morse Cutting Tool raise many questions concerning why local development efforts were concentrated on saving a plant that accounted for less than 2 percent of total city employment and had poor future prospects. The emotional attachment to Morse seemed to far exceed its economic value. The dramatization of events at Morse and exaggeration of the potential impact of the plant closing appeared to undermine other revitalization efforts and to reinforce adversarial relations between labor and management and business and government in the city.

State and local development resources might have been better deployed, attracting new industry with better growth potential into the city, providing support to businesses in New Bedford with brighter prospects, or encouraging other development activities in New Bedford, such as WHALE. Concerted action to saving jobs at Morse appeared to reinforce unrealistic expectations and perceptions that fundamental changes in the local economy were unnecessary.

With local development efforts focused on Morse during the period from 1982 to 1985, New Bedford's positioning in product and process life cycles continued to deteriorate, and the local economy continued to decline (as documented in the shift-share analysis in Chapter 3 and in the introduction to this chapter).

Economic Development Task Force

The mayoral election in November 1985 resulted in the defeat of the incumbent Brian Lawler by John Bullard. Bullard prevailed in a close election (16,337 to 15,377) without the support of the city's labor leaders, who had supported Lawler after his actions with Morse. When Bullard took office in January 1986, he organized several task forces.[33] The task force with the greatest visibility was focused on economic development.[34] The economic development task force was dominated by representatives from the private sector. Many members of the task force were from the Chamber of Commerce board, which comprised the city's business elite. Notably absent from the task force were representatives from organized labor or from women's or minority groups.

The specific purpose of the task force, as defined by Mayor Bullard, was to determine how New Bedford could better organize and coordinate its development activities and how any new organizational structure should relate to the existing public and private groups already involved in development. The mayor defined the ultimate purpose of the task force (and other local efforts in economic development) as the creation of jobs for city residents.

Most of the task force members selected by the mayor knew each other quite well. Many had served on other development bodies together, including the New Bedford Economic Development Corporation (EDC) and the Chamber of Commerce.[35] The economic task force, however, did not include representatives from all the agencies working on economic development in the city. For instance, in the summer of 1986, the city planner indicated that he had heard about the task force, but he was not on it and had not even been asked about it.

The economic development task force held its first meeting in April 1986. At the first meeting, the mayor put up a list of fourteen agencies that were involved in economic development in New Bedford. Other task force members then added seventeen more groups to the list. Ten of the agencies listed were local agencies which the mayor had some control over; the other twenty-one were organized efforts that the mayor did not control. The task force was surprised at what the mayor referred to as the "alphabet soup" problems of the city's development efforts. Bullard stated that he believed the city had all the tools necessary for development already in place. The problem lies, he said, "in how the city organizes and uses these tools."

The mayor's plan for the economic development task force was to divide it into five working subcommittees. Two of the subcommittees would deal with alternative approaches to structure: public and public-and-private partnership approaches. The remaining three subcommittees would focus on three need areas identified by the mayor, including organization, image, and priorities.

After six months of task force meetings and input from the five subcommittees, the mayor went public with his plan for reorganization of economic development activities in New Bedford. The mayor's plan incorporated many of the recommendations put forward by Jim Mathes from the New Bedford Chamber of Commerce and the partnership subcommittee. It called for an economic development partnership between the mayor and the Chamber. This would involve the creation of a new position in city government for an economic development assistant to the mayor and the hiring of an economic development vice president at the chamber. The economic development assistant to the mayor and the economic development vice president of the Chamber of Commerce would coordinate the city's economic development.

The mayor noted that it would be critical to keep the partnership balanced over time. However, no suggestions on how to maintain a balance between private and public sector interests were forthcoming from the mayor or task force members. Another problem—as revealed in the minutes and reports of the priorities and public sector subcommittees—was that the recommendations of the task force and the priorities and actions of the city council were likely to conflict.

It was unrealistic for the task force members to believe that the proposed economic development partnership could circumvent the city council. The city council had to approve any publicly supported development project. The task force members continually raised the issue of the potential conflicts between the development partnership and the city council; however, their recommendations did not offer any strategy to deal with the potential problems.

Efforts by the economic development task force (pushed by an aggressive executive director at the Chamber of Commerce and adopted by an ambitious mayor) appeared to pose a threat to the city council and to neighborhood groups with vivid memories of previous development efforts in the city that had been insensitive and overly ambitious. Instead of pulling the community together, efforts by the economic development task force appeared to be pushing it further apart. Neighborhood groups and city council members felt left out. They did not participate in the task force, were not informed of the discussions that transpired, and were given no clear role in the proposed economic development partnership. The organization of development activities in New Bedford in the 1980s is reflective of Kantor's view of development decision making. Decision making authority was removed from representative bodies and dominated by local business interests.

It is difficult to come to any definitive conclusions about the effectiveness of the economic development task force. However, there are several indications that it did not accomplish its objectives. Although Mayor Bullard continued working to bring the city together to revitalize New Bedford, the economy continued to stagnate.[36]

The task force appeared to be poorly conceived and directed. Bullard seemed to have been overly optimistic and attempted too much too fast. The mayor and private sector leaders were not sympathetic enough to New Bedford residents' apprehension of development efforts organized by the city and dominated by the private sector. Before forming the task force, the mayor might have reduced citizen concerns by holding public meetings in neighborhoods, engaging city residents in the process, and getting more input about development priorities and concerns. In addition, membership on the task force appeared to be too exclusive; more broad-based representation on the task force might have allayed fears among New Bedfordites that the task force and partnership, as proposed, were not in their best interest. Finally, the task force's mission—to increase job opportunities for New Bedford residents—appeared to be too narrowly conceived to generate citywide support for its efforts. The task force did not consider broader development priorities, such as increasing educational and training opportunities and expanding municipal services, that might have generated consensus support among different interests in the city. The limited nature of the task force priorities appears to have inhibited its potential to build broad-based support for city economic revitalization and generate useful suggestions.

Conclusion: A Summary of "Lessons" from New Bedford and Lowell

The local development initiatives in New Bedford in the period 1977 to 1986 (as represented by the efforts to save Morse Cutting Tool and Mayor Bullard's economic development task force) highlight the lack of several elements that we observed in Lowell and that seem, in part, to explain the failure of the New Bedford efforts. Those elements that may be critical to successful city development efforts include the following:

1. A crisis situation, or perception of a crisis, to motivate local action, as was the case in Lowell.

2. A broad conception of economic development that can generate citywide support, as we observed in Lowell with Pat Mogan's vision for Lowell and the plans put forward by the Central City Committee and the Lowell Plan.

3. Sensitivity to citizen pessimism, acquiescence, and fear of change; the experience in Lowell suggests that city resistance to organized development efforts may be overcome by engaging citizens in development activities, as happened under the Model Cities program.

4. A strategy to improve city positioning in product, process, and factor price cycles, as we saw developed in Lowell by the Central City Committee and then the Lowell Plan.

5. Institutional innovation to enhance local development capacity and insure balance and cooperation between the public and private sectors, as was true in Lowell with the concerted activities of the city planning and development department, LDFC, and the Lowell Plan.

6. An organization to get neighborhood-based groups involved in larger city development activities, such as the Coalition for a Better Acre in Lowell.

These hypotheses are refined and tested and others are suggested in the analysis of revitalization activities in Jamestown and McKeesport in the next two chapters.

Six

Jamestown: Attempted Preservation

THE SHIFT-SHARE ANALYSIS in Chapter 3 suggests that Jamestown's economy, relative to McKeesport's, endured quite well through the 1970s. The city appears to have benefited from cooperative and consensus-based policy making among the public, private, and nonprofit sectors. This chapter documents the two most significant local development initiatives in the past two decades: the formation of a Jamestown area labor and management committee in the early 1970s to alleviate labor and management conflict that appeared to have a positive influence on local industry and helped the city attract new industry; and the organization of an economic development committee in the late 1980s by area foundations to address a broad range of emerging development issues in the city that the labor and management committee did not address.

Jamestown is the twelfth largest city in New York State with a population of 34,710 in 1986.[1] It is located seventy miles south of Buffalo, approximately halfway between New York City and Chicago. While Jamestown benefits from its proximity to urban centers in the industrial belt, including Buffalo, Rochester (137 miles to the northeast), Pittsburgh (150 miles south) and Cleveland (155 miles west), it is not a satellite city; Jamestown is the principal urban center for Chautauqua County and the southern tier of New York. Jamestown serves as the industrial, commercial, financial, and recreational hub of a metropolitan area of more than 70,000 residents and a market area of nearly 175,000 people.[2]

Development Environment

As had Lowell and New Bedford, Jamestown benefited from water access, natural resources, and location (between the industrial Midwest and major markets in the Northeast). The abundant forests in the Jamestown area were first utilized as a cash crop. Commencing in 1811, the water power at Lake Chautauqua's outlet was used to power the region's first dam and sawmill. In 1812 a small wood furniture operation, the forerunner of Jamestown's renowned furniture industry, was established.

In 1815, the hamlet at the foot of Lake Chautauqua was named Jamestown in honor of its first industrialist, James Prendergast, who built and operated the region's first dam and sawmill. In 1886, with a population of approximately 10,000, Jamestown received its charter as a city by the state of New York.

Jamestown residents benefited from the city's location at the base of Lake Chautauqua, a site of many recreational and cultural activities, including boating, fishing, golf, skiing, and concerts and seminars at the world renowned Chautauqua Institute. In addition to the activities on the Lake, Jamestown established a reputation for quality public services. For example, by 1900 Jamestown residents were reported to enjoy "every urban amenity at the time."[3] At the turn of the century, Jamestown's children had been educated in city schools for over 85 years, a public library had been opened, the first hospital had been started, the city's streets were already paved and lighted with electricity, there were municipal water and sewer systems, and electrical street cars operated on city streets.

Between 1900 and 1930, Jamestown's population doubled, rising above 45,000 in 1930. New crafts and skills were brought into the region by Swedish, Italian, Irish, and English immigrants. Swedish immigrants skilled as wood craftsmen made Jamestown famous for quality furniture making and other woodworking. By the early twentieth century, many small family craft shops grew into medium-sized establishments employing two to three hundred workers. English immigrants started up textile and apparel shops and were responsible for the village's early reputation as a worsted manufacturing center. The Italians and Irish, as in many other industrial areas, were employed mostly in lower skilled and lower paying industrial and service jobs.

Jamestown, in spite of an employment concentration in manufacturing industries, maintained some of the characteristics of a rural community, including a relatively low population density and a high proportion of single unit houses. The dispersed nature of the population appears to have contributed to fewer neighborhood-based activities in Jamestown than in New Bedford or Lowell. Many civic activities were focused at the workplace and organized by unions and other worker organizations. When political, religious, and cultural activities were organized outside the workplace, they are usually organized on a city or countywide basis, not a neighborhood basis. Reflective of Peterson's view in *City Limits*, city development activity has been organized mostly on a consensus basis. However, extended negotiation was often required to achieve consensus, particularly between laborers and managers/owners of industry, as will be discussed in detail below.

By 1914, approximately 7,800 manufacturing workers were employed in the city of Jamestown. Employment was concentrated in furniture and textile manufacturing. Manufacturing employment increased through the first half of the twentieth century. Jamestown's manufacturing employment did not decline during the Depression, as it did in Lowell and New Bedford. Between 1925 and 1932 manufacturing employment in Jamestown increased slightly, 1 percent, from 8,763 to 8,857. During the 1930s, however, there was a shift in Jamestown's industrial composition, since many local firms in declining industries did not survive the Depression. Worsted mills were the hardest hit and, as the national economy recovered from the Depression, metal manufacturing, primarily metal furniture manufacturing, replaced textiles as Jamestown's second largest industrial employer.

After the Depression, Jamestown manufacturing employment increased rapidly, rising to 12,070 in 1947—an increase of over 36 percent from 1932. In 1950, Jamestown became the largest office furniture supplier in the nation. At the time, nearly half of Jamestown's total employment was in manufacturing, approximately double the national average, with employment in furniture and metals manufacturing related industries alone accounting for over 30 percent of total employment in the city (see Tables 6.1 and 6.2).

The immediate post–World War II period proved to be the pinnacle years. After nearly a century of increasing manufacturing employment, Jamestown's economy entered a period of decline in the 1950s, as its two primary industries, furniture and metals product manufacturing, entered their mature phase. Between 1950 and 1970, total employment declined by over 20 percent, manufacturing employment declined by 41 percent, and employment in furniture and metals manufacturing declined over 44 percent. In addition, during this period Jamestown's unemployment level exceeded the national average and median family income (for the first time since the United States complied statistics) fell below the national average (see Table 6.1).

As suggested by the shift-share analysis in Chapter 3, Jamestown's economy, even when controlling for base period industrial mix and regional industry growth, significantly underperformed the United States and the regional economy in the period from 1950 to 1970.

As employment opportunities declined, so did Jamestown's population. Jamestown's population peaked in 1930 at 45,000 and was fairly stable through World War II; however, after 1950 the city's population began to decline. Between 1950 and 1970, Jamestown's population declined 8 percent, while the population in New York state increased by 23 percent.

TABLE 6.1
Jamestown Profile

Jamestown	1950	1960	1970	1980	Index Relative to the United States 1950	1960	1970	1980
Population	43,354	41,818	39,795	35,775				
Total Employment	18,846	16,550	15,253	14,599				
Percent Manufacturing	48.0%	45.0%	39.6%	33.2%	184.6	166.1	152.3	148.2
Unemployment Rate	5.2%	6.9%	4.5%	7.5%	106.1	135.3	102.3	115.4
Median Family Income	$3,463	$5,607	$8,624	$15,973	112.7	99.8	87.4	78.9
Percent H.S. Graduate	20.7%	22.9%	32.5%	37.3%	60.5	55.7	62.1	56.1
Percent Over 65	12.0%	14.5%	15.9%	18.0%	148.1	157.6	160.6	159.3

Source: U.S. Census Bureau, Population and Housing.

In 1972 unemployment in Jamestown hit 10.2 percent, compared with the national average of 5.9 percent. The major immediate factor contributing to Jamestown's high unemployment level was the decision of Art Metal Manufacturing, makers of office furniture and one of the city's largest manufacturers, to shut down its plant and thereby eliminated 700 jobs (5 percent of Jamestown's total employment at the time).[4] Following the news about Art Metal, Crescent Tool, a hardware and tool manufacturer that employed 800 in Jamestown, announced its intention to move to South Carolina.

These were not isolated incidents; for eighteen consecutive years Jamestown had been losing manufacturing jobs. As one local observer commented in 1973, "most companies were either going broke or going South."[5] The primary factor hindering Jamestown's development was a rise in factor and production costs. The reasons most frequently cited for Jamestown's decline were labor and management strife and declining worker productivity.[6] During the 1960s, Jamestown experienced two and a half times as many lost days per industrial worker due to strikes as the average in New York state. Business and union leaders (80 percent of Jamestown's manufacturing workers were unionized) rarely spoke outside of the collective bargaining process.[7]

Given the condition of the local economy and the labor-management environment in 1972, it is impressive that Jamestown was able to survive the decade without an economic collapse, as occurred in McKeesport and other cities throughout the industrial belt bounded by Pittsburgh, Buffalo and Cleveland. The shift-share analysis in

TABLE 6.2
Jamestown Employment 1950 to 1980

	1950	1960	1970	1980	Percentage Changes 1950–1960	1960–1970	1970–1980	1950–1980
Total Employment	18,846	16,550	15,253	14,599	(12.2)	(7.8)	(4.3)	(22.5)
Manufacturing	9,051	7,446	6,047	4,824	(17.7)	(18.8)	(20.2)	(46.7)
Total NonDurable	1,833	1,211	519	558	(33.9)	(57.1)	7.5	(69.6)
Total Durable	7,218	6,235	5,528	4,284	(13.6)	(11.3)	(22.5)	(40.6)
Furniture & Wood	3,112	2,684	1,422	1,167	(13.8)	(47.0)	(17.9)	(62.5)
Metal Industries	2,619	1,641	1,599	1,014	(37.3)	(2.6)	(36.6)	(61.3)
Machinery	1,161	1,528	1,795	1,318	31.6	17.5	(26.6)	13.5
Trans., Com. & Util.	823	561	651	677	(31.8)	16.0	4.0	(17.7)
Wholesale & Retail	3,932	3,212	3,186	3,219	(18.3)	(0.8)	1.0	(18.1)
F.I.R.E.	531	691	808	666	30.1	16.9	(17.6)	25.4
Services	3,107	3,283	3,525	3,960	5.7	7.4	12.3	27.5

	Percentage Breakdown			
	1950	1960	1970	1980
Total Employment	100.0	100.0	100.0	100.0
Manufacturing	48.0	45.0	39.6	33.0
Total NonDurable	9.7	7.3	3.4	3.8
Total Durable	38.3	37.7	36.2	29.3
Furniture & Wood	16.5	16.2	9.3	8.0
Metal Industries	13.9	9.9	10.5	6.9
Machinery	6.2	9.2	11.8	9.0
Trans., Com. & Util.	4.4	3.4	4.3	4.6
Wholesale & Retail	20.9	19.4	20.9	22.0
F.I.R.E.	2.8	4.2	5.3	4.6
Services	16.5	19.8	23.1	27.1

Source: U.S. Census Bureau, Population and Housing.

Chapter 3 and other statistics comparing the 1970s with the previous two decades in fact suggests that, in spite of its economic difficulties, Jamestown's economy endured quite well through the 1970s. After declining by 12 and 8 percent in the 1950s and 1960s, employment decline in Jamestown slowed to 4 percent in the 1970s (see Table 6.2). Of significant note, employment in nondurable manufacturing and wholesale and retail trade reversed two decade declines and increased by 8 and 1 percent respectively.

Part of the relative resiliency of Jamestown's economy in the

1970s, compared to McKeesport's, could be attributed to its more diversified industrial composition and greater concentration in growing industries. Even after controlling for industry mix, however, Jamestown's economy significantly out-performed McKeesport during the decade.

The analysis in Chapter 3 suggests that the 1970s would be a useful period to compare and contrast local development efforts in Jamestown and McKeesport. This chapter documents and examines the most significant local effort to retain employment during the 1970s in Jamestown—the establishment of areawide and in-plant labor and management committees to improve labor and working conditions in Jamestown commencing in 1972.

Labor and Management Committees

The most direct benefit of the labor and management committees in Jamestown was the establishment of a neutral local forum to encourage cooperative (labor, management, and local government) efforts to revive local industries. The committees appeared to help improve Jamestown's positioning in the factor price cycle by promoting steps to increase worker productivity and reduce strike days. The labor and management committees also helped to change the image of Jamestown from "a bad labor town" to that of a city where labor and management cooperated. The most visible and immediate result of Jamestown's changed labor relations was the introduction in 1974 of Cummins Engine—the first major new industrial employer in the area in over fifty years. Jamestown's experience contrasts sharply with the situation in McKeesport, where confrontation between labor and management and declining worker productivity were two of the key factors contributing to an acceleration in economic decline during the 1970s, as will be discussed in Chapter 7.

In November 1971, Mayor Stanley (Stan) Lundine, pledging to help restore economic vitality to his home town, was re-elected by greater than a 2-to-1 margin. Right after his re-election, the Art Metal company (one of the largest industrial employers in the city) closed its doors. The crisis situation, caused by the shut down and double digit unemployment, together with the strong public support demonstrated in his re-election, convinced Lundine to pursue a novel approach to alleviate Jamestown's economic problems. In his second inauguration address, Mayor Lundine announced, "We have the capacity to reverse the trend toward economic stagnation and decline. It will take the active participation of labor leaders and manufacturing executives as well as the total support of the local government to achieve our fundamental objective."[8]

Lundine chose to address the most critical and visible problem in the city—labor and management relations—putting it at the forefront of his administration's city revitalization efforts. In the 1960s, thirty-nine strikes at Jamestown plants had accounted for 1,442 strike days.[9] Efforts to attract new business and maintain the viability of many industrial firms were hampered by the city's poor labor and management climate and by low worker productivity. Between Lundine's re-election and inauguration, he had meetings with experienced labor mediation officials in western New York state and Jamestown to discuss what to do to improve labor and management relations in the city. In these meetings, the idea of organizing a Jamestown Area Labor and Management Committee (JALMC) was first raised.

Labor and management committees were not a new concept; they had been in practice since the 1920s. The first labor and management committees in the United States were small in-plant committees which dealt with productivity and working condition issues in individual factories. One of the best known early committees was at the Baltimore & Ohio Railroad (B&O). The B&O committee was formed in 1923 and, over a fifteen-year period, helped to implement nearly 31,000 worker and management recommendations. Area-wide committees, which included labor and corporate leaders from more than one local firm, started later. The first area-wide labor and management committee was begun in Toledo, Ohio in 1946 with forty-eight members, sixteen labor representatives, sixteen management officials, and sixteen citizens from the community. The Toledo "model" was adopted by Louisville, Kentucky in 1947.[10]

One of the officials Lundine consulted after Art Metal closed was Sam Sackman of the Federal Mediation and Conciliation Service field office in Buffalo. Before his assignment to western New York, Sackman had worked with labor and management committees in several Pennsylvania cities. Sackman stressed in his conversations with Lundine that he thought Jamestown was no different from other cities. What Jamestown suffered most from was its reputation for strikes. Sackman emphasized that it would be critical to change the image of Jamestown; he advocated labor and management committees principally to alter Jamestown's "bad labor town" image.

Sackman put Lundine in contact with Alvin Mardon of the Jamestown Manufacturers Association and Raymond Anderson, a Jamestown attorney who represented local manufacturers. Together they mapped out an outline of an area-wide labor and management committee for Jamestown and a strategy for its implementation. They agreed that any labor and management committee in Jamestown would have to remove itself from collective bargaining, grievance procedures, and arbitration. The consensus among Lundine and the three mediation experts was that a committee divorced from collective bargaining issues would be less prone to bog down in the ritual of traditional labor and management negotiation in the city.

After mapping out a strategy, Lundine and Sackman took the lead in organizing a labor and management committee in Jamestown. Lundine called the chief executive officers from the largest industrial employers in the greater Jamestown area together in January 1972. Lundine emphasized in the first meeting that, if "we are going to reverse Jamestown's economic decline, private business has to be the cornerstone of revitalization efforts."[11] The very next day, Lundine met with labor leaders called together by Sackman to tell them that they were the cornerstone of revitalization efforts. Early the next month, Lundine and Sackman arranged for the two groups to meet together with Lundine as the self-appointed moderator. The mayor invited fifteen top labor officials, representing a majority of the metropolitan area's manufacturing workers, and fifteen corporate leaders, representing local industrial firms. The labor and management representatives had seen one another before, but only on different sides of the bargaining table.

The initial discussion was not encouraging, particularly when one union leader used it as an opportunity to accuse the manufacturers association of systematically trying to keep all new business out of the area in order to keep area wage rates low. Joseph (Joe) Mason, a business agent for the International Association of Machinists and Aerospace Workers and eventual union co-chairman of the JALMC executive committee, described the initial meeting:

> Everybody was pointing a finger at everybody. Nobody wanted to take the blame for Jamestown having the reputation of a strike-happy town. But the more we talked and listened, the more we understood that everything came down to the same thing: every company has to make a profit because they (private businesses) are not in business for their health and when we (labor) got involved with the problems they were having, we could understand how to get what we wanted.[12]

In subsequent meetings between labor and management leaders, with Lundine as moderator, it was resolved that a Jamestown Area Labor Management Committee (JALMC) be formed that would work with the mayor and the Chautauqua County Industrial Development

Agency to stabilize and support existing businesses and help attract new industry to the area.

The JALMC was formally established as a private nonprofit corporation in 1972. The purpose of the JALMC was to foster a climate of positive labor and industrial relations throughout Jamestown and adjacent areas. A twenty-member executive governing board was created with nine union, nine management, and two government members (the mayor and the ombudsman for the city). The executive board was to meet on a regular basis to hear labor and management complaints and offer suggestions. The executive board employed the Quaker decision-making method: issues would be discussed until a consensus was reached, and votes were not taken out of concern that they would encourage committee members to take sides instead of forging workable compromises.

Labor and management officials in Jamestown agreed that the labor relations would improve if they concentrated on areas where business and labor had common goals and where mutual benefits could be derived. With strong persuasion from Lundine and Sackman, the committee decided it would devote its attention to areas of cooperation apart from the collective bargaining process.

It was determined that the first area of committee activity would be improving productivity in existing industry. To make the productivity issue less controversial, it was agreed that productivity be broadly defined and not involve simply a speedup of worker effort. Such objectives as reducing absenteeism, improving product quality, and eliminating waste would be recognized as productivity advances. Moreover, it was agreed that the financial benefits resulting from productivity improvements should be shared between labor and industry and that no jobs would be lost in an industry as a result of efforts to improve productivity. Management accepted the concept that those workers whose jobs were eliminated as a result of productivity improvements would be transferred to other jobs within the same enterprise.

The Jamestown Area Labor Management Committee became Jamestown's most visible agent in city economic development efforts. During its organization, the JALMC got labor and management to communicate and reflect on how their actions influenced each other and the city as a whole. The Committee was able to establish increasing productivity, improving the skills of the labor force, and attracting new industry, not only as management and union objectives, but also as citywide goals.

Although it had established citywide goals and Committee objectives, the JALMC was still a long way from an action program. It became increasingly clear to both labor and management representatives that any practical efforts (e.g., efforts to increase productivity and reduce absenteeism) would have to take place at individual work places and that, given the recent history of hostility between labor and management, this would require outside professional assistance. Such assistance, however, required more money than the JALMC had at the time. To overcome the financial deficiency, Mayor Lundine went to Washington D.C. with a local delegation to apply for a federal grant to fund consulting assistance for implementation of in-plant labor and management committees. In 1973, Jamestown was able to secure a $22,500 grant from the federal Economic Development Administration (EDA) of the United States Department of Commerce. The grant, which was supplemented with $7,500 from the city, was made specifically to support JALMC programs to increase industrial productivity and promote the "quality-of-work-life" concept.

The reasons for giving the grant to the JALMC were summarized by Verna Richardson, an EDA official at the time:

> We felt that Jamestown was the right place for a pilot project on quality of life (QWL) because the city had such tremendous problems, it was a city effort and didn't involve just one plant, and the cooperation that had already been established between labor and management showed that it had a very good chance of succeeding.[13]

The experience of working together for something they both could directly benefit from, federal aid, seemed to help bond labor and management in Jamestown. As Lundine commented, "this period of repeated trips to Washington had a benefit beyond providing funding for consultants; it worked to unify labor and management representatives."[14] The federal grant represented the first time labor and management cooperation had real dollar benefits in Jamestown. This reinforced the feeling that it was possible to work together for mutual gain.

The EDA grant enabled Jamestown to recruit Dr. James McDonald of Buffalo University as the first coordinator of the JALMC. Additional help came from the National Commission on Productivity which brought in Dr. Eric Trist, who had established a reputation at the Wharton School for his studies in the "quality of work" field. These individuals helped establish six in-plant committees at plants where both labor and management were receptive to the concept. After organizing the committees, McDonald and Trist continued to work closely with workers and management. Their approach was to seek suggestions from workers and encourage them to speak up about the way they worked, how the production process was managed, and what could be improved.

The forms of labor and management cooperation devised by the in-plant committees in Jamestown were varied. They were designed to address the particular needs and problems at individual plants. Forms of labor and management cooperation included reduction of waste and breakage, implementation of quality control systems, cooperative design of new products, joint effort towards improved bidding procedures, and collaborative factory design.

The JALMC and the in-plant committees appeared to have a significant positive impact on Jamestown's economy in a relatively short period of time. In two years, the JALMC reported that it had helped to prevent six plant closings, saving over 1,300 jobs. Labor relations improved markedly; there were no strikes in 1972 and 1973, and grievances and absenteeism were also significantly reduced.[15]

The most visible indicator of the improvement in Jamestown's labor climate took place in the spring of 1974, when Cummins Engine Company of Columbus, Indiana, bought the abandoned Art Metal factory. Cummins purchased the facility for a plant to manufacture diesel engines and components. This was the first time in over fifty years that Jamestown had attracted a major new company. In 1975, the Cummins Engine plant started production with over 400 production workers in well paying jobs.

Because the production process planned for the plant required team work and work floor flexibility, Cummins had sought a city where workers and managers trusted each other, could work together, and had a favorable attitude toward quality-of-work-life approaches.[16] The labor environment and image projected in the city by the JALMC appeared to have a positive influence on Cummin's decision to locate in Jamestown, even though Cummins' workers were not unionized and Cummins could not therefore participate in the JALMC.

Cummins Engine conducted extensive research and interviews before selecting Jamestown. Company officials spent months and thousands of dollars deciding where to locate their new plant, considering not only the capital and operating costs of different locations but also examining social and cultural characteristics of cities and their labor environment. In the end, the change in labor and management relations was an important factor. Jim Muhlfedler, director of personnel at the Cummins Engine Jamestown plant, com-

mented, "If the labor and management climate of the 1960s had prevailed when we were deciding where to open a new plant we would
not have moved here [to Jamestown]."[17]

Cummins is satisfied with its decision to locate its diesel engine
plant in Jamestown. Cummins Engine management has been particularly happy with the quality of the workforce in Jamestown. The
Jamestown plant, which is one of Cummins's most productive and
profitable, expanded its operations steadily over time.[18] In 1987 employment at Cummins in Jamestown reached 1,100.

There are other examples and indicators suggesting the JALMC's
contributions to the local economy. In the mid-1970s the Committee
helped to revive two nearly bankrupt companies, Chautauqua Hardware (a manufacturer of furniture hardware) and Jamestown Metal
Products (a manufacturer of cabinets, sinks and counter tops with
over 300 jobs). Owners of both companies cited the improved labor
situation since the JALMC was formed as an important factor that
helped their companies survive difficult times.[19]

The opening of the Cummins plant in Jamestown and the survival
of companies like Chautauqua Hardware and Jamestown Metal
Products helped Jamestown avoid the worst aspects of the national
recession in the 1974–76 period. During the recession period, Jamestown's unemployment remained well below state and national averages.[20] Prior to the organization of the JALMC, it had been said that
"when the nation's economy catches a cold Jamestown gets pneumo-
nia."[21] Thanks in part to the efforts of the JALMC in the mid-1970s,
this was no longer the case. The JALMC appeared to contribute to
the Jamestown economy's resiliency in the face of national economic
recession by encouraging greater flexibility in management and work
practices, allowing for mutual (labor and management) adaptation to
changing circumstances in increasingly competitive industries, and
contributing to improvements in worker productivity. The JALMC
during the 1970s seems to have provided the institutional base for
identifying and helping implement some of the invisible factors in
local economic development (discussed by Doeringer et al.) that contributed to Jamestown's improved positioning in product, process,
and factor price cycles and its superior economic performance in the
1970s.

The affect of the JALMC on Jamestown's economy cannot be fully
quantified; however, the discussion above suggests that its influence
was positive and not insignificant. The most obvious benefit of the
Committee was the establishment of a forum for labor, management,
and local government officials to identify and pursue opportunities
for mutual gain. The JALMC established increasing productivity, im-

proving the skills of the labor force, attracting new industry, and good labor and management relations as city-wide goals. After labor and management committees were established in industrial plants, they were organized in the Jamestown school system, the municipal utility company, and the public hospital. As an article in *The Economist* (1980) commented, "In Jamestown labor and management ranked with apple pie and motherhood."[22] The experience in Jamestown suggests (as did the development efforts in Lowell) that consensus action on city interests in economic growth often require extensive discussion among local institutions representating different sectors. It also suggests that city interests in economic growth have to be operationalized through local organizations, political suasion, and negotiation.

The JALMC's impact appeared to be most significant in improving Jamestown's positioning in the factor price cycle by promoting measures to increase worker productivity and reduce strike days. However, the influence of the JALMC on turning around Jamestown's poor "labor town" image was also profound. The image projected by the JALMC appeared to help Jamestown attract new industry and motivate Jamestown residents, who became more positive about themselves and more optimistic about their future. The efforts of the JALMC gave Jamestown favorable national press, including national television stories and articles in *Newsweek*, *The New York Times*, *The Wall Street Journal*, and *The Economist*. In addition, Jamestown was named an "All American City" by the National Municipal League in 1974. The award was based on evidence that "Jamestown people from all sectors of the community were working together to improve their city."[23]

In spite of the favorable press and its initial success in bolstering the Jamestown economy, the labor and management committees did not arrest employment decline or stop deterioration in socioeconomic conditions (see Table 6.1). In 1980 Jamestown's unemployment rate was 7.5 percent, 15 percent above the national average, and median family income was nearly one-quarter below the national average (after being at or above the national average prior to 1960).

Jamestown in the Mid-1980s

It appears that Jamestown's economy lagged behind the "rust belt" economy in the 1980s. Jamestown's unemployment rate in the 1980s was consistently above the national and state averages. For example, in 1986 Jamestown's unemployment rate was 8.2 percent, compared to the New York state average of 7.3 percent. In addition, per capita income in 1985 was $8,785, less than 75 percent of the New York state average.

Jamestown's development problems in the 1980s cannot be understood with employment and income statistics alone. In 1987, over 20 percent of Jamestown residents were on some form of public assistance and over 40 percent of the students in the Jamestown public school system came from families living below the poverty level.[24] Adding to Jamestown's problems was a dying downtown business district (wholesale and retail establishments in the city declined by over 31 percent between 1972 and 1982) and inferior housing stock (over 75 percent of the city's housing units had been built prior to 1940, compared to the New York State average of 40 percent).[25]

A 1987 survey of the twenty-four largest employers in the greater Jamestown area was quite revealing about the economic condition of the city and its future prospects.[26] One-third of the chief executives interviewed indicated that employment at their establishments had declined between 1980 and 1987. Three-quarters expected no growth in employment over the next ten years. Over sixty percent rated Jamestown as an average or below average place to operate a business establishment. Many of the chief executives and plant managers interviewed commented that if they could do it all over again they would *not* locate in Jamestown. Still they had too much invested in Jamestown to move operations.

The most significant problems in operating a profitable business in Jamestown identified in the survey were (1) shortages of high-skilled workers, mostly in engineering and management; (2) shortages of low-skilled workers with basic literacy, numeric and interpersonal skills; (3) the negative image of the city; (4) and the deteriorated condition of the downtown. The latter two problem areas were identified as factors making it hard to operate a profitable business in Jamestown, primarily because they made it difficult to attract high skilled workers to the city.

The ability of the JALMC to sustain positive industrial relations can be questioned, given the comments from those corporate executives interviewed. Not atypical were the comments of one local plant manager who despaired of the labor situation in 1987. There was, he said, "a kind of ingrained learned incompetence among workers and foremen that could not be changed without some sort of trauma."[27]

While the labor and management committees helped Jamestown confront the fundamental problem that was affecting economic growth in the early 1970s, the JALMC's ability to continue as the leading local institution on economic development matters seemed to fade over time. In the 1980s, Jamestown businesses and residents were discovering that economic development success is not forever. A city can solve selected economic problems for a limited time, but dynamic institutions and active citizens may be required to maintain a vibrant city.

The JALMC seemed to be burdened by its early success and not amenable to changing its orientation (identified as critical to the development of Lowell in Chapter 4 and in the Lowell update in Chapter 8). The focus of the JALMC appeared to be too limited to deal with the broad nature of Jamestown's development problems emerging in the 1980s. Perhaps, if the JALMC had followed the example of Toledo's area-wide committee and included as many community representatives as management and union representatives, it might have been able to adapt over time and expand its agenda. Instead the JALMC became more limited in focus, concentrating on worker training, mainly because of the availability of generous federal Job Training Partnership Act (JTPA) training funds.

In addition to the problems associated with the declining effectiveness of the JALMC, Stan Lundine's move to Washington in 1977, as the area's congressional representative, created a leadership void in the city. There were individuals in the city who tried to take the lead on local development issues, such as Lundine's successor, Steven Carlson, and Lundine's disciple, David Dawson, the director of the Chautauqua County Industrial Development Agency (IDA).[28] However, the efforts of the new mayor and Dawson were limited. They were not well coordinated and failed to address the slow steady economic and social decline in Jamestown.

There was widespread criticism of Mayor Steven Carlson. He was described by many business and labor leaders in the city as a competent and honest public official but lacking the charisma of his predecessor.[29] Carlson and his colleagues in local government, in turn, found business and labor leaders uninformed about public sector activities, focused only on their own problems and indifferent to the general welfare of the city.

David Dawson (at the Chautauqua County IDA) had established an agenda of his own directed at encouraging industrial recruitment and entrepreneurial efforts. Dawson's plans included the establishment of a regional venture capital fund, a business incubator center, and a cooperative research and training center at Jamestown Community College.

Many in the city were concerned about gaps in the organization of local development activities. Paul Benke, the president of Jamestown

Community College, worried that no one was focusing on the important "less tangible" problems facing the community, including problems of spirit, image and leadership.[30]

The general feeling among Jamestown residents was that, while the Jamestown economy was staggering, it was not at a crisis or trauma level. Without such trauma, many wondered how the city could be organized to work towards expanding economic opportunities.

Community Foundation Efforts

In 1986, eight local foundations, together with the Chautauqua Region Community Foundation (CRCF), began to cautiously pursue involvement in local economic development.[31] They formed an Economic Development Committee with representatives from each member foundation to explore the possibility of entering the economic development arena. Their concern about the social and economic decline in the city was tempered by a trepidation that any of their contributions to local development activities not violate their IRS status as independent nonprofit foundations or their fiduciary responsibilities.

The local foundations participating in the Economic Development Committee included the Gebbie, Sheldon, Hultquist, Carnahan, Clarke, Darrah, Lenna, and Peterson Foundations.[32] Collectively, as of 1986, these eight foundations had over $100 million in endowments. Over 90 percent of donations by these Jamestown foundations were made locally. In 1986, through the community foundation and individually, the eight foundations made grants of over $4.2 million in the greater Jamestown area, or well over $30 per capita.[33] These grants were concentrated in cultural and educational activities and social services.

Part of the caution in entering the economic development field on the part of foundation administrators was out of concern in the city's nonprofit sector about the "net effect" of foundation contributions to economic development activities. For example, Murray Bob, the director of the Jamestown library, expressed fear that foundation contributions to economic development might come at the expense of traditional philanthropic gifts, like those to his library.[34] Foundation directors wondered how any economic development role they undertook would relate to their more traditional involvement in the city.[35]

The foundations' formation of an economic development committee was in part a response to another effort organized in 1986 in which the foundations believed their generosity was abused. In 1986 an Economic Development Committee of the greater Jamestown area Chamber of Commerce began a vigorous fund-raising campaign and had, in the judgment of local foundation leaders, intimidated the foundations into sponsoring redevelopment in the central business district and a study of the city's tourism potential. The unilateral promotion of these activities by the Chamber had, according to Francis Grow (the managing director of the Chautauqua Region Community Foundation), threatened to undermine the fragile coalition that favored an expanded role for foundations in economic development activities.

In May 1987, the Chautauqua Region Community Foundation requested that Mayor Steven Carlson and Harold (Hal) Bolton, the chief executive at Dalhstroms Inc. (a local manufacturer of computer castings) and former management co-chair of the JALMC, chair a steering committee to help the foundation's Economic Development Committee establish priorities. Local foundation leaders and administrators wanted to create an institutional vehicle to build city consensus on how they should proceed on economic development matters. Mayor Carlson and Hal Bolton agreed to chair the citywide steering committee. It was decided that within an eight-month period the steering committee would submit a report with recommendations to the foundation's Economic Development Committee. Carlson and Bolton selected a twelve-member committee, which included eleven local people and one outsider, Winthrop Knowlton, director of the Center for Business and Government at Harvard University, who had previously (in 1987) been hired as a consultant by the Community Foundation. The local persons selected for the committee represented, in the co-chairs eyes, an emerging leadership group of creative and vigorous individuals in the city who had little direct personal stake in the foundation grants that would be effected by the committee's recommendations.

The steering committee included representatives from the private, public, and nonprofit sectors; it included the president of Jamestown Community College, the plant manager of Blackstone (a manufacturer of automobile radiators and the second largest industrial employer in Jamestown), a retired grocery store owner, a lawyer in private practice, a labor leader and JALMC official, the marketing director of the Chautauqua Institute, a foundation administrator, the director of the local arts council, an assistant to the state assembly representative, a self-employed business consultant and former director of the city's development office, and a businesswoman whose family owned and operated a metal furniture manufacturing company in Jamestown.

Starting in May 1987, the steering committee held breakfast meetings focusing on different aspects of local development problems, including education, industrial promotion, downtown development, and social and human services. The steering committee, under the direction of Mayor Carlson and Hal Bolton, adopted a broad view of economic development, primarily out of concern for the sensitivities of foundation administrators.

The breakfast meetings were designed by the co-chairs, in consultation with Winthrop Knowlton, and organized primarily by Bolton, with some assistance from the mayor. There were seven meetings, approximately one meeting each month. The principal purpose of the meetings was to enable the committee members to make an informed and realistic appraisal of the city's current position. At these sessions, local experts and administrators in the different development areas were invited by the committee to highlight ongoing efforts, issues of concern, and prospective new programs where the foundations could provide meaningful support.

In December 1987, a two day retreat was organized at the Chautauqua Institute with a group facilitator. According to co-chair Bolton, "The purpose of the retreat was to allow committee members to collectively digest the discussions from prior meetings and to consider whether there was a positive role that foundations could play in local development efforts and if so to identify priority areas and programs for local foundations to fund."[36]

During the retreat, the committee unanimously agreed that foundations should play a role in economic development.[37] More specifically, committee members supported the view that a significant addition of quality jobs was critical and that this would require a program of action in a number of different areas in which local foundations could be particularly helpful, including education, competitive effectiveness, health and human services, cultural and recreational enrichment, housing and community pride. These were not meant to be mutually exclusive areas of attention, but interrelated.

The Committee, in its report to the Community Foundation, cited specific programs deserving of consideration in each substantive area. Specific programs and initiatives cited for foundation consideration included support of new businesses with high growth potential (through a loan fund established by local foundations), an institute that could serve as a model for community-based delivery of human services, a local civic center, a riverwalk project in the down-town that would serve as the centerpiece for renewal efforts in the downtown, the establishment of a low-income homeownership loan program, and a city public relations program.

Update

As of this writing, it was too early to assess fully the influence of the recommendations of the steering committee. The foundations were still proceeding cautiously with their involvement in economic de-velopment matters. The reluctance of local foundations to fund de-velopment activities is in part reflective of the "shopping list" nature of the projects the steering committee recommended. If the steering committee had highlighted one or two priority projects that did not venture far from traditional foundation activities (e.g., an institute for community-based delivery of human services), foundation sup-port might have been more forthcoming. The steering committee should have considered gradually moving foundation leaders to-wards sponsorship of less traditional activities (e.g., the businesses loan fund), rather than starting with an extensive list of projects for the foundations to sponsor.

Nonetheless, the efforts of local foundations and the steering com-mittee seem to indicate progress. The initial efforts represent the re-alization that the JALMC is no longer effective as the leading local development institution, and that city economic development in-volves more than just job growth, worker training, and productivity improvements. It also represents recognition that local foundations can be a valuable resource that should be part of development efforts in Jamestown and awareness that multi-sector, not just governmen-tal or private sector, effort may be necessary to insure the city's eco-nomic vitality.

Seven

McKeesport: Decline and Struggle

RESIDENTS of municipalities across the Mon Valley have suffered from extended economic decline. Local development efforts in the Valley have had to confront poor positioning in product, process, and factor price cycles, a history of dependence on a single industry and single employer, poorly functioning local government, and resident acquiescence and inexperience with local development activities.

This chapter documents the economic decline in the Valley and efforts at revitalization. The focus is on large-scale and ambitious efforts that have not been successful and have seemed at times to worsen problems. The development initiatives documented include national steel industry and labor and management efforts in the 1970s to improve labor relations and efforts to assist economically and socially depressed cities in the Valley by Allegheny County in the mid-1980s. The chapter concludes with a description of a recent (1987) and novel initiative that attempts to engage local residents in small-scale development activities. This effort, co-sponsored by the Allegheny Conference and the Local Initiatives Support Corporation (LISC), operates with a different philosophy than previous development efforts—it is premised on the belief that vitality can only be restored by increasing the capacity of local residents to help themselves and that change will have to take place incrementally.

Introduction

The Monongahela (Mon) Valley has a rich industrial history, dating back to the opening of the first steel mill in 1851. The development of the Valley was strongly influenced by national economic growth and federal government infrastructure and military expenditures. The steel mills and the people of the Mon Valley helped build twentieth century America supplying rail for railroads, tubes for oil and gas pipelines, beams for bridges and skyscrapers, sheet steel for automobiles, and appliances and iron for ordnances.

The Mon Valley comprises boroughs, townships, cities, and urban neighborhoods on both sides of the Monongahela River, stretching from the city of Pittsburgh in Allegheny County up river (south) to the city of Brownsville in Fayette County, Pennsylvania. The Valley is more than forty miles long, as the river turns, and contains seventy-one municipalities.

Development Environment: McKeesport and the Mon Valley

In the mid-eighteenth century the Mon Valley was part of a pioneer settlement that usurped land from native Indians. Pioneer settlers were first attracted to the land as a transportation center and for its natural resources. Many of the early pioneers were from Scotland and Ireland and were attracted to the area by special incentives provided by the government of the province of Pennsylvania. The Valley, located at the confluence of the Monongahela and Youghiogheny Rivers and Turtle Creek, was a desirable area in which to settle because of its access to natural resources to the south (including coal and natural gas in West Virginia) and expanding markets to the north and east.

In the eighteenth and early part of the nineteenth century, the Mon Valley's economy was dominated by river trade, which was significantly enhanced by the development of the local coal industry. By the 1850s, industry related to coal mining and transport began to prosper throughout the Valley, including sheet iron, coal wagon, freight car, locomotive, and barge manufacturing. The Valley's economy was further stimulated by the completion of the railroad that connected McKeesport with the city of Pittsburgh and eastern markets in 1857.

In 1901, with the incorporation of the U.S. Steel Corporation, one company came to dominate the fate of the municipalities in the Valley.[1] Although U.S. Steel controlled the economic fate of the Valley, it was headquartered in the city of Pittsburgh. By the early 1900s, U.S. Steel operated eight major steel plants along the Mon River between Pittsburgh's South Side and the city of Donora. The scale of U.S. Steel operations in the Valley could be compared to a gigantic assembly line with each plant, including three McKeesport plants, being a work station along the river serviced by subsidiary lines.[2] Iron ore, coal, and hundreds of other supplies moved up and down the Valley, by water, rail, and road lines connecting all the plants in an interlocking system.

The scale of U.S. Steel operations in the Mon Valley grew to awesome proportions. At its peak in the late 1940s, U.S. Steel employed over 60,000 United Steel Worker union (USW) members in production, maintenance, and clerical jobs in the Valley. Adding managerial and supervisory jobs at the plants, Mon Valley steel industry employees totaled 80,000 right after World War II. U.S. Steel was possessive about the pool of labor in the mill towns. There were stories of the company actively discouraging other industries from entering the area. The second largest local employer in the mill towns was most typically the municipal government, public hospital, or the school district, employing a mere fraction of the numbers of workers employed in the U.S. steel mills.

As was true of other "one-industry towns," the major company, U.S. Steel, dominated city hall, city councils, local chambers of commerce, school boards, and city political activities in municipalities across the Valley. In recent years, as will be discussed below, these institutions, particularly municipal governments and local unions, have been unable to adjust to U.S. Steel plant closings and confront local economic problems.

The "dependent city" that Kantor and other critical urban theorists critique typifies the municipalities in the Mon Valley throughout most of their history. The livelihood of municipalities was dependent on employee and property taxes derived from steel facilities. Therefore the municipalities gave priority to the steel industry. For example, McKeesport, soon after incorporation, adopted a "zones of activity" concept in planning, whereby industry had first choice over any land parcel. Thus if U.S. Steel required land for expansion, municipal officials would make arrangements to transfer the land, even if that required displacing residents or nonindustrial businesses.

Local public services were also geared to serving the steel industry. Transportation systems, including bus and street car routes and city streets, were designed to move workers to and from the mills at shift changes. Many area high schools developed curricula encouraging students to specialize in industrial skills. For example, in the 1930s, McKeesport opened one of the nation's first vocational high schools with mechanical and electrical shops.

Mon Valley steel workers and their family members actively supported local policies favorable to the local steel mill and supported candidates for office who promised to do everything that they could to keep mills operating near capacity and "keep U.S. Steel happy." While the national organization, the United Steel Workers union (USW), adopted mostly confrontational tactics with U.S. Steel (see discussion below), local union officials and rank and filers realized that their fate was closely linked to the success of local steel facilities and were most supportive of local policies which met industry demands.

U.S. Steel appeared to benefit greatly from its virtual monopsonistic position in the Valley. Company officials frequently pitted municipalities in the Valley against each other in competition for the expansion and retention of facilities. Municipalities competed by offering free land, public services (roads, water and transport), and special tax treatment. Because of competition among the cities, which each had its own steel mills, interests, and traditions, the Valley lacked organizational structure or collective political will for addressing common problems.

The first industrial workers in the Valley came from the stock of Scots-Irish, German and English who initially settled the area in the mid-eighteenth century. As production at the steel mills expanded and the initial pool of workers was exhausted, Andrew Carnegie and other U.S. Steel magnates became aggressive in their recruitment of immigrants. U.S. Steel sent agents to recruit workers at Ellis Island and placed advertisements in European newspapers offering "good opportunities in the steel mills of America."[3] Although some skilled workers, such as machinists, came from England and Germany, the great majority of immigrants were unskilled. The unskilled came in succeeding waves, starting in the 1870s and lasting through the 1920s. Included in these groups were large numbers of Hungarians, Poles, Serbs, and Russians.

Immigrants came to the Valley hoping to find their versions of the American dream, often fleeing repressive regimes and limited economic opportunities in their mother countries. Many immigrants realized their dreams, since wages in the mills allowed them to purchase their own homes, provide for their families, and educate their sons and daughters. Later, Afro-Americans from the South were recruited to the Valley, often as strikebreakers after the unionization of steelworkers in the 1940s.

The great ethnic diversity of the population in the Mon Valley is suggested by the Census statistics for McKeesport, the largest city in the Valley. In 1930, 58 percent of McKeesport's residents were either foreign born (coming from thirty different countries) or native born of foreign or mixed parentage.[4] Each ethnic group tended to work in the same mill department and live in the same enclave. Segregation in the mills and residential neighborhoods appeared to keep the Valley divided. Lacking democratic traditions and accustomed to authoritarian leaders, many of the immigrant workers accepted corporate control over their civic life. Mon Valley residents were never as well organized and active in civic affairs as at the workplace.

John Lewis and other national Congress of Industrial Organizational (CIO) leaders were successful in organizing Mon Valley steel workers to fight for higher wages and improved working conditions.[5] Worker concern about unemployment and recurring depression appeared to subordinate their fear of company reprisals and led to the organization of the Steel Workers Organizing Committee (SWOC) as the first official bargaining agent for U.S. Steel Company employees.[6] In 1942, six years after the formation of the SWOC, the USW was established.

The USW was constituted as a highly centralized organization, in part, to countervail the great political and social power of U.S. Steel. The strong national union proved to be a substantial force, helping steel workers become (according to some reports) the highest paid industrial workers in the world. Since the national union and the major steel companies were constant adversaries, major strikes and contested negotiations occurred throughout the thirty-year, post–World War II period.

As the steel industry in the Mon Valley and throughout the nation declined, labor and management each blamed the other. Union officials blamed management for failing to invest in new plants and equipment, planned obsolescence, redirecting corporate resources to other endeavors (one example of this being U.S. Steel's $6 billion purchase of Marathon Oil in 1982), and outdated management practices. Management blamed workers for getting too greedy, demanding unreasonably high wages, and failing to support programs to increase productivity.

McKeesport: The Central City in the Mon Valley

Located thirteen miles south of Pittsburgh at the junction of the Monongahela and the Youghiogheny rivers, McKeesport emerged in the late nineteenth and early twentieth century as the central city of the Mon Valley. McKeesport's position emanated from its being the site of the first steel mill, the first stop on the railroad line connecting the Valley with Pittsburgh, and the municipality with the largest population in the Valley.[7]

McKeesport's history is representative of cities throughout the Valley. McKeesport's development evolved around three steel mills that all become part of the U.S. Steel Corporation.[8] The first steel mill in McKeesport was an iron sheet mill owned and operated by W. Dewees Wood and known as the Wood Works. In 1872, the National Tube Works was established in McKeesport and, by 1901, it was the largest steel pipe producing plant in the world. Before long McKeesport took on the title "Tube City." Peak employment at National Tube exceeded 10,000 in the late 1940s. The third steel mill in

TABLE 7.1
McKeesport Profile

| McKeesport | 1950 | 1960 | 1970 | 1980 | Index Relative to the United States | | | |
					1950	1960	1970	1980
Population	51,502	45,489	37,977	31,012				
Total Employment	19,543	15,538	13,309	10,892				
Percent Manufacturing	49.2%	43.8%	43.6%	33.2%	189.2	161.6	167.7	148.2
Unemployment Rate	6.5%	9.2%	5.5%	12.0%	132.7	180.4	125.0	184.6
Median Family Income	$3,186	$5,309	$8,566	$17,129	103.7	94.5	86.8	81.5
Percent H.S. Graduate	20.4%	22.9%	31.0%	40.8%	59.6	55.7	59.3	61.4
Percent Over 65	8.4%	12.0%	14.5%	18.0%	103.7	130.4	146.5	159.3

Source: U.S. Census Bureau, Population and Housing.

McKeesport, the Christy Park Works, commenced production in 1897. The Christy Works made specialty tube products and ordnance used in two world wars and the Korean War. In World War II, the plant's employment peaked at 7,500 when it became a prime producer of bombs.

Right after World War II and the immediate postwar national economic boom, McKeesport's economy began to decline. Between 1950 and 1960, population declined nearly 11 percent and total employment declined 21 percent (see Table 7.1). Employment decline was concentrated in metals manufacturing, which declined by one-third during the 1950s (see Table 7.2). Metals manufacturing employment dropped from 42 percent to 33 percent of total city employment over the course of the decade. As in Lowell at the turn of the century, the economic decline in McKeesport in the 1950s can be attributed to the compounding effects of unfavorable positioning in product, process, and factor price cycles, including employment concentration in mature product manufacturing, uncompetitive production processes, and cyclical rises in factor prices. Demand for steel products declined with the end of the post-war boom period and with the introduction of lower cost substitute materials, including ceramics and hard plastics. Compounding problems with declining product demand, steel manufacturing facilities throughout the Valley employed an outdated technology, open hearth processing, which could not compete effectively with new basic oxygen furnaces and mini-mills in the United States and abroad. Local factor prices, most notably wages, which had risen rapidly with increasing production and employment

TABLE 7.2
McKeesport Employment 1950 to 1980

	1950	1960	1970	1980	1950–1960	Percentage Changes 1960–1970	1970–1980	1950–1980
Total Employment	19,543	15,538	13,309	10,892	(20.5)	(14.3)	(18.2)	(44.3)
Manufacturing	9,609	6,804	5,801	3,617	(29.2)	(14.7)	(37.6)	(62.4)
Total NonDurable	605	598	465	333	(1.2)	(22.2)	(28.4)	(45.0)
Total Durable	9,004	6,206	4,616	3,284	(31.1)	(25.6)	(28.9)	(63.5)
Furniture & Wood	15	86	77	47	473.3	(10.5)	(39.0)	213.3
Metal Industries	8,183	5,055	3,375	2,537	(38.2)	(33.2)	(24.8)	(69.0)
Machinery	452	589	518	372	30.3	(12.1)	(28.2)	(17.7)
Trans., Com. & Util.	1,269	789	682	732	(37.8)	(13.6)	7.3	(42.3)
Wholesale & Retail	4,195	3,049	2,881	2,539	(27.3)	(5.5)	(11.9)	(39.5)
F.I.R.E.	424	513	512	437	21.0	(0.2)	(14.6)	3.1
Services	2,488	2,594	3,038	2,815	4.3	17.1	(7.3)	13.1

	Percentage Breakdown			
	1950	1960	1970	1980
Total Employment	100.0	100.0	100.0	100.0
Manufacturing	49.2	43.8	43.6	33.2
Total NonDurable	3.1	3.8	3.5	3.1
Total Durable	46.1	39.9	34.7	30.2
Furniture & Wood	0.1	0.6	0.6	0.4
Metal Industries	41.9	32.5	25.4	23.3
Machinery	2.3	3.8	3.9	3.4
Trans., Com. & Util.	6.5	5.1	5.1	6.7
Wholesale & Retail	21.5	19.6	21.6	23.3
F.I.R.E.	2.2	3.3	3.8	4.0
Services	12.7	16.7	22.8	25.8

Source: U.S. Census Bureau, Population and Housing.

in the Valley, did not decline with local product demand but continued to increase.

During the post–World War II period, employment at the three steel mills in McKeesport fell from approximately 20,000 to 500. The Wood Works closed in the early 1950s. In the early 1980s, the Christy Park Works was sold to CPM Industries, a specialty steel manufacturer which employed 500 workers in McKeesport. The National Tube Works was closed down in 1987 and plans were made to raze most of the buildings at the site.

The drop in employment at the three mills had a dramatic impact on McKeesport throughout the post–World War II period. By 1980, metal industry employment in the city accounted for less that one-quarter of total employment in the city (see Table 7.2). As metals industry employment declined, so did population, total employment, and median family income. Between 1950 and 1980, metals industry employment declined by nearly 70 percent, while the city's population declined by 40 percent and total employment declined by 45 percent (see Tables 7.1 and 7.2). During the thirty-year period, unemployment was significantly above the U.S. average, rising to nearly double the U.S. average in 1980. In addition, median family income, which until 1950 had been above the U.S. average, fell to 84 percent of the national average in 1980.[9] The city continued its pronounced decline in the 1980s. Between 1980 and 1990, the city's population decreased another 16 percent, falling to just above 26,000, and the city continued to lose total and manufacturing employment. These data indicate the dramatic nature of McKeesport's decline and suggest an inability to revitalize or stabilize the local economy during the post–World War II period. The shift-share analysis in Chapter 3 suggests that, even when controlling for declines in the metals industry in the nation and region, McKeesport underperformed Jamestown in the 1970s.

In contrast to the situation in Jamestown, an analysis of labor and management relations in McKeesport identifies an intensification of adversarial relations between labor and management during the 1970s that appears to have contributed to accelerated economic decline. In particular, adversarial labor and management relations at U.S. Steel plants in McKeesport appeared to significantly inhibit local adjustment to changing economic conditions.

Labor and Management Conflict in the U.S. Steel Industry

There were efforts at improving labor relations in Mon Valley and McKeesport steel mills, but these tended to be imposed on the local plants by the national union and corporate management and were insensitive to local conditions. In 1971, the Nixon administration, determined to avoid a steel strike on the eve of wage-price controls, pushed the steel industry to grant a generous wage settlement to the United Steel Workers union. In return, the Nixon administration encouraged the two parties to adopt a productivity program that the government could point to in justifying its support of a hefty wage increase. The result was a provision in the national contract requiring that each local union and plant management set up productivity committees. These committees were supposed to "advise with plant management concerning ways and means of improving productivity and promote orderly and peaceful relations with employees."[10] Although hundreds of productivity committees were established across the country, most, including those at the National Tube Works and the Christy Park Works in McKeesport, collapsed without accomplishing their objective.

Giving the name productivity to the committees apparently doomed them from the start. The average Mon Valley steelworker (and steelworkers in mills across the country) viewed the productivity committees "as another speed-up, crew-cutting program which inevitably would mean more layoffs."[11] And, in point of fact, that is exactly what the committees became. According to a USW report, plant managers mistook the productivity committees as a mandate to negotiate crew reductions and refused to listen to other suggestions for improving productivity or quality of work life.[12] This resulted in increased conflict and tension between labor and management, as plant managers used the committees to justify layoffs.

In contrast to the labor and management committees in Jamestown, the 1971 national steel industry contract provision calling for the establishment of in-plant committees was imposed on the locals from the national union. It did not involve rank and filers, did not focus on activities with potential mutual benefits, and demonstrated little sensitivity to local concerns and implementation issues. The productivity committees only called for local and union and management officials to sit on the committees. There were no guidelines for ensuring that substantive worker participation took place and no provision for outside assistance to help organize in-plant committees that could work to overcome over forty years of adversarial relations.

Again in 1980, the national steel industry contract included a provision intended to improve labor and management relations. The 1980 labor and management provision, however, appeared, at least on paper, to encourage local organization more similar to the Jamestown in-plant committees than the 1971 settlement. The 1980 contract included a clause recommending the implementation of Labor-Management Participation Teams (LMPTs). The LMPTs were conceived as an experiment to help address lagging productivity growth. Unlike the (1971) productivity committees, implementation of LMPTs was to be voluntary, requiring agreement for such a committee between the local union and plant management.

The LMPTs failed to turn around adversarial relations between labor and management. As one USW staff official described management's reaction to the LMPT's, "Management was absolutely hysterical about union 'encroachment' on management rights. They wanted no part of the union having any rights in the production process. They wouldn't let us near it. The plant superintendent would tell me 'you run the union, I'll run the plant, and we'll get along just fine.'"[13]

On the other side, USW locals focused their energies on establishing strict rules in order to protect their membership against what they feared would be autocratic dictates of plant managers on the LMPTs. This suggests that the LMPTs, unlike the Jamestown in-plant committees, tended to encourage a furthering of the formal contractual relationship between labor and management instead of promoting cooperation, trust, and workplace innovation.

The LMPT concept turned out to be more form than substance, particularly with regard to their influence on labor and management relations in McKeesport and the Mon Valley. Labor and management at National Tube and Christy Park refused to set up LMPTs. The locals' reluctance was mainly due to lack of encouragement from the national union, ideological opposition to cooperation with management after years of adversarial relations, and the unwillingness of local union officials to encourage their ranks to accept a program which appeared to involve significant risk. On the other hand, local plant managers turned down the idea mainly out of what appeared to be arrogance, thinking that steelworkers could not tell them anything about making steel that they did not already know. Labor relations in McKeesport and throughout the Valley continued to be highly adversarial, leaving little opportunity for cooperative efforts to improve productivity and the competitiveness of local mills. As Mike Bilcsik President of Duquesne Local 1256 (who attempted unsuccessfully to install an LMPT in the Duquesne U.S. Steel plant), commented about the situation in the 1970s and early 1980s in steel mills across the Mon Valley, "We're living with 40-year old union practices and 40-year old management practices. . . . The alienation runs clear from the top all the way down."[14]

The "all-knowing" management and "uncompromising" union officials in the 1970s appeared to contribute to an accelerated loss of market share throughout the U.S. steel industry, with concentrated loses in McKeesport, as suggested by the shift-share analysis in Chapter 3. Many observers cited McKeesport and the Mon Valley as exemplifying what went wrong with the U.S. steel industry and how labor and management worked to destroy an industry. While that is too strong and does not reflect other contributing factors including product and process cycle factors and trade and macroeconomic policies over which local labor and management had little control, the fact remains that, during the 1970s, in contrast to the situation in Jamestown, labor and management were not able to identify any common ground and appear to have contributed to McKeesport's poor economic performance.

The decline of employment accelerated with continued poor positioning in product and process cycles and adversarial labor relations that compounded problems in positioning in the factor price cycle. Several noteworthy attempts were made in the 1980s to revitalize McKeesport and other cities in the Mon Valley. Exploration of these efforts may add insights into local development; in particular, it may shed some light on how severely depressed cities may begin to engineer economic and social recovery.

Allegheny County Development Efforts

Allegheny County encompasses a large portion of the Valley and is the second largest county in the state.[15] It has been in the lead in development efforts in the Mon Valley during the post–World War II period. The County's leadership position emanates in large part from the belief held by many political leaders and development professionals in the area that the problems confronting the Valley are too great and cities in the Valley too small and inexperienced to undertake effectively any economic development initiatives on their own.

Opinion regarding who should lead development efforts in the Valley is consistent with the historical role of the County in economic development in the greater Pittsburgh metropolitan area. Allegheny County has been by far the most aggressive governmental unit in economic development in the region.[16] Allegheny County, through its Department of Development, positioned itself as the conduit for economic development monies, with the initiation of the federal Urban Renewal program in the early 1950s. The County's position as the leader in regional development efforts heightened under the new federalism. Allegheny County has been the primary conduit for federal community development block grants (CDBGs) and other grants and has been the primary regional agent for state economic development programs.

Taking a leadership role in the mid-1980s, the County undertook three major development initiatives in the Valley. These include the organization of a Mon Valley Commission (MVC) in 1986 to analyze development problems in the Valley and make policy recommendations; the formation of a multiple city state enterprise zone to receive special support from the state; and the funding of an American Institute of Architects (AIA) study of the Valley.

One of the major efforts by Allegheny County regarding the revitalization of the Mon Valley was the organization of a Mon Valley Commission (MVC) in May 1986. The stated purpose of the MVC was to "develop a strategy which would include recommendations for immediate actions as well as long range plans, and would make a cohesive whole out of the many fragmented studies and reports already in existence."[17]

The MVC consisted of sixteen individuals appointed by Allegheny County Commissioners, including two co-chairs.[18] The Commission was supported by staff and divided into seven task forces, including manufacturing, nonmanufacturing, transportation, education and labor, environmental systems, housing and human services, and local government. Allegheny County administrators and staff had a strong presence on the MVC. One of the two co-chairs of the Commission was Joseph Hohman, the director of the Allegheny County Department of Development; the other co-chair was James Taylor, chairman and CEO of McKeesport National Bank (at the time, before it was taken over by a larger bank holding company, the largest locally headquartered bank in the Valley). The Commission's staff director was Raymond Reaves, the director of the Allegheny Planning Department. And five of the seven task forces of the Commission were staffed by County employees.[19]

There were representatives from the Mon Valley on the MVC; however, their influence is questionable. Many of the MVC recommendations appeared to be strongly influenced by well placed County officials, including County staffers who were responsible for writing the final Commission report. The strong influence of the County on the MVC can be inferred from the commission's recommendations. The MVC recommendations positioned the County, in particular the County Department of Development, as the leader in Valley revitalization efforts. The highlight of the MVC's recommendations was, for example, the conveying of the McKeesport National Works and the Duquesne Works from USX (the reorganized U.S. Steel company) to the county which would then be responsible for redeveloping the sites. The following quote from a press report is reflective of the lack of input local Mon Valley officials had in the recommendations of the MVC: "The announcement (sic. that USX would convey the property to the County) surprised elected officials in those cities."[20]

The package of recommendations from the MVC carried a price tag of $333 million—most of the money was to come from the state and most of the responsibility for administering its use was assigned to the County. The proposal called for over $307 million in funding from the state. The bulk of the funds, $298 million, would come from the PA Department of Transportation for expressway and other road improvements ($246 million) and from the PA Department of Community Affairs and Commerce for economic studies, planning, site demolition, and public housing modernization ($52 million). The MVC report recommended that the County contribute less than one-tenth of one percent ($265,000) of all monies, primarily for economic data gathering and analysis by the Allegheny County Planning Department.

While the MVC recommendations called for Allegheny County to contribute a very small fraction of the funds, it positioned the County at the forefront of development efforts. In all seven policy (task force) areas, the County was assigned implementation responsibility, including responsibility for the $20 million redevelopment of the Duquesne and National Works, establishing a Mon Valley Education Consortium, undertaking a steel retention study, conducting a pre-engineering study of the proposed Mon Valley Expressway, and providing targeted incentives for local government modernization. There was not one single local municipality listed as primarily responsible for any priority action in the Commission's 152-page report.[21]

Newly elected (November 1986) Governor Robert Casey, along with the three County Commissioners and state elected officials, was at the McKeesport campus of Penn State University for the release of the Mon Valley Commission report in March, 1987. Interestingly, in all the hoopla, Governor Casey did not commit a single state dollar to the proposed revitalization strategy. In his speech, he only commented that "I come here today to pledge my personal commitment to work with the individuals and organizations who put this report together."[22]

In another effort to lead and orchestrate economic development efforts in the Valley, The Allegheny County Department of Development in early 1988 filed a novel proposal with the state Department of Community Affairs. The County proposed to create and oversee an enterprise zone made up of thirty-seven Allegheny County cities in the Valley to receive special state economic and community development program support. The thirty-seven cities proposed for inclusion included some suburban cities that could hardly be categorized as depressed, including Monroeville, which experienced over a 70 percent increase in earned income tax revenue from 1980 to 1986.[23]

Reflective of the feelings of local citizens toward the enterprise zone proposal were the comments made by the thirty-ninth district democratic state representative, David Levadansky, in a letter to the Pennsylvania Department of Community Affairs. His comments included the following:

> I believe that the effort to combine cities into an area-wide enterprise zone is really an attempt to remove decision-making ability from the business and government leaders at the local level. Though some County officials believe they know what is best for Mon Valley cities, I feel that the County is simply seeking state funding for their efforts to gain full and total control of economic development initiatives. . . . Imposing top-down lines of authority and control over communities will only exacerbate the problem of weakened economies.[24]

In still another effort by the County, it supported a Regional Urban Design Assistance Team (RUDAT) study of redevelopment issues in the Mon Valley. RUDATs are organized by the American Institute of Architects (AIA) "to help cities identify issues, develop action plans and move forward to new horizons."[25] In the Mon Valley, the AIA was asked to investigate the "remaking" of four U.S. Steel mill sites in the Valley that had been abandoned and represented over 1,000 acres of steel mill property. These included the Homestead Works, the Carrie Furnace in Rankin, the Duquesne Works, and the National Works in McKeesport. The RUDAT team spent five days in Mon Valley cities hearing presentations by citizens, government, and local industries. It identified and analyzed issues, developed alternative courses of action, prepared specific recommendations, and produced an action plan in a 120-page document. The RUDAT team made the following recommendations:[26]

> 1. Use of existing buildings at the Homestead Works for an international garden festival to be held in 1992. This would involve stripping the buildings' steel shell and enclosing in glass to provide a central exhibition area, restaurants, theaters and a winter garden ("the equivalent of a Crystal Palace");
>
> 2. Reuse of the National Tube Works in McKeesport as a flea/trade market and for recreation;
>
> 3. Construction of a trash recycling plant at the Duquesne Works and

retention of the (Dorothy Six) blast furnace as an industrial heritage museum;

4. Preservation of the Carrie Furnace in Rankin as a steel museum;

5. Formation of a Mon Valley Historical District in order to inventory and preserve historic sites throughout the Valley;

6. Establishment of a River Zone District with common zoning for all riverfront property in the Valley.

The recommendations did not include retention of any of the mills for industrial production. The plan simply stated that "outdated mill buildings that cannot be used again should be torn down."[27]

The RUDAT team report got a mixed reception. County representatives were particularly pleased by the report. County Commissioner Tom Foerster, for example, was excited about the report. He was particularly pleased by the suggestion to have common zoning for all the Mon Valley River property. Forester commented that "common zoning would be a lift for any developer."[28] He also announced that he had already received numerous calls from potential investors and developers regarding carrying out some of the report's recommendations.

In spite of the County's enthusiasm, many local residents worried about what would become of their cities without the steel industry. Representative of the opinion of many long-time residents with strong emotional and economic ties to the steel industry were the comments by the president of United Steelworkers Local 1397 Pensioners Association, Babe Fernandez: "The young people will leave and we won't have anyone here but old people unless steel mills are reopened."[29]

The RUDAT team presented its findings and plans for the Valley to 350 international participants at the AIA "Remaking Cities" conference held in Pittsburgh in March 1988. There was much media attention (including an article in the *New York Times*, March 6, 1988) surrounding the Conference. A large part of the national interest in the conference was generated by the attendance of Britain's Prince Charles as honorary chairman of the four-day conference. The Prince, in a speech to the Conference on its final day, endorsed the recommendations of the RUDAT study. However, he also urged the international AIA representatives "to help people help themselves in rebuilding industrial cities. It is the residents who should be consulted about their city, who should take part in rebuilding their city and who should benefit—psychologically and economically—from their city."[30]

The Prince's message regarding the need to build local capacity to address development issues could have been just as, if not more, appropriately delivered to Allegheny County officials, who at times appeared to be more concerned with maintaining their control over development activities and funding than with meeting the needs of residents in the depressed cities in the Valley. The efforts by the County appeared to have little effect on conditions in the Valley. They seemed to take more effort in documenting problems than ameliorating them. The County's approach to development in the Valley demonstrated little sensitivity to local needs and resident concerns.

Community-Based Development Efforts

As an alternative to the County's approach, a new effort, which attempted to involve residents of municipalities across the Mon Valley in their cities' development, was initiated in 1985. The initiative was designed to help local residents confront a new economic, social, and institutional reality.

As described earlier, having been dependent on one industry and one corporation for over a century, citizens in the Valley had been prone to equate local efforts in development with providing inducements to U.S. Steel to continue, or delay reducing, operations. Prevalent throughout the Mon Valley was the feeling that U.S. Steel would always be there and one way or another provide for their economic well-being. If that failed, Mon Valley residents assumed that, as they had in the past, the federal and state government and Allegheny County would provide for them with macroeconomic and trade policy and with special programs and development funds.

There was little history of locally initiated economic and community development efforts. This was reflected by the absence of local development planning bodies equivalent to the Lowell Plan or the economic development steering committee in Jamestown and the lack of any community development corporations (CDCs) or nonprofit development groups in the Valley, such as the Coalition for a Better Acre in Lowell and WHALE in New Bedford. There appeared to be no perceived need and little will to develop capacity within cities that would allow local citizens to initiate economic development efforts on their own.

The Allegheny Conference on Community Development (Allegheny Conference), a group of corporate and civic leaders in the greater Pittsburgh area, became increasingly concerned with the declining economic and social situation in the Valley and the lack of progress made in improving conditions.[31] The leaders in the Allegheny Conference were disturbed by what they perceived as poorly designed and implemented public programs, the confrontational tactics of a small but vocal group of local ministers in the Valley, and the absence of initiative by the majority of local residents.

In 1985 the Conference began to consider alternative approaches for alleviating deteriorating conditions in the Valley. The Conference hired Michael Eichler, who had spent his earlier years as a community organizer in Buffalo and the city of Pittsburgh, to look at the Mon Valley and make recommendations for a development strategy. Eichler spent his first four months on the job interviewing people in the Mon Valley and federal, state, county, and local government officials and came to the following conclusions:[32]

1. Existing local political leaders had risen to power at a time when the paternalistic employer and union were dominant and were incapable of effectively responding to the massive loss of tax base from the closing of the steel mills.

2. Local people currently not in leadership positions were eager to do something and to work on producing a success. They were frustrated by the inaction on the part of elected local leaders and their own lack of ability to get economic development efforts off the ground.

3. The cities throughout the Mon Valley were isolated from Pittsburgh, Harrisburg (the state capital), and each other.

4. A wide range of individuals in the public and private sectors were genuinely concerned about the Mon Valley and were prepared to help once a local agenda was articulated. Potential development partners included national and regional foundations and state and local government.

Based upon these findings, Eichler devised a strategy that was designed to facilitate the creation of locally based human and organizational capacity in economic development throughout the Mon Valley. The strategy was to use funds from the Local Initiatives Support Corporation (LISC) as an organizing tool—a tangible resource that could set parameters for local development and which placed responsibility on the shoulders of the local citizenry to form coalitions, organize development corporations, and formulate specific development project ideas.[33]

LISC funding required that development projects have local partners and investors and be implemented by community development corporations (CDCs). It also required that projects generate both economic benefits in the community and some profit for the CDCs so that LISC funds could be leveraged into future CDC projects. Eichler's strategy was to use LISC funds as an incentive to mobilize the local citizenry and to begin the difficult task of building city-based development capacity.

Eichler's tactic was to employ a development team of young committed professionals who would work closely with local people in individual cities in the Mon Valley. The staff of the Mon Valley Development Team (MVDT) was to take the following pragmatic actions:

1. identify local citizens for participation in development efforts;
2. organize community development corporations; and
3. work with local people to conceive project ideas, turn ideas into specific projects, and implement projects.

The intent of the MVDT was to provide a vehicle for local people to learn about development by doing it. The strategy was to start with small-scale projects in individual cities and gradually build development capacity and knowledge within and among Mon Valley cities. The objective was to help Mon Valley citizens to help themselves, by increasing their understanding of the dynamics of the local economy (i.e., the position of the Mon Valley in the larger regional and national economy), increasing their awareness of the resources (public and private, technical and analytic) available to them, and helping them learn the basics of "doing development," including the right questions to ask private developers and governmental officials.

The MVDT was established in January 1987 with two full-time organizers. Organizers followed the "development team model" designed by Michael Eichler.[34] Organizers first went into cities and identified potential local leaders by observing the existing power structure, social networks, and credibility patterns. The organizers then used their knowledge of the cities, along with the incentive of LISC funding, to persuade residents to form community development corporations. Next, organizers used the credibility they established during their information gathering to identify and suggest project ideas and bring in development professionals to work with the CDCs on development projects. The MVDT and the local citizens then worked together with the Pittsburgh area LISC program officer to produce a tangible success (i.e., develop a project). The objective was to find projects with benefits to the community and a relatively high probability of success.

The cost of the initial efforts of the MVDT were low, especially when compared to other efforts that had been proposed for the Valley, including the $333 million plan put forward by the Mon Valley Commission in 1987.[35] The Heinz Endowment (a Pittsburgh-based foundation) provided initial operating funds for the MVDT. In its first year, the team had an operating budget of $150,000. In its second year, the budget was increased to $340,000.

Initially Eichler hired two young professionals with masters degrees in social work as organizers. The organizers were later supported by architects, attorneys, and other experienced development professionals with specific areas of expertise critical to undertaking development projects in the Valley, including finance, marketing, and housing. The technical experts were employed as consultants and brought in by organizers to assist CDCs with specific projects on an "as needed" basis. Later on, as the demand increased, the MVDT hired two full-time technical experts in addition to two more organizers. By the fall of 1988, the MVDT included a head organizer and development expert, three staff organizers, and two staff technical experts—one in finance and one in housing.

The MVDT started its work in cities that had been identified as the most in need. The most needy cities were the industrial cities along the Monongahela River (including McKeesport) that were suffering from severe industrial abandonment and dislocation. These were also the cities that had the least capacity and experience in terms of financial, organizational, and human resources to deal with economic and community development problems.

In each city, the MVDT organizers recruited fifteen to twenty CDC board members who would be capable of collectively delivering citywide support for development project ideas. CDCs were organized initially in fourteen cities (expanding to seventeen by 1984) throughout the Mon Valley including: McKeesport, Braddock, Charleroi, Clairton, Duquesne, Elizabeth, Glassport, Homestead, Monessen, Monongahela, Rankin, Swissvale, Turtle Creek, and Wilmerding.

The CDCs have been remarkably active, especially in light of the paucity of local initiatives prior to their organization. In less than two years, the CDCs initiated economic development projects with an estimated value of over $10 million, and LISC money was committed to six projects. Projects involved a mix of housing, commercial, business, and industrial development, which included the conversion of a building in downtown Homestead from a fire damaged shell to the site of the Pittsburgh High Technology Council's Mon Valley satellite office, renovation and conversion of a old movie theater in Charleroi into a performing arts center, and the opening of a twenty-two–room Inn with restaurant and banquet facilities in a historic building in Monongahela.

The locating of the Pittsburgh High Technology Council satellite office in the Mon Valley reflects the potential transom effects of recent growth in high technology and medical services from the University district just east of Pittsburgh and north of the Mon Valley. This is somewhat similar to what happened in Lowell in the mid-

1970s, which benefited from the build-up of the Route 128 corridor and entrepreneurial activity emerging from nearby research institutions. In Lowell, M.I.T. and Harvard produced many of the entrepreneurs that stimulated the revitalization of the area, including Dr. Wang. There is potential that the Mon Valley can benefit from its proximity to the University of Pittsburgh and Carnegie-Mellon University in a similar way. The major attractions of the Valley, similar to Lowell's in the early 1970s, are its proximity to research institutions and related industries, low rents, and available labor supply.

The individual CDCs in 1989, decided to join together in a larger regional organization, the Mon Valley Initiative (the Initiative). The purpose of the Initiative is to enable the CDCs to work more closely together, to engender more cooperation between the cities, and to institutionalize the MVDT. The Initiative houses the MVDT (as common support staff), shares funding, and is an advocate for development activities throughout the Valley. The Mon Valley Initiative staff provides assistance to the individual CDC's, in much the same way the MVDT did during its two years of existence, except without the extensive organizing activities required at the MVDT's inception. Community organizers on the Initiative staff help facilitate CDC activities and help recruit new volunteers.

With the formation of the Initiative, the pool of funds available for Mon Valley development projects expanded beyond the original LISC funds. Mon Valley CDCs, by demonstrating their unified purpose with the organization of the Initiative, were able to get an increased commitment of $16 million from area foundations and banks for development projects. Pittsburgh area foundations that financed the MVDT were impressed with Eichler's initial efforts and willing to commit $6 million of equity funding to development projects in the Valley, contingent on the creation of a mechanism to distribute project money among the CDCs.[36] The Initiative created a financial committee with representatives from individual CDCs that served that purpose and insured that the foundation money would be forthcoming.

As with the MVDT, the strategy to get increased bank funding of projects in the Valley was conceived by Michael Eichler. First Eichler made an agreement with Alfred Wishart, the executive director of the Pittsburgh Foundation, to make the new $6 million equity commitment from local foundations for Mon Valley projects contingent on area banks committing loan money to the Valley. Eichler then used his connections with Pittsburgh Foundation officials and his position as a staff member of the Allegheny Conference to arrange meetings with chief executive officers at Pittsburgh's leading banks.[37] He went to the four largest banks in Pittsburgh—the Mellon Bank, Equibank, Pittsburgh National Bank and Union National Bank (all of which had branch offices in the Valley)—and asked them each to make $2.5 million in loan money available for development projects in the Mon Valley. At these meetings, Eichler highlighted the progress that had been made in the Valley, including the organization of CDCs, the undertaking of small development projects, and the increasing sense of collective purpose among the residents of the Valley, as demonstrated by the organization of the Initiative. Eichler also emphasized that the bank money could leverage $6 million in foundation investment. Eichler pointed out that all the Mon Valley was missing was capital, since the residents now had the organizational capacity and initiative to undertake development projects. Eichler also suggested that the banks might be concerned that their lack of investment in the Valley might be in violation of the Community Reinvestment Act. He did this without threatening to expose them (even though he had the data in hand that documented their lack of investment).

The $2.5 million commitment Eichler eventually got from the four banks did not require a radical departure from standard bank operating procedures. The "Mon Valley money" would be administered by loan officers at the individual banks. The money would be regular loan money, and the banks were not asked to make loans available at below-market rates for Mon Valley projects. The objective was not to get a pool of subsidized below-market-rate loan monies or to create a new financial development corporation for the CDCs, only to gain some commitment from regional financial institutions to economic and community development in the Valley. Along with the commitment of the four large regional financial institutions to set aside funds for projects in the Valley, a system of accountability was established. This included periodic meetings with bank CEOs, foundation heads and the Allegheny Conference executive director to review potential CDC projects and to work on problems at "roll up the sleeves" meetings in the Valley with Initiative board members.

It is too early to reach definitive conclusions about the efforts of the MVDT and the Initiative. The CDCs in the Valley are not a panacea, but that was not their intent. Their purpose was to help local citizens develop awareness and capacity to address development issues in an informed and organized manner. The organization of CDCs and the Initiative around city development issues appears to have engaged and empowered local citizens, changed attitudes and perceptions, increased local awareness of development issues, helped cities to develop the (organizational, technical and financial) capacity that will be critical to addressing development issues in the future, and engendered a collective sense of purpose among Mon Valley cities that had been lacking.

Conclusions

The development in McKeesport and across the Mon Valley over the past decade and a half, when compared and contrasted to the experience in Jamestown, Lowell, and New Bedford provides insights into the dynamics of city economic development. The lack of any tradition of initiative by local governmental bodies and the strong conflicts in labor and management relations in the face of severe industrial decline in the Mon Valley suggests that local institutions established in earlier eras can become significant barriers to city revitalization. The experience in the Mon Valley indicates that it may be necessary at critical points in a city's development to create new institutional arrangements to circumvent old institutions that have proven to be ineffective in adapting to changing circumstances. New local institutions can provide useful symbols and change attitudes and behavior of citizens and organizations.

The JALMC was a local institutional innovation that overcame development problems in Jamestown similar to those that burdened the Mon Valley in the 1970s. The JALMC helped local workers and management perceive each other in a new light. It encouraged cooperation, helped reduce strike days, and facilitated programs to improve worker productivity, thereby contributing to improved city positioning in the factor price cycle and local economic growth. The JALMC was also a symbol of new city priorities and attitudes and provided a signal to outsiders, including Cummins Engine, that problems in the city were being addressed and changes were taking place.

In contrast to the JALMC, the productivity committees and the LMPTs in the Mon Valley steel plants were by-products of negotiations dominated by national organizations, U.S. Steel and the USW, which appeared incapable of adjusting to changing circumstances or promoting labor and management cooperation. Neither the productivity committees nor the LMPTs were responsive to local needs; nor were they designed to change attitudes or behavior—both perpetuated poor relations and reinforced old prejudices and failed to improve work practices or city economic positioning.

In contrast to the steel industry productivity committees and LMPTs, the Mon Valley Development Team was designed to address development problems in the context of the realities of the local development environment. The incremental tactics of the MVDT reflected not only a strategy to build local development capacity, but also recognition of the limited economic opportunities in the region and a politically sensitive approach designed to overcome potential resistance from existing institutions and city leaders. Whereas an ambitious development program led by aggressive political leaders appeared to be successful in Lowell, in the Mon Valley the incremental approach undertaken outside of the political arena seemed more appropriate.

The failure of city political leaders in the Mon Valley to use a crisis situation to put forward new development initiatives (as we observed with Tsongas in Lowell) can be attributed not only to limited economic opportunities in the Mon Valley in the late 1970s and early 1980s (especially when compared with Lowell in the mid-1970's), but also to the political culture in the Mon Valley. Residents of the Mon Valley appeared to have limited expectations of local government and local officials lacked the experience, political savvy, and independence to initiate new development efforts.

A curious similarity between development efforts in Lowell, Jamestown, and the Mon Valley is that outside financial assistance appeared to be critical in all these areas in fostering the creation of innovative local development initiatives. Given city inertia in the face of extended economic decline and internal resource limitations, outside assistance may be necessary to start depressed cities on new paths and get development momentum generated. The in-plant labor and management committees in Jamestown were funded by an EDA grant; Mogan's vision for Lowell would never have been formalized without Model Cities funding; and the efforts of the MVDT were dependent on the contributions of the Allegheny Conference and Pittsburgh-based foundations. In Jamestown and Lowell, federal grants at the initial stages of development efforts proved to have noteworthy multiplier effects since development momentum was generated after initial success. In the Mon Valley, it is still too early to tell what the multiplier effects of Heinz Endowment's initial $150,000 contribution to the MVDT might be.

In the next chapter, we will expand on the discussion here and review the key findings from the city development analyses.

Eight

Critical Factors in City Revitalization

THE CITY DEVELOPMENT ANALYSES suggest that local leadership and organization of selected city economic development activities can be beneficial. It can change the attitudes and behavior of individuals and organizations, a city's image, and city positioning in product, process, and factor price cycles.

This chapter summarizes the findings from the city development analyses and considers their relevance. Characteristics of successful local development efforts are listed, and the key conclusions from the city analyses are presented with reference to the theories of urban politics and collective action introduced in Chapter 2. Then the broader significance of the findings are considered—first, in light of recent developments in one of the study cities, Lowell, and then with respect to theories of local market and government failure.

Findings from the City Development Analyses

Chapters 4 through 7 were most concerned with inductive theory building, as contrasted with much of the analysis of local economic development that tests hypotheses and existing theory. The methodology—case study and comparative case study—produced data and evidence of the particular economic history and conditions, political culture, and traditions in each city that shaped their development. The city development analyses indicated the value of individualized responses to circumstances initiated by local leaders and implemented through local decision-making agencies that are broadly conceived. The comparative study of the four cities produced some general conclusions which suggest hypotheses about local economic development.

Key components and characteristics of successful local economic development efforts as suggested by the city analyses include the following:

1. *Local leadership* able to engage the citizenry and to relate to federal, state, private, and foundation groups;

2. *Strategic development agencies* designed to address key problems and opportunities in local development (including positioning in product,

process, and factor price cycles) and serve as forums for negotiation and consensus-building;

3. *Institutional arrangements* (e.g., public and private partnerships, labor and management committees, community development corporations) that can foster new relations, motivate participation, and circumvent failing local institutions that have not been effective in adjusting to changing circumstances. These institutions are most effective if they can engender trust and cooperation among the public, private, and nonprofit sectors;

4. *Local development capacity* that can work toward lowering the costs of implementing development projects. Local development capacity could include technical expertise and an ability to coordinate activities between different levels of government and the public, nonprofit, and private sectors;

5. *Regional analysis* to determine city development assets and liabilities, to assess city positioning in the regional economy and product, process, and factor price cycles, and to identify opportunities for growth along with potential bottlenecks;

6. *Sensitivity to labor force characteristics and dynamics*, including skill levels, training requirements, and socialization and how they relate to economic development;

7. *Broad conception of economic development.* Local economic development involves more than industrial attraction and employment training. The potential role of education, health care, housing, and social services in economic development and their influence on city positioning in product, process, and factor price life cycles should be considered.

8. *Positive city attitude towards development efforts.* Part of local development involves instilling residents and local institutions with a positive attitude about themselves, their city, and the future;

9. *Sensitivity to city history, and political and social culture.* Early development history of a city can uncover a single or several important historical events that shape its political and economic culture and strongly influence its development.

10. *Recognition that economic success is not forever* and that development is a dynamic process subject to cycles. Cities will therefore require continuous revitalization.

Politics and Collective Action Reconsidered

It appears that the workings of the larger political economy and the nature of development policy do not uniquely shape local politics or determine the specific kinds of development policies pursued. In all the cities, we observed that the type of development policies undertaken and the distribution of benefits from development are to a significant degree politically determined at the local level. Local political leaders in Jamestown, Lowell, and New Bedford strongly influenced city development policies. Political leaders in each city pursued a different strategy with considerably different distributional impact. In the Mon Valley, the notable absence of local public officials from city development activities also had a profound influence on development in the Valley, as Allegheny County officials dominated the economic development agenda in the area.

With regards to consensus politics and collective interest in local development policy, the analysis supports public choice theory and contradicts the city limits view. It is suggested that citywide interest in economic growth is not a sufficient condition for collective action in local development. Congruent with Olson's view of the logic of collective action, the city development analyses indicate that selective inducements and/or political entrepreneurship are often necessary to induce collective effort in local development. We observed this most strikingly at the beginning stages of development efforts when coalitions were first being organized (e.g., Senator Tsongas threatening banks that did not participate in the LDFC and the political savvy employed by Lundine to get labor and management to cooperate in a novel local development effort). In addition, the analysis concurs with Axelrod that repeated interactions, particularly when institutionalized in local organizations, such as the community development corporations organized in the Mon Valley in the late 1980s, can motivate mutually beneficially cooperative activities.

The city development analyses also demonstrated the variety of local development coalitions, as do Mollenkopf, Stone, Swanstrom and BMT. Not all development coalitions are elite (either economic or political elite) dominated. The Lowell Plan and LDFC were dominated by economic and political elites. The economic development task force in New Bedford was dominated by economic elites. The JALMC in Jamestown included local labor leaders and was a more inclusive organization than the dominant development institutions in Lowell or New Bedford. The Mon Valley Commission was dominated by regional political elites, while the CDCs in the Valley had local residents as board members.

The analysis is inconclusive with regard to the efficacy of nonelite and citizen organization. There are no indications of nonelites being empowered through incorporation in dominant local development coalitions, as BMT suggest took place in Berkeley. A lack of citizen group participation in city development politics seems to generally describe the situation in development policy making in all four cities. Nonetheless, Long's view that citizens can benefit from political and social organization is supported by the influence of the CBA in Lowell and CDCs throughout the Mon Valley. In particular, the organization of the Mon Valley Initiative and the increase in resources available to CDCs in the area suggests—as does Swanstrom's observation of development policy making in Cleveland—the utility of forming a metropolitan area coalition of neighborhood groups based on common interests. This contrasts with the more common view of Peterson, Mollenkopf, and Katznelson that local politics and citizen action is incidental and potentially disruptive to development policy making. Regardless of the validity of the more common view, it can have the unfortunate consequence of being self-fulfilling, as we observed most distinctively in the Mon Valley prior to the efforts of the Mon Valley Development Team. A "rational" response to the perception of powerlessness by citizens and community groups can be to assume even less control, and responsibility for their lives.

The significance of noneconomic factors in inspiring local development coalition building and citizen mobilization appears to be limited. In local development policy making, solitary and purposive incentives appear to be significantly less important than self-interest. Economic self-interest appeared to be the primary motivation for all the significant local economic development initiatives documented, ranging from the banks in Lowell organizing the LDFC to citizens in the Mon Valley forming CDCs. Perhaps one of the most enlightening phenomenon observed, however, was how individual and organizational perceptions of self-interest could be altered by local development leaders. We observed how Mayor Lundine transformed perceptions of self-interest of labor and management in Jamestown. We also observed how public discourse, the documentation of the city's history, and the actions of Mogan and Tsongas changed the perceptions of self-interest of Lowell citizens and bankers. Finally we observed how leaders of the CBA changed the perceptions (and reality) of residents in the Acre neighborhood regarding their personal efficacy.

Further Consideration of Local Development Hypotheses

An Update of Development Activities in Lowell

An update of the development experience in Lowell allows for consideration of some of the hypotheses generated from the comparative analysis. It provides an opportunity to test for the importance of (1) leadership, (2) local development institutions, and (3) citizen mo-

TABLE 8.1
Lowell and New Bedford, 1975 to 1990

	1975		1986		1990		1975 to 1986 Percent Change		1975 to 1990 Percent Change	
	Lowell	N.B.	Lowell	N.B.	Lowell	N.B.	Lowell	N.B.	Lowell	N.B.
Manufacturing	12,592	19,487	18,723	18,325	15,233	13,517	48.7	(6.0)	21.0	(30.6)
Wholesale & Retail	6,114	12,174	7,495	7,914	6,209	8,184	22.6	(35.0)	1.6	(32.8)
Services	5,770	5,806	9,218	8,131	9,447	9,076	59.8	40.0	63.7	56.3
Total Private	28,304	38,370	40,435	40,376	34,925	36,436	42.9	5.2	23.4	(5.0)

Source: Mass. Department of Employment and Training.

bilization. It may also give an indication of whether similar factors contribute to managing local economies during periods of general economic decline as well as during periods of revitalization.

Lowell experienced impressive growth from the mid-1970s through the 1980s. Over the fifteen-year period—1975 to 1990—manufacturing employment increased by 21 percent and total private employment increased by 23 percent. (In contrast, during the same time period manufacturing employment in New Bedford declined by over 30 percent and total employment declined by 5 percent [see Table 8.1].) Since its period of economic revitalization (as identified in Chapter 3) from 1975 to 1986, however, Lowell's economy has contracted and unemployment has increased. Between 1986 and 1990, total private employment in the city declined by nearly 14 percent, manufacturing employment declined by 19 percent and unemployment reached 13 percent in July 1991, its highest level in over 15 years.

Lowell's economy was adversely effected by numerous factors, some of which might have been predicted by dynamic cycle and regional economic theories and others by factors not as predictable. The major factors contributing to Lowell's economic downturn in the late 1980s included pronounced economic decline throughout New England, regional banking difficulties, and declining profitability and employment in mini-computer manufacturing.

Lowell was still mired in economic difficulties at the time that this update was written; nonetheless, the discussion here suggests that unexpected strength in manufacturing, access to capital (including recycled development funds), and local capacity to adjust development efforts to changing circumstances appear to have benefited Lowell and favorably positioned the city for future growth.

TABLE 8.2
Lowell and New Bedford: Differential Employment Shifts 1980 to 1990

| | 1980 – 1986 | | 1986 – 1990 | | 1980 – 1990 | |
	Lowell	N.B.	Lowell	N.B.	Lowell	N.B.
Manufacturing	3,925	(3,058)	(500)	(1,881)	3,426	(4,939)
Services	(711)	(191)	(964)	(107)	(1,676)	(299)
Wholesale & Retail	(1,179)	(952)	(1,201)	360	(2,380)	(592)
F.I.R.E.	643	(144)	(586)	(438)	57	(582)
Trans., Com. & Util.	79	(520)	(119)	163	(39)	(357)
Total	3,720	(5,789)	(3,002)	(2,067)	718	(7,857)

Source: Massachusetts Department of Employment and Training.

LOWELL IN THE LATE 1980S

Between 1986 and 1990, Lowell suffered a decline in employment relative to the state and to New Bedford (see Table 8.2). The negative differential shift in employment of approximately 3,000 suggests that, if Lowell's employment sectors had grown (or decreased) at the same rate as the state's, Lowell's employment, instead of declining by 5,000, would have fallen by just 2,000. This is in sharp contrast to the early 1980s, when Lowell's economy significantly outperformed the state's and New Bedford's economy (see Chapter 3). A large portion of the city's negative shift in employment was in services, wholesale and retail trade, finance, and real estate employment.

It is significant that, despite layoffs and substantial financial losses at Wang Laboratories Inc. and despite the city's employment concentration in an industry in the mature stage of the product life cycle (mini-computer and related manufacturing), the city experienced a relatively small negative shift in manufacturing employment, particularly compared to the decline in New Bedford. In addition, the average wage in Lowell remained above the state's and New Bedford's—$26,614 in Lowell compared to $25,220 in the state and $19,782 in New Bedford. Furthermore, the city continued to attract new residents—Lowell's 1990 population was 103,439, an 11 percent increase from 1986.[1] This suggests underlying strength in Lowell's economy in the late 1980s and indicates some capacity in the city to counteract negative economic fundamentals.

During the late 1980s, Lowell appears to have replaced employment lost at Wang and related industries with employment in expanding or new manufacturing industry. While Wang was reported to have reduced its workforce in Lowell by approximately 2,500 between 1986 and 1990, total manufacturing employment in the city declined by only 2,900.[2] This is less than what might have been expected, given the employment decline at Wang and other mini-computer and related manufacturers in the city and their multiplier effects in the local economy.

Lowell appears to have been most negatively affected by weaknesses in secondary industries. While the causes of employment decline in the secondary sector are not difficult to identify, they have proven difficult to overcome. The weakness in wholesale and retail trade (in which employment declined by 17 percent between 1986 and 1990) can be attributed in large part to increased competition from suburban malls and retail outlets in New Hampshire (a state with no retail sales tax), as indicated by Jordan Marsh closing its store in downtown Lowell. The 13 percent employment decline in the finance, insurance, and real estate (FIRE) industries can be attributed in large part to Lowell's position as a regional banking center— a position that was particularly beneficial in supporting initial revitalization efforts but apparently became a vulnerability when regional financial difficulties set in during the late 1980s, development activity slowed down, and some local banks were taken over by larger regional banks.[3]

The city's high unemployment rate in the late 1980s and the early 1990s can be attributed both to a decline in local employment opportunities and to increased labor supply. For the first time since the 1920s, Lowell's population increased during the 1980s. Lowell's reputation for economic revitalization and support of immigrants served as a magnet, even when economic growth in the city subsided in the late 1980s.[4] In addition to contributing to increased unemployment, increases in the city's population put a strain on the city's fiscal resources, as many new residents required significant public services without making comparable contributions to the city's financial base.[5] However, the city once again (similar to the situation in the middle 1970s) had a supply of low-cost labor that could be used as a "selling point" to attract new industry.

WANG AND BEYOND

While the warnings that "as goes Wang so goes Lowell" appear to have been exaggerated, there is no question that the problems experienced at Wang Laboratories had a profound influence on the city. Wang suffered, as did other mini-computer manufacturers in the state, including Digital Equipment Company (DEC), Prime Computer, and Data General, from rapid technological change and product maturation.[6] Most significant were the increased capabilities and declining cost of micro-computers, which effectively reduced the demand for mini-computers.

Major restructuring at Wang was required in light of losses of nearly $1 billion in fiscal years 1989 and 1990 and revenue declines approaching 20 percent annually. The company moved away from hardware manufacturing to software development, consulting services, and marketing. The "new" Wang in Lowell operated with significantly fewer workers. Between 1986 and 1990, Wang decreased its worldwide labor force from 31,000 (its peak employment) to 17,500 and, in June 1991, announced that it would lay off an additional 3,000 to 4,000 workers. Approximately 40 percent of the company's layoffs and current workforce are in Massachusetts.[7] A majority of Wang's employment in Massachusetts is in the Greater Lowell area, approximately 4,600 in 1991.[8]

The composition of the Wang workforce also changed substantially. Wang in the 1990s employed a greater concentration of skilled, marketing, and technical support employees and fewer manufacturing workers. This is reflected in the company's "office 2000 strategic thrust for the 1990s," which focused on improving the productivity of client companies by providing an array of technology and consulting services and by an agreement to sell equipment made by IBM.[9] With its repositioning, Wang entered the 1990s in a relatively high-growth and high-margin segment of the high-technology industry. This change portended a more positive future for the company and the city.[10]

As Wang was transformed from a durable goods manufacturer to a software and computer marketing and consulting services company, it appeared that the employment multiplier effect of Wang in Lowell was reduced. The local business that seemed to suffer the most from Wang's decline was the Hilton Hotel, whose viability was premised on Dr. Wang's commitment to fill hotel rooms with trainees. As part of its initial downsizing and re-positioning, Wang closed its Corporate Education Center in downtown Lowell. Without Wang clients coming to Lowell for training, the Hilton experienced occupancy rates of approximately 50 percent, which were below the Hotel's breakeven point, and the Hilton's owners were forced into bankruptcy.[11] The lead bank with a first mortgage position, Coast Federal Bank of Los Angeles (formerly Coast Savings and Loan), foreclosed on the property and took over the operation of the hotel in June 1990.

Coast's actions after foreclosure suggest that it believed a hotel in downtown Lowell was viable. The bank contracted Interstate Hotels

Inc. of Pittsburgh to manage the facility and committed to keeping the hotel open and maintaining employment.[12] The bank invested $500,000 toward renovation of the hotel and, in August 1991, canceled the franchise with Hilton and signed a new agreement with Sheraton. Coast believed that the hotel would fare better as a Sheraton franchise, because of its stronger name recognition as a Boston-based company compared to that of Hilton, which was headquartered in California.[13]

While Coast Federal Bank kept the hotel operating in the downtown, the Lowell Plan and city government worked with state officials to ensure that the Wang Corporate Education Center did not go unutilized. The Education Center was sold by Wang to the state's largest community college, in 1990 for $13 million, or approximately $100 a square foot. The former Education Center re-opened in the fall semester of 1991 as the downtown Lowell campus for Middlesex Community College (MCC). The new use of the facility is substantially different from its intended purpose as an international training center for one of the world's largest computer services companies, and public ownership of the facility results in no property tax revenue for the city. However, the facility still attracts people to downtown Lowell—approximately 1,300 commuter students now attend community college classes at the former Wang Education Center. In addition, there are plans for MCC to expand its Lowell campus.[14]

Even though the hotel in downtown Lowell remained open, the Lowell Inn Associates, the original developers of the Hilton, defaulted on their second mortgage UDAG loan administered by the Lowell Development Financial Corporation (LDFC). The loan default meant that $2.8 million less money would be recycled for local development projects. The developers first stopped payments in February 1988 and subsequently defaulted on the loan.[15] The LDFC made loan loss provisions of $2.8 million for the Hilton loan in fiscal year 1989. The Hilton loan default was the largest of four loan defaults out of a total of 160 loans in the sixteen year history of the LDFC—a remarkable record given the organization's mission as an innovative finance vehicle for risky development loans.[16]

It could be (and has been) argued that, even with the default on the Hilton UDAG loan, the city was better off than it would have been without the Hilton deal in 1985. If the Hilton UDAG had been administered as most other UDAGs were at the time, the federal money would have been used as an outright grant rather than a loan. In the city's view, as Jim Cook the new (1990) LDFC director and assistant city planner in 1985 argued, "Any money we got back on the UDAG was gravy . . . when the Hilton owners defaulted the city still had a new Hotel in the downtown."[17]

The LDFC remained financially secure. The LDFC's capital base by 1990 had increased to $28 million (see discussion below) and, in fiscal year 1989, the LDFC disbursed over $1 million in new loans to twenty-five local recipients, mostly small- and medium-sized local businesses. According to the director of the Lowell Plan, the city leaders in the early 1990s were in the process of "shifting back to the bread and butter of economic development."[18] It was a shift away from the city's earlier focus on cultural and educational activities, outside of traditional economic development toward a renewed focus on finding new uses for underutilized local facilities and industrial recruitment. The (new) 1990s economic development vision for Lowell was to position the city as "the first in the region to recover from the recession and to make Lowell the most economically viable and physically attractive city of its size in America."[19]

The centerpiece of the new development strategy for Lowell was similar to the revitalization strategy of the 1970s—the recruitment of high growth companies into the area. Toward these ends, the Lowell Plan funded research by University of Lowell faculty on the biotechnology industry and the writing of a city ordinance for biotechnology companies. Through the efforts of the University and the Lowell Plan, Lowell was well-positioned to attract biotechnology industry, as one of the first cities in the state and region to have an ordinance in place. Lowell Plan and LDFC officials began aggressively recruiting biotechnology industry to the city, visiting several growing firms in New Jersey. In addition, the city and the Lowell Plan, in partnership with the University of Lowell, offered incubator space to fledgling biotechnology companies.

The University of Lowell also planned to develop a support program for manufacturing firms. According to Harvey Kahalas, the Dean of the University's school of management, "The objectives of the support program are to try to provide small- and medium-sized manufacturing firms with support to enhance productivity and exporting, an important sector for the future of the country and the region."[20]

While the Lowell Plan and the University of Lowell gave renewed priority to industrial recruitment and business development that could improve the city's economic positioning, the LDFC and the city, under pressure from community groups (see discussion below), expanded their activities on housing and related issues in the city's downtown and low income areas.[21]

In 1989 the city arranged for the LDFC to administer a HUD Housing Development Grant (HoDAG) in a manner similar to the way in which the LDFC administered the city's UDAG loans in the 1980s.

The city advanced $4.6 million in HoDAG funds to the LDFC, which then loaned the funds to a private developer (Joseph R. Mullins Company) for the rehabilitation of an old textile mill facility, the Massachusetts Mills building, in the downtown. The "rehab" project involved conversion of an old mill to a 160 unit apartment building, with 27 percent of the units designated for affordable housing. The HoDAG loan, like the UDAG loans, is being recycled through the LDFC to support future development activity. The repayment proceeds from the Massachusetts Mills loan are designated for loans to develop additional low and moderate income housing in the city.

In 1990 the LDFC established a separate First Mortgage Loan Pool Program (FMLPP) to make loans available for affordable housing for low and moderate income families. Twelve local banks committed a total of $15 million for this purpose. This effectively doubled the LDFC's capital base, to $28 million. The affordable housing fund is administered by the same nine-member LDFC executive committee that makes decisions on all other LDFC loans.

As occurred in the Acre Homeownership program in 1985, city interest and public and private sector cooperative efforts in affordable housing were instigated by an aggressive grass roots campaign, which included tenant and community organizing by the Coalition for a Better Acre (CBA). The organization of the FMLPP was in large part the public and private sector leadership response to persistent demands by the CBA. The CBA used a combination of political activity—including voter registration, involvement in city council elections, contacts with U.S. Senators Kerry and Kennedy, and threats of CBA action—to inspire local action. Organizing and political efforts were strengthened by "bankable" projects, conceived and marketed by the CBA, for which affordable housing funds could be put to immediate use.

FMLPP funds were committed for below-market rate, long-term, fixed rate mortgages for two projects: $14 million for the renovation of the North Canal Apartments (NCA), with 265 low-income rental units located in the Northeast corner of the Acre community; and $.9 million for the Merrimack Street Housing Limited Partnership, with twelve low-income residential and six commercial units across the street from City Hall in downtown Lowell.[22]

Both the NCA and Merrimack Street projects were conceived and sponsored by the Acre Triangle Community Development Corporation (ATCDC)—the development subsidiary for the Coalition for a Better Acre. The NCA was initially developed in 1968 for low and moderate income families under HUD's Section 221(d)(3) below-market-rate mortgage program. The NCA was built and owned by private local developers. The facility was poorly constructed and inadequately maintained and, soon after the project was completed, the owners filed for bankruptcy.[23] The project mortgage was assigned in 1975 to HUD as the insurer of the property with an obligation to pay off the mortgage holder once a pattern of default became apparent. HUD initiated foreclosure proceedings in 1981 and announced plans to auction the property to the highest bidder in 1983, which is when the CBA first got involved.

The CBA saw the HUD auction plans as a threat to their efforts in the Acre to retain affordable housing. In the booming Lowell real estate market, the twelve acres of downtown real estate occupied by NCA would be more valuable to a private developer as market-rate, rather than affordable, housing. As described by CBA chairperson, Charles Gargiulo, "If we spent 4 years building 70 units in the Triangle and at the same time we lost 267 units at North Canal, then we were not doing our job as a community organization. We resolved then and there to put the full force of the organization behind saving the North Canal."[24]

In 1983 the CBA organized the North Canal Tenant Council (NCTC) and began to work toward community control of the NCA. In 1985 the CBA and NCTC contracted with a Boston-based development consultant to outline a redevelopment plan and a strategy. The long-term redevelopment plan included a $15 million repair program and retention of the facility as affordable housing for low-income residents. The strategy to gain community control over the property involved, first, insuring that the property got legally transferred over to HUD and, then, negotiating with HUD to sell the property at reasonable cost to the tenants group. In 1986 a 93(A) consumer action suit (for owner negligence) was used to pressure the original owners to turn over the property title to HUD instead of risk additional liability. Then in 1989, the ATCDC negotiated a purchase of the property from HUD. ATCDC also received from HUD a commitment of fifteen years of section 8 subsidies for all of the units.

Once again, community leaders and the city of Lowell helped facilitate federal program innovation, just as they had on the urban national park and the use of an UDAG as a loan. The NCA was the first HUD-assisted 221(d)(3) project sold to a community group in order to avoid foreclosure and displacement of low and moderate income tenants.

The last, but surely not least important, piece of the CBA-NCA effort was securing project financing. Financing at below-market rate was necessary to repair the apartments while insuring that the units remained affordable to low income tenants. With the momentum from the community organizing efforts in the Acre and continued support from state political officials—including the Governor and both U.S. Senators—the CBA instigated the establishment of the First Mortgage Loan Pool. The NCA project provided immediate use for a large portion of the FMLPP funds and provided the LDFC with a viable project that could help sponsoring banks meet their CBA requirements. At the same time, the establishment of the FMLPP could enhance the public image of the LDFC, which had been blemished by the Hilton loan default.

The CBA's efforts with the NCA and FMLPP furthered its reputation and positioned the organization to get involved in "more traditional" local economic development efforts. When a foreign company, Pellon/Freudenberg Nonwovens (Pellon), decided it no longer had use for a 155,000 square-foot warehouse bordering the Acre community, it asked one of its board members, a Lowell resident, for suggestions. It was recommended that the company contact the CBA and consider turning over the property to the nonprofit organization.[25]

In 1991 Pellon donated the warehouse to the CBA in a mutually beneficial arrangement. Pellon got United States tax benefits from its donation to a nonprofit organization, and the CBA extended its control over local land use. The CBA's preliminary plans for the old warehouse are for 110 units of affordable housing and 30,000 square feet of community and/or commercial space.

CBA's activities with the North Canal Apartments and Pellon support the conclusion that community groups can influence local development policy to insure that the needs and priorities of their constituents get addressed. The experience of the CBA furthermore indicates the value of local citizen organization and the potential role of nonprofit groups in local development efforts. Even though elite organizations (such as the Lowell Plan and the LDFC) dominate development activities in Lowell, the CBA is increasingly able to affect policy and the distribution of benefits from local development. In addition, the CBA's efforts in Lowell suggest that citizen group activities can work in the city interest. Without the CBA in Lowell the NCA might now be vacant—another victim of extended legal negotiations and real estate speculation—and Pellon's options would have been limited and its industrial space underutilized for an extended period of time. Through the efforts of the CBA, 1,100 low and moderate income tenants reside comfortably in the NCA, and there are plans for reusing the Pellon warehouse building.[26]

LOWELL IN THE 1990S: BENEFITING FROM THE
   DEVELOPMENT LEGACY

Lowell in the late 1980s was profoundly affected by the declining regional economy and loss of competitiveness of Wang Laboratories
and the mini-computer industry. Yet the city has endured impres-
sively and the worst effects of Wang's decline appear to be over. The
general strength in the primary local employment sector, manufacturing, suggests that, despite a downturn in the economy, the city is
well positioned for future growth. The loss from Wang's declining
competitiveness and regional economic problems have been mini-
mized by actions taken by city leaders and local development institutions—actions similar to those suggested as beneficial in the comparative analysis at the beginning of the chapter.

Lowell has drawn on development leaders, capacities, methods,
and resources established during the city's revitalization era to confront its present difficult economic situation. The city has benefited
from expedient and focused actions by committed local leaders, including City Manager Jim Campbell and CBA board member Charlie
Gargiulo, and by strong local organizations, including the Lowell
Plan, LDFC, and the CBA. Most notably, the LDFC continues to be
an invaluable local resource. It's main value is in leveraging and
recycling public and private investment in the city.[27] The fund insti-
tutionalizes public and private cooperation and support of local development. The LDFC allows for collective private and public investment in development and for resources to be recycled from a more
prosperous economic era and an era when the federal and state government were more generous with grants for local development.
This is particularly valuable during difficult economic times when
capital is not readily available.

Lowell policy makers also continue to use analysis of economic
and social conditions to inform development strategy. Diagnosis of
the local and regional economy in the early 1990s provided a realistic
reassessment and guidance for a new vision for Lowell—to be the
first city in the region to recover. Unlike other cities in similar situations (e.g., New Bedford in the 1980s), Lowell did not focus development efforts in the early 1990s on saving struggling local firms in
mature industries. Instead local efforts in Lowell are focused on
identifying creative new uses of underutilized facilities (such as the
Wang Education Center), leveraging financial and political resources, supporting fledgling firms, and attracting new high growth
industries (at a more advantageous stage in the product cycle) to the
city.[28] In addition, community-based efforts continue to advocate for

housing and neighborhood development that appears to be in the long-term interest of the city.

Finally, Lowell benefits from the culture of innovation and public, private, and community cooperation established during the revitalization era, as reflected in the use of a HoDAG grant as a loan, the selling of a HUD 221 (d)(3) project to a community group, and a foreign company's donation of property to a community organization.

Local Market Failure and City Revitalization

This section further considers the generality of some of the hypotheses put forward. It speculates on the potential economic value of some of the local development acts identified in the city development analyses and the Lowell update. It suggests a framework for identifying useful local development practices—development activities that can increase local economic output through better allocation and more productive use of existing city resources. Along with Chapter 2, this section provides the theoretical foundation for the discussion in the concluding chapter, which offers strategic as well as practical guidelines for city renewal.

It will be argued, in discussion meant to be suggestive rather than comprehensive, that local market failure can limit the potential for private market activities alone to stimulate economic revitalization. The value of local development acts and "alternative" (to market and government) organization of development activities will be considered in (1) internalizing local development externalities; (2) motivating initial revitalization activities; (3) overcoming problems of free riders; (4) reducing uncertainty and information failure; and (5) correcting local labor market failure. No new theory is offered. Familiar concepts of public finance, institutional economics and organizational theory are related to some of the findings from the city development analyses.

EXTERNALITIES AND ORGANIZING DEVELOPMENT ACTIVITIES

There can be substantial externalities associated with local development activities. Development externalities can be both positive and negative and are often difficult and costly to take account of in private market transactions. Consider a bank in Lowell in the early 1970s determining whether to make a loan to a firm interested in locating in the city. For purposes of simplicity, let's assume that the firm is an exporting firm and has no local competitors; therefore, it will not take market share from a competing local firm. When the bank and the firm transact, the industrial firm's major concern is whether the cost of the loan (the interest rate) is less than the expected private net benefit from the loan (the profit that can be generated from investing the loan money in the business). On the other side of the transaction, the bank's major concern is the risk and return of the loan and the opportunity cost of the loan (could the loan monies be invested elsewhere with the same return at lower risk or with higher return at the same level of risk?).

A profit maximizing bank would also consider the portfolio effects of the loan. If the bank had other loans outstanding locally, it would consider how its loan to the single firm may effect its other loans (will it reduce the risk of outstanding business loans, mortgages, and consumer loans?). The individual bank would not, however, have an incentive to consider how its loan might affect the loan portfolio of other banks in the city or the income and wealth of owners of other industries and property in the city who were not customers (or potential customers) of the bank.

With such a "simple" activity as an industrial loan, there can be significant external effects that are not considered. This can result in a misallocation of resources.[29] When there are net positive (negative) externalities with a private market transaction there is a tendency for underinvestment (overinvestment) in that activity compared to the optimal level.

The theory of social cost suggests that, even without the assignment of property rights, the market would effectively account for externalities.[30] The third parties benefiting (suffering) from development activities would make payments reflecting the benefits (costs) they derived (suffered). There can be significant transaction costs associated with the pricing of externalities, however, that can inhibit the undertaking of development projects in which external benefits exceed external costs and also increase the likelihood that projects with net negative expected value will be undertaken.

The failure of markets to consider externalities adequately in development activities can result in a misallocation of local resources and inhibit a city's economic development. Some alternative institutional arrangement may work toward correcting market failure by more effectively internalizing externalities. We observed an example of this in Lowell. A private nonprofit organization, the Lowell Development Financial Corporation (LDFC), appeared to provide a local institutional vehicle to internalize some of the externalities in development finance at lower transaction cost than interbank arrangements. The LDFC encompassed a pooled loan fund for local development with contributions required from all local banks. The LDFC encouraged local investment by enabling local banks to share the risks and benefits of local development activities. Before the LDFC was created, loan originations were minimal; after the organization of the LDFC, investment in the city by the LDFC and individual member banks increased at a steady rate. LDFC funds appeared to supplement and encourage private financing in the city, most notably at the initial stages of revitalization efforts when the external benefits of development projects were particularly significant.

MOTIVATING THE INITIAL REVITALIZATION EFFORTS

Increasing returns (declining costs) to development activities are an externality associated with city revitalization efforts that private markets may not price effectively. The experience in Jamestown and Lowell (as well as the more recent experience in the Mon Valley) suggest that, with the first couple of successful development undertakings, city development, officials and residents learn about development, including the private, state, and federal resources available and how to put a development deal together. With the undertaking of projects, new contacts are established, relationships developed, and experience gained, and the effort and cost of development activities can decline. Without a mechanism to internalize the decreasing cost of development projects, there might be a tendency to invest at less than an optimal level in the initial, what may be termed "momentum-generating," development activities.

Private markets are not likely to fully account for the longer term benefits that may result from initial revitalization efforts. This emanates from the unlikely prospects of private investors and developers capturing all the benefits from the initial development activities.[31] A potentially advantageous arrangement might provide initial development investors with some guarantee, either through a series of contracts or some institutional arrangement, that they would benefit "downstream" from their initial project investment in a city. For instance, one method to internalize the increasing returns from the initial development activities might be to give a developer the right of first refusal on development projects in a city over a specified period of time.[32] The functional equivalent of this type of arrangement might occur when a single corporation dominates city development activities and owns a large share of city real estate, or when private companies cannot move their operations and are, therefore, more concerned with the longer term implications of their development efforts. Examples of companies which fit the former description are large private corporations headquartered in smaller cities such as Cummins Engine in Columbus, Indiana, and Procter & Gamble in

Cincinnati. These multinational companies seem to take a longer term and more active interest in their headquarter cities than corporations that are less prominent in their cities.[33] Examples of the later type of corporate involvement in local development are utility companies that have a restricted service area and whose revenue and profitability are highly dependent on the economic health of the cities they service. The Georgia Power Company is a utility company that is particularly active in city development activities throughout its service area, the state of Georgia.[34]

In some situations, community development corporations that represent a collective commitment to undertake related development projects over time might be vehicles for internalizing increasing development returns. CDCs can allow for consideration of increasing returns to development activities by a collection of individuals and institutions with an interest in maximizing development benefits over an extended period of time.

FREE RIDERS AND LOCAL LEADERSHIP

Similar to the failure to internalize positive development externalities, a problem with free riders can result in a less than optimal level of effort in city revitalization activities. The development analyses suggest that strong leadership can work toward overcoming problems with free riders by creating selective benefits from development and changing individual and institutional perceptions of self-interest. For example, fear of the imposition of "selective costs" for not participating could explain why banks contributed to the LDFC in Lowell. It seems that local bank presidents were concerned that Tsongas might use his position on the congressional finance committee against them (or, at least, not to their advantage) if they did not participate in the LDFC. An example of the latter role of local leaders in overcoming problems of free riders is Mayor Lundine's efforts in putting together the area-wide labor and management committee in Jamestown by persuading local labor and management leaders that their collective contributions were necessary to revitalizing the city. It appears that Lundine was able to convince labor and management leaders that their commitment to development efforts were essential—that there would be no benefits from development activities without their collective contribution (see Chapter 9 for more discussion).

The influence of Tsongas, of Lundine and, perhaps even more instructively, of Mogan at the early stages of revitalization efforts in Lowell suggest that local leaders can overcome problems of free riders and motivate the identification of common objectives and the organization of collective action. In essence, local leaders may be critical in making operational Peterson's notion of consensus action on common city interests, especially at the critical beginning stages of revitalization efforts. While the particular catalyst or reason for broad participation in development activities will vary by city, leadership will often be necessary. For example, Model Cities designation in Lowell in the mid–1960s engaged citizens and gave them the opportunity to think collectively about the future of their city; however, it did not have a similar effect in New Bedford. Lowell's favorable experience with Model Cities appeared to be attributed in large part to the inspirational leadership and vision of Pat Mogan. Similarly, much of Jamestown's success with labor and management cooperation can be attributed to the efforts of a single individual, Mayor Stan Lundine. Labor and management involvement in local development was a rallying point in Jamestown in the early 1970s, while it was a source of division in New Bedford and McKeesport.

UNCERTAINTY AND LOCAL ORGANIZATION OF
   DEVELOPMENT ACTIVITIES

The transaction costs (contractual expense) of writing contingent claims between parties for each potential contingency can prevent a desirable (in the sense that the net expected value of the venture was positive) project from being undertaken.[35] This suggests that there may be advantages to institutional arrangements that reduce the transaction costs associated with deal making under uncertainty by facilitating trust between parties, allowing for negotiation of payments as development project contingencies unfold, and providing regular opportunities for adaptive decision making.[36]

It appears that community development corporations, in addition to having potential to capture the benefits from increasing returns from development activities, have potential to serve as local institutional vehicles for mutual adjustment and adaptive decision making. CDCs, by institutionalizing long-term commitment to economic development efforts, can support risk sharing and mutual adjustment to development contingencies among the public, private, and nonprofit sectors. We observe the seeds of such an organization in McKeesport and throughout the Mon Valley, with the organization of the Initiative. The Initiative was organized as part of a long-term commitment among CDCs and greater-Pittsburgh-area foundations and financial institutions to undertake development projects in the Valley.

The Initiative appears to represent an institutional vehicle for CDCs, regional banks, and foundations to make a collective commitment to the revitalization of the Mon Valley and share the risk and responsibility for area revitalization activities. For example, the Initiative has instituted regular meetings between foundation, bank, and CDC officials that will provide opportunities for mutual adjustment to contingencies in economic development efforts. The potential value of undertaking high risk development projects through an organization, such as the Initiative, is to increase the likelihood that city development activities with great uncertainty yet with positive expected value get undertaken.

INFORMATION FAILURES

Information failures represent another area of local market failure that alternative organization of local development activities might help overcome.[37] There can be significant benefits from gathering data, analysis, and planning as the efforts of the Central City Committee in Lowell and the efforts of the economic development steering committee in Jamestown indicate. The local public good character of development information (e.g., nonexcludability and nonrival consumption), however, suggests that an efficient level will be gathered only when mutual benefits are recognized and costs are shared. Information collection is often not undertaken collectively, but by individual firms, government agencies, nonprofit organizations, and consultants on contract. There are frequently *ad hoc* and overlapping efforts in information collection, as we observed in the Mon Valley with the efforts of the MVC and RUDAT team, and a tendency to collect data that provides little new and useful information. This occurs because individual data collectors often consider their data collection in isolation from the information gathering and needs of others.

Institutions with representatives from different sectors (such as the CCC in Lowell and the economic development steering committee in Jamestown) can make the gathering of development information more of a collective enterprise and help to overcome, what Stiglitz refers to as, "overhead information costs."[38] Benefits from collective information gathering efforts can emanate from savings in the cost of collecting any given level of development information (including the reduction of overlap), from collection of more appropriate and informative data, and ultimately from better allocation decisions that may result from increased availability of more and higher quality information.

LOCAL LABOR MARKET FAILURE

The city analyses, particularly the comparison of development activities in Jamestown and McKeesport, suggest that there may also be opportunities to enhance city renewal by correcting for what might be identified broadly as local labor market failure. Workers often lack the financial means to undertake the training that changing economic and industrial conditions require or the foresight to accept wages below the marginal value product of their labor during training periods.[39] On the other hand, employers may not have the foresight and confidence to make the appropriate investment to train workers when there is no guarantee that firms will stay competitive and that workers will stay long enough to justify the investment (and might, in fact, sell their skills to local competitors). Even with perfect foresight on the part of workers and employers, there may be prohibitively high transaction and enforcement costs associated with writing employment contracts that require employees to stay for a given period of time (and not join a competitor) after receiving company subsidized training.

Labor market failure can be particularly relevant in cities experiencing rapid change, including changing industry composition and the introduction of new industrial processes. This suggests that mechanisms to correct local labor market failures may be beneficial. In Jamestown the JALMC served, in part, as a collective forum to identify, fund, and conduct worker training programs that were beneficial to a large number of local firms and workers. The JALMC provided an institutional vehicle for area employers and workers to disseminate their needs and concerns to each other, identify opportunities for collective effort, and pursue those opportunities. Collectively financed training programs, such as those undertaken by the JALMC, can be more effective in capturing the benefits from increases in worker training than training by individual employers. It is more likely that workers within any given city will use their training within that city than at any individual employer.

MARKET FAILURE AND LOCAL GOVERNMENT INTERVENTION

Local market failure, as discussed above, is a necessary, but not sufficient condition, for justifying on economic efficiency grounds the organization of local development activity outside of the market. It is necessary in that, without a market failure, economic theory suggests there would be no efficiency or economies of organization gain from removing the activity from the market. Market failure is not a sufficient condition, however, because there is the chance that employing an alternative (to the market) structure may impose greater costs and produce more harm than the original deficiency.

Local political leaders and public officials often advocate government involvement on the grounds that government effort can remedy market failure. Arguably the most prominent justification for governmental involvement in local economic development is the failure of private markets to account for the external benefits (multiplier effects) from the attraction of new industry. The external benefits from exporting industry is often used to justify large public subsidies to new and relocating industrial firms.[40]

Local government involvement in private market activities can be highly problematic, as suggested by the effort in New Bedford by local and state government to save the Morse Cutting Tool plant. There is risk that local government action that attempts to remove a market deficiency may impose greater costs and efficiency loss than the original deficiency.[41] Government involvement in economic development activities can suffer from several limitations, including exaggeration of market failure to promote government involvement, public officials acting in their self-interest (rather than the public interest), domination of government policy by special interests, and a lack of information and expertise on development matters.

The existence of government failure, along with local market failure, suggests potential benefit from alternative organization of some development activities. This supports the conclusion of the analyses of development efforts in Lowell, New Bedford, Jamestown, and McKeesport, which indicated that selective local development activities undertaken outside the dominant jurisdiction of private markets and local government by city leaders, community development corporations (CDCs), and multi-sector development institutions and committees may promote better use of city resources and contribute to local economic growth.

The discussion here of local market failures suggests that the relative effectiveness of private markets, local governments, and alternatives will vary with the nature and scope of activity. In the development analyses we observed many development activities—most notably at the initial stages of development efforts—that involved much uncertainty and significant externalities. This suggests that alternative agents and organizational structures may be particularly advantageous in revitalization situations. The benefits of alternative organization of local development activities, however, must be weighed against the costs. There can be significant costs associated with organizing development activities outside the market and local government.

LOCAL MARKET FAILURE AND ECONOMIC GROWTH

Various types of local development activities have been identified as having potential to enhance local economic performance—primarily through more efficient allocation and productive use of existing resources—without requiring significant new resources from outside. All development initiatives, including the "reshuffling of internal resources" and "transaction cost reducing" types highlighted here, will result in some transfer of economic activity between areas. At the margin and in the absence of cities competing for development by offering distorting subsidies, economic activity will relocate where production costs are lower (profits are greater) and where resources are deployed in a more efficient manner. This suggests that increased economic activity in any single locality resulting from the kinds of local development initiatives suggested here may have potential not only to contribute to local economic growth but also to net national economic growth.

Nine

The Renewal Process

Overview

As the economy becomes more global and dynamic, processes of economic adjustment at all levels—individual, firm, city, state, and nation—are increasingly important.[1] The development analyses explored processes of adjustment in four medium-sized cities in the Northeast. We observed that cities, particularly those with concentrated employment in a single industry, are highly vulnerable to changes in global industries and in the national and regional economy.

Economic theory suggests that a significant part of local economic adjustment will occur through private market forces, including movement of industry and factors of production and changes in local factor prices to reflect changes in local supply and demand conditions. Trade and price equalization theory, as discussed in Chapter 2, suggests some natural or automatic process through which local economies adjust to changes in economic circumstances. We observed tendencies towards a market adjustment process in each of the four cities—as indicated by declining population, employment, and incomes during periods of economic recession—but there was substantial stickiness and local market failure in the process. The city development analyses indicated that market forces and economic self-interest were not the only determinants of city growth and change. The value of place (beyond its function as a site to pursue economic self-interest) was suggested by the discussion of each city's historical development and the observation that in none of the cities, not even in McKeesport, did population decline as dramatically as manufacturing employment.

In each of the cities there were extended periods of high unemployment and underutilization of local resources. In none of the four cities did factor inputs, most notably labor, migrate out of the declining areas at the rate or scale predicted by equalization theory. In addition, local factor prices did not adjust to local supply and demand conditions to the degree suggested by economic theory. The failure of local economies to adjust to changing market conditions resulted in extended periods of decline with substantial personal, social, psychological, and economic loss.

This suggests that market forces cannot be relied on alone to facilitate adjustment of local economies to industrial changes and changes in the national and regional economy. It has been suggested (in Chapter 8) that, under certain conditions, city leaders and institutions can facilitate beneficial adjustment to changing economic circumstances through the reorganization of local resources.

Insights into city revitalization, while instructive, require contextual discussion to inform practice usefully. The effectiveness of any development effort will depend in large part on how the effort addresses local needs, opportunities, and vulnerabilities and how it is coordinated with other efforts. This concluding chapter attempts to give coherence to the various insights provided and to propose strategic guidelines for local economic development practice. Again, as throughout the text, the analysis will be related most closely to turnaround situations in economically depressed cities and to the four study cities.

A Framework to Guide Local Development Practice

The city analysis and local market failure discussion suggested the importance of different agents in local economic development (see summary of development agents in the four cities in Figure 9.1). Motivating, diagnostic, and organizational agents were identified as crucial. The key motivating agents identified were local leadership, as suggested by the efforts of Lundine in Jamestown and Tsongas in Lowell, and city visions, such as the vision for a new industrial future in Lowell. Examples of diagnostic agents included regional economic analysis and surveys of local firms, such as those undertaken by the Central City Committee in Lowell. Organizing agents also took different forms in the study cities, including public and private partnerships, such as the Lowell Plan, and city-wide development committees, such as the JALMC and the economic development steering committee in Jamestown.

To be effective motivating, diagnostic, and organizational agents must be carefully deployed and coordinated. When deployed inappropriately (or simply not deployed), these agents can inhibit local development. In the Mon Valley and New Bedford, we observed several development agents that inhibited revitalization efforts. In the Mon Valley, one of the most prominent development inhibitors

FIGURE 9.1
Revitalization Agents in the Four Cities

	Lowell	New Bedford	Jamestown	McKeesport
MOTIVATING				
Crisis Situation	Mid–1970s		Early 1970s	Throughout the 1980s
Leadership	Tsongas/Mogan	Bullard	Lundine	CDC board members
Vision	Historical Park		L & M Cooperation	
	New Industrial Future			
DIAGNOSTIC				
Local Planning	City Planning Office			M.V. Dev. Team
Outside "Experts"	American Cities Corp.		Mediation Service	AIA RUDAT
ORGANIZING				
Dominating Institution	Lowell Plan, CBA	Econ. Task Force	JALMC	M. V. Initiative
Implementing Agencies	City Planning Office			CDCs
				(Developing)

was the lack of local leadership. We also observed in the Mon Valley that outside expert diagnosis was not useful when it lacked any local organization or individuals to work with. In New Bedford, we observed a lack of critical and objective diagnosis, particularly of the long-term prospects of Morse Cutting Tool and the machine tool industry. It appears that the city would have benefited from dynamic cycle analysis before local and state development efforts were concentrated on saving the Morse plant.[2]

Motivating, diagnostic, and organizing agents are not mutually exclusive. As we observed most strikingly with the efforts of Lundine and Tsongas, local leadership can both help motivate and organize local development activities. City visions, such as Jamestown's vision of itself as a "model city" for labor and management cooperation, involve diagnosis and can be highly motivational. Organizing agents such as the Lowell Plan can motivate public and private cooperation; at the same time, they can help to coordinate activities on particular development efforts.

Guidelines for purposive action in local economic development will be outlined. The guidelines will be presented by "phase of city revitalization" and around key agents in local development—including crisis situations, leadership, vision, planning, and multisector development organizations. It is suggested that (1) motivating agents are particularly relevant at the beginning stages of revitalization when the mobilization and cooperation of public, private, and citizen resources and actors is critical; (2) that the importance of diagnosis increases with city-wide interest level and mobilization; and

(3) that organizing agents are most important at the implementation phase of revitalization efforts, when specific programs and plans identified as being useful are implemented.

Crisis Situations: Creating a Climate for Change

We observed across the city development analyses that, counter to Peterson's view, collective city action on common development problems is not automatic. Motivating agents such as a crisis situation, local leadership, and vision are often necessary. The most problematic stage in city economic development efforts appears to be at the outset, when changes in relationships and city priorities are first proposed and when the foundation for identifying opportunities and organizing activities is being laid. Resistance to change can occur on many levels, in personal relations, private markets, local government and community affairs, and has been documented by psychologists, sociologists, political scientists, and policy analysts.[3] Especially in cities that have experienced extended economic decline, it appears that a general reluctance to consider change and enter new relations has to be recognized and overcome before new economic initiatives can be pursued.

The experiences in Jamestown and New Bedford, in particular, suggest that a sense of crisis is often necessary to pave the way for city-wide mobilization around development issues and commitment to new proposals in economic development. It appears that a crisis situation can also be used to get local citizens engaged in development efforts and to accept change. The *status quo*, not change, can be threatening when a feeling of crisis prevails in a city. It appears that a crisis, or a perception of crisis, can be used to instill a sense of urgency in a city and a belief that, if changes are not made, conditions in the city will deteriorate even further.

In Jamestown, in 1972, Mayor Lundine came forward in the local press and in a series of meetings with city groups and described labor and management relations as being at a crisis level. At the time, Jamestown had the most strike days per worker of any city in the nation and little was being done to improve labor and management relations. Existing industries in Jamestown were struggling to survive, and it was exceedingly difficult to attract new industry into the city because of its reputation as a "bad labor town." Lundine's pronouncement paved the way for discussion and cooperative effort to improve labor and management relations. Lundine's actions appeared to motivate labor and management to recognize that their confrontational attitude toward each other was destructive, and that they would both benefit from cooperation.

The experience in Jamestown suggests that a crisis can be used to motivate collective action. Lundine convinced local labor and management leaders that all of their cooperation was essential to improve local economic conditions. The incentive to free ride seemed to have been reduced by selective benefits to participation in the JALMC, including more secure employment for workers and managers and increased profits for firms. Over time, however, as labor and management cooperation and commitment to local development efforts became a norm throughout the city, selective benefits seemed less important, as suggested by Cummins Engine's decision to locate a plant in the area but not participate in the JALMC.

Unlike Jamestown during the early 1970s, New Bedford has never experienced a sense of economic crisis. While the economy has been declining since the early 1920s, the decline has been slow and steady and has not been precipitated by a particular problem, such as labor and management conflict, or a dramatic decline that could be used to inspire collective action. The lack of a crisis situation in New Bedford appears to have resulted in citywide complacency and (together with the memory of the failings of Urban Renewal and Model Cities) a general reluctance to participate in collective development efforts.[4]

Leadership

The contrasting experience in Jamestown and New Bedford suggests that a crisis situation may be a necessary condition for citywide mobilization on development issues and receptivity to new proposals in economic development. The development history of McKeesport suggested that it is not a sufficient condition. In McKeesport, the economy has been in a crisis condition (according to most informed observers) throughout the late 1970s and 1980s. However, the city appears to have suffered from a lack of local leadership to motivate and coordinate efforts. This is similar to the situation in Jamestown prior to 1972, when Lundine came forward and assumed a leadership position in local economic development efforts.[5] The experiences in Jamestown and McKeesport suggest that, for mobilization to emanate from crisis situations, local leadership may be required.

Unfortunately, local individuals are often reluctant to step forward and define city socio-economic conditions as being at a crisis level unless they have a plan of action to put forward and prospects for success are reasonable. Frequently local political leaders practice the credo "if there is no solution, there is no problem." In Jamestown, Mayor Lundine conceived of the idea of bringing labor and management together in a Jamestown Area Labor and Management Committee before he went public and declared that labor and management conflict was ruining the city and scaring away industry.

The willingness of local leaders to declare that a crisis exists and come forward with new development proposals may be related to the political and other capital they can draw on and their perception of the potential efficacy of their efforts. For example, Lundine came forward with his labor and management proposal only after being re-elected by a large margin in November 1971. The Lowell experience and the efforts of Tsongas further indicate that the aggressiveness and effectiveness of city leaders in local development efforts depend on their access to political and other resources. Tsongas's efforts as the leader in revitalization efforts in Lowell were greatly enhanced by his position in Washington D.C., including his seat on the Congressional Finance Committee. Tsongas was instrumental in securing Department of Interior and HUD funding for Lowell and in gaining commitment from local banks to increase their level of investment in Lowell through the LDFC. Tsongas, however, did not conceive of the strategy for obtaining and using funds. Pat Mogan, the superintendent of the schools in Lowell, was "the dreamer" who provided a vision for Lowell that defined how the city could use federal and private funds in local development efforts.

City Visions

Mogan was the first to identify Lowell's industrial past, its abandoned mills, canals, and underemployed labor force as economic development assets. His idea was to promote development by taking advantage of resources in the city that many local people had devalued. He saw potential in Lowell's history, its old mill buildings, its waterways and its hardworking ethnic work force. His novel idea was a national urban park that would tell the story of Lowell's men and machines and provide a boost to the city's dormant economy.

Visions, as described here, are general strategies in local economic development. The vision in Lowell was to leverage federal grant money to create a new industrial future based upon Lowell's heritage and location right outside the Route 128 high technology corridor. Lundine's vision in the early 1970s was to establish Jamestown as a model city for labor and management cooperation and to develop a national reputation for Jamestown as a city where labor and management worked together.

The experiences in Lowell and Jamestown suggest that new visions can help mobilize citizens and encourage collective effort by altering public perceptions and overcoming negative responses and inertia to economic decline. From the seeds of destruction a visionary may create hope for the future, stimulate a change in attitudes and behavior, and generate a level of excitement and broad commitment to local development efforts. The dramatic change in labor and management relations in Jamestown appeared to increase city pride and made workers and businesses more willing to engage in cooperative efforts. New visions it appears also can serve as a "marketing tool," a signal to outsiders that conditions have changed in a city that make it attractive for investment.

Local development visionaries, like Mogan and Lundine, through extensive diagnosis can often see advantages where others see only liabilities. Pat Mogan viewed the decaying mills and canals and local industrial work force as assets in Lowell's revitalization. After Mogan's efforts with the Model Cities project team, Lowell citizens began to appreciate their history and work constructively toward creating an industrial future, instead of rejecting and denying their industrial past. Similarly, Mayor Lundine in Jamestown recognized that labor and management conflict could be turned on its head and used to motivate citywide cooperation on a matter critical to Jamestown's economic future.

Based on the contrasting experience in New Bedford (compared to that in Jamestown and Lowell), a thematic and general vision might be preferred to more detailed plans, particularly at the initial stages of revitalization efforts. In New Bedford, Mayor John Bullard ran into difficulties with his economic development task force when he defined the objective of the task force as "job creation". The narrow definition of the objective of the task force (and city development efforts in the Bullard administration) appeared to inhibit collective effort. Businessmen on the task force started worrying that job creation would reduce their labor pool and drive up wages. Local workers asked Bullard who the new jobs were for and what kinds of jobs they would be. Also in New Bedford (during the same time period), it appeared that the committee formed to save Morse Cutting Tool presented too narrow a mission—to save jobs at a single plant—which inhibited citywide cooperative effort.

The actions of Mayor Bullard and local union 277 (to save the Morse plant) appeared to reinforce existing controversy in the city, instead of creating consensus and encouraging collective effort. The objectives of job creation and saving jobs at a single plant differed markedly with the broader visions presented in Lowell and Jamestown. In Lowell and Jamestown, most residents could perceive some benefit from the realization of development objectives and were therefore willing to contribute toward their realization, but this was not the case in New Bedford.

City-Based Planning

Not all citizens and local institutions will be motivated by general visions. A well documented diagnosis of problems and a development plan might make believers out of those who are not convinced by simple themes. For example, in Lowell, the American Cities Corporation report appeared to be both a diagnostic and motivating agent adding detail to and building support for many of the visionary ideas first put forward by Pat Mogan.

The experience in Lowell with The American Cities Corporation study suggests that local development diagnoses and planning can produce a variety of benefits well beyond the end product of the process, a detailed plan of action. In Lowell, collective inputs in the drafting of the development plan appeared to open up new channels of communication between different sectors in the city, change the perceptions of individuals and organizations about the city, themselves, and towards each other, and lay the foundation for long-term collaborative effort between leaders in the private and public sector.

Lundine's experience in Jamestown and Mogan's in Lowell support the desirability of undertaking a development diagnosis that considers a broad range of local development attributes and liabilities, including cultural, political, social, and institutional factors. Along with more traditional physical and economic factors, the diagnosis might usefully document and assess labor force characteristics, relations between management and labor, city psychology (including attitudes toward change and economic development), fiscal conditions, quality of public services, political relationships in the county, state and federal government, groups active in economic development and their relations with each other, and local leadership in the public, nonprofit, and private sectors.

The Lowell experience suggests that diagnoses should not only evaluate existing resources in their present application, but also consider how existing resources may be strengthened and utilized in more effective and productive ways. Cities undertaking new development efforts might usefully ask the question whether new assets can be created by using old assets in new ways. The development experiences in Lowell and Jamestown support the view that development assets are not fixed. Significant new assets may emerge out of local development diagnosis. For example, the very conditions that local development efforts are targeted to ameliorate—including high unemployment, low wages, and vacant buildings—can become assets once development objectives and plans are defined.

Multi-Sector Local Development Institutions

There are several examples from the city development analyses of how organizing agents are necessary to complement diagnostic and motivating agents. For example, the plan put forward in Lowell by outside experts, the American City Corporation, was commissioned and strongly endorsed by the Lowell Plan. Individual board members of the Lowell Plan, including local bankers, the city manager, and the director of the City Planning and Development Department, took responsibility for the implementation of American City's plan. In a 1986 report, the Lowell Plan proudly reported that nine of the twelve projects identified by the American City Corporation had been completed.[6]

Lowell by the early 1980s not only had in place a vision, an action plan and strong local leadership, but also had developed the organizational capacity to use resources—most notably outside resources—effectively. Lowell's turnaround would have been significantly less dramatic without the injection of federal UDAG and Department of Interior funds. The influence of federal funding in Lowell suggests that outside resources can be a critical factor in the revitalization of depressed areas (see Chapter 4). However, competent local institutions were essential to the dramatic positive influence of federal grant-in-aid in Lowell. The experiences in McKeesport and New Bedford during the 1970s and early 1980s and New Bedford's experience with the Urban Renewal and Model Cities programs indicate that the availability of outside resources is not a sufficient condition for city revitalization. Neither McKeesport or New Bedford suffered as much from a lack of federal or state financial assistance as from a lack of local development organizational capacity to use outside assistance effectively.

In sharp contrast to the experience in Lowell with the American City Corporation, in McKeesport (and throughout the depressed steel towns in the Monongahela Valley), the American Institute of

Architects consulting team study in 1988 lacked competent local institutions and individuals to make their recommendations workable. This suggests that, if outside experts cannot (or do not choose to) work with local individuals or institutions, their efforts may have less chance of having a positive influence.[7] An alternative, or corollary, to outside experts in the Mon Valley is the Mon Valley Development Team (MVDT) organized in 1986. The MVDT consists of community organizers and development professionals whose primary objective is to build local development capacity—to educate local citizens on development matters and help organize community development corporations (CDCs) to undertake development projects. The Allegheny Conference and the greater-Pittsburgh-area foundations funding the MVDT could have directly funded the development projects in the Valley that were recommended by the team of Architects, but they determined that it would be in the Mon Valley cities' best long-term interests to develop local capacity and leadership first before disparate development projects in the Valley were undertaken.

New development organizations, such as the CDCs in the Mon Valley, can provide cities with new capacities to undertake development projects and also help break bottlenecks in development by supplanting existing institutions that have failed. Throughout the Mon Valley, local government has failed to take the initiative in leading development efforts. Local mayors and city councilors have often been mentioned as the leading source of development inertia and resistance to new development programs. The CDCs in the Valley are beginning to initiate development projects in areas such as affordable housing, small business development, and historical preservation that in many other cities would have been undertaken by local government.

The experience in Jamestown in the 1980s further supports the hypothesis that new local development institutions may be required when existing ones fail. In Jamestown in the "post–labor-and-management-conflict era," city image, aesthetics, and worker training emerged as critical development problems.[8] The Jamestown Area Labor Management Committee appeared to lose its effectiveness in serving as a vehicle for promoting local economic development, because its focus and governance structure were too narrow, and it did not adapt to changing circumstances and needs in the city. The economic development steering committee supported by the local foundations seems to have potential to replace the JALMC as the leading development organization in the city. The steering committee broadened the concept of development to include social services, the arts, and cultural activities. Jamestown economic development steering committee members, including representatives from private industry, local government, and nonprofits, are focusing their efforts on engaging established city organizations in local development efforts. They are proposing to use existing organizations, including local foundations, health service providers, and educational institutions, in new ways to change public attitudes and behavior toward development and create new development capacities and opportunities.

The comparative case studies suggest that, in some situations, the presence of a dominant institutional arrangement representing the core of a local development strategy can be advantageous as an organizing and coordinating agent. During the 1970s, the dominant local development institution in Jamestown was the JALMC. The JALMC represented recognition by labor and management that they had similar concerns and interests in the future of Jamestown and that efforts coordinated through a joint committee could be mutually beneficial. Currently the economic development steering committee is emerging as the dominant development institution in Jamestown. In Lowell, a local private and public partnership, the Lowell Plan, serves as the dominant development institution. The Lowell Plan represents recognition by leaders in the public and private sectors that they have similar interests and can both benefit from collaborative effort. Not surprisingly, in New Bedford and McKeesport, which lack any clear vision for their future, dominant development institutions have been lacking.

In Jamestown and Lowell, dominant development institutions appear to have provided highly useful symbols of new initiative at the initial stages of development efforts. Most importantly, however, they have served as the coordinating base for local development efforts. The experiences in Jamestown and Lowell suggest that dominating development institutions are most effective if they engage parties with significant resources and a significant financial, professional, and personal stake in local economic development.

The experience in both cities also suggests the potential value of dominant development institutions having board-based representation. The Lowell Plan ran into difficulties when its objectives became too focused on the downtown and business development and did not consider the interests of low income and minority residents. In Jamestown, the effectiveness of the JALMC declined as it failed to address issues apart from labor and management relations. It appears that the continuity and sustained effectiveness of dominant development institutions might be related to how they address different city interests. This suggests that there may be a relationship between functionality and accountability—that more representative organizations will be better able to serve the long-term development interests of cities. Both the Lowell Plan and the JALMC might have benefited from copying the structure of precursor institutions, the Central City Committee in Lowell and the Akron Labor and Management Committee. Both these (precursor) organizations included community group representatives that broadened their scope and made the organizations more representative of diverse interests.

It appears that the effectiveness of the dominant local development institution also depends on a supporting organizational capacity to take action and implement development projects. As indicated most pointedly by the experience in Lowell, implementing organizations must be capable of coordinating development efforts and packaging development projects to attract private, nonprofit, and public sector investment. This suggests that a single, lead implementing organization may be beneficial.

The core implementing organization will take different forms in different cities. The particular agency that takes a leadership position in development deal making (and the likelihood that such an organization will emerge) depends on the capacities of local individuals, organizations, government, and politics. For example, in cities such as Lowell, with strong local government and highly influential local public officials, the leading implementing organization may reside in a local governmental department. In cities with influential actors outside of government, such as Jamestown, the core implementing agency may be independent of city government. In cities in which development is highly divisive, establishing a single implementing agency may be problematic.

In Lowell, the leading implementing organization is the city's Planning Department. In Jamestown, the comparable organization is a nonprofit, private Industrial Development Agency (IDA). In the Mon Valley, the Initiative has emerged as the lead implementing organization for cities across the Valley. In contrast, New Bedford's competing development agencies and lack of a single lead implementing organization represents a significant deficiency.[9]

Core implementing organizations appear to be most effective when promoting mutually beneficial deals and the sharing of resources and information between economic development groups in the public, private, and nonprofit sectors. The experience in New Bedford suggests that independent actions by development agencies that lack sensitivity to other development groups can result in confrontation and waste of local resources.

Leading implementing organizations appear to work well when they are given authority and flexibility in structuring development deals. These organizations have to be prepared not only to respond to new opportunities, but also to anticipate and create opportunities. For example, in Lowell, the most visible economic development success in the early 1980s—Wang Laboratories locating in the city—would not have occurred without the persistence of Lowell's City Planning Department. Wang was attracted to Lowell with the novel use of a federal UDAG that the City Planning Department helped to devise.

The evidence suggests that implementing organizations can have the additional value of attracting and retaining talented individuals to work on local development. Core implementing organization can serve as training grounds for future city leaders and a good place for talented young people to start careers. Many of the skills in local development are learned on the job, "doing deals" with private developers, and interacting with federal and state officials. "Learning about development activities" as staff to a lead implementing organization can be particularly helpful in cities that have experienced extended periods of economic decline.[10] Career opportunities and opportunities for visible success can help the implementing organization attract and retain quality staff who build continuity into local development efforts.

Implementing agencies can serve a variety of purposes. They can be effective vehicles for undertaking development diagnostics, organizing development activities, and building continuity into development efforts.

Epilogue

PERHAPS one of the least practiced but most critical contributions that development diagnoses can make is to increase local awareness that economic success is not forever—that local development is a dynamic process subject to cycles. It appears that, to remain vital over time, cities must continuously update their assets and liabilities and redefine their unique qualities, capabilities, areas of comparative advantage, vulnerabilities, and positioning in product, process, and factor price life cycles and in the regional economy. New institutional arrangements must be created, or existing ones, refined to stimulate development opportunities, overcome unforeseen bottlenecks, and deal effectively with critical points in development as they arise. Local development institutions have to create new capacities, linkages, and expertise to undertake development projects in new areas and develop relations with a broad network of actors involved with economic development. Local leaders must respond to changes in the regional and national economy and to the needs and priorities of private businesses, developers, and community groups. Unless it responds effectively to citizen concerns and economic opportunities and difficulties, local development can easily break down.

The focus of the text has been on turnaround situations in medium-sized industrial cities. Many of the findings, including the importance of leadership, vision, and building local development capacity, may apply more broadly to other subnational units, including inner city neighborhoods and larger metropolitan areas. However, some of the development guidelines proposed, such as the desirability of a single dominant development institution and core implementing organization, may be most relevant to turnaround situations in smaller cities and problematic in other situations.

This research has been fundamentally exploratory. It suggests that there are benefits from detailed observation, inductive theory building, and analysis of thoughtful hypotheses. The research indicates that no single theory or analytical construct can fully capture the essence of local economic development. It also demonstrates the value of reaching across traditional disciplinary boundaries. A challenge for future research will be to expand on the empirical and intellectual foundation established here.

The value of motivating, diagnostic, and organizing agents in local development, as strongly suggested here, cannot be evaluated by static and short-term performance measures such as Lowell's economic situation in 1991. Their value must be considered in the context of the local development environment and changes in the larger economy, over which individual cities have little control. One potential fruitful direction for future research would be to dissect the experiences of a larger and more diverse number of cities. Another potentially valuable line of inquiry would be to continue tracking the development experiences in the four study cities as a way to further test and refine the original hypotheses, as was done in the Lowell update in Chapter 8.

Notes

Chapter One
Renewing Industrial Cities

1. Helen F. Ladd, "Introduction to Symposium on Managing Local Development," *Journal of Policy Analysis and Management*, Vol. 9 No. 4, Fall 1990, p. 484.

2. The changes in the federal system with the intergovernmental policies of the Reagan and Bush administration, represent a new version of the New Federalism programs put forward during the Nixon administration. However, Nixon increased the budget for programs in which administrative responsibility shifted from the federal government to state and local government, while Reagan and Bush have pursued policies that simultaneously shift responsibilities and reduce federal expenditures. See Timothy Conlon, *New Federalism* (Washington D.C.: Brookings, 1988), Chapters 1 and 11, for more detailed discussion of federal program changes in the Reagan and Bush administrations. The proliferation of public-private development partnerships is documented in Brooks, Liebman and Schelling, *Public-Private Partnerships* (Cambridge: Ballinger Publishing Company, 1984). The increased number of local development corporations, currently estimated at over 2,000, is documented in Avis Vidal, *Community Economic Development Assessment*, Community Development Research Center, New School for Social Research, 1991.

3. Lowell is located approximately thirty miles northwest of Boston. New Bedford is sixty miles southeast of Boston. Jamestown and McKeesport are 150 miles apart. Jamestown is seventy miles south of Buffalo, and McKeesport is twelve miles southeast of Pittsburgh.

4. All the study cities have a history of employment concentrations in single manufacturing industries—textiles (and later mini-computer manufacturing) in Lowell, garments and apparel in New Bedford, furniture and wood products in Jamestown, and steel and steel products in McKeesport.

5. Notable exceptions include John Gaventa's *Power and Powerlessness* (Champaign: University of Illinois Press, 1984), a study of development in Appalachian communities, and Daniel Elazar's studies of cities in the American prairie in *Cities of the Prairie* and *Cities of the Prairie Revisited* (Lincoln: University of Nebraska Press, 1970 and 1986). The paucity of consideration given to locally based development activities emanates in part from the view that local development initiatives represent a zero, or even negative, sum competition for shares of national industry. See Kotlowitz, Alex and Dale Buss, "Localities' Giveaways to Lure Corporations Cause Growing Outcry," *Wall Street Journal*, September 24, 1986. Glickman, Norman and Douglas Woodward, *The New Competitors* (New York: Basic Books, 1989).

6. Examples of analyses of development efforts in larger cities, which will be discussed in some detail in Chapter 2, include Clarence Stone, *Regime Politics* (Kansas: University Press of Kansas, 1989), an analysis of Atlanta; John Mollenkopf, *The Contested City* (Princeton: Princeton University Press, 1983), a study of development efforts in San Francisco and Boston; and Todd Swanstrom, *The Crisis of Growth Politics* (Philadelphia: Temple University Press, 1985), a study of Cleveland.

7. According to the U.S. Census Bureau, as of 1980 there were 600 cities with populations between 25,000 and 100,000, compared to fifty-five cities with populations of over 250,000. Eighteen percent of the U.S. population lives in the 55 largest cities. Source: U.S. Bureau of the Census, *Statistical Abstract of the United States*, (Washington, D.C.: U.S. Government Printing Office, 1984). Smaller cities tend to have more concentrated employment in single industrial sectors and are particularly vulnerable to declines in U.S. industrial competitiveness. Some of the smaller cities that are most vulnerable to decline are older industrial cities, such as Lowell, New Bedford, Jamestown, and McKeesport, that have concentrated employment in declining industries, such as textiles, apparel, furniture, and primary and fabricated metals manufacturing.

8. U.S. Census Bureau, *Census of Population and Housing* (Washington D.C.: U.S. Government Printing Office, 1900).

9. U.S. Census Bureau, *Census of Manufacturing* (Washington D.C.: U.S. Government Printing Office, 1914, 1925, 1938, 1948, 1954, 1958, 1964, 1968, 1972, 1977, 1982).

10. Brooks, Geraldine, "The Road Back: Old New England City Heals Itself; Can One in Midwest Do So Too?," *Wall Street Journal*, February 1, 1985. Butterfield, Fox, "In Technology, Lowell, Mass., Finds New Life," *New York Times*, August 10, 1982. "High Tech Ends a Long Slump in an Old Mill Town," *U.S. News and World Report*, April 6, 1981. Adams, Jane Meredith. "High-Tech Credited with Revitalizing Old Mill City Lowell," *New England Business*, November 7, 1983. Spring, Suzanne, "Dying 'City of the Future' Reborn in Effort by Townspeople, Business," *The Miami Herald*, February 10, 1985.

Chapter Two
Theories of Local Development

1. Representative studies of business location include: John Blair and Robert Premus, "Major Factors in Industrial Location: A Review," *Economic Development Quarterly*, Vol. 1 No. 1, 1987; Dennis Carlton, "The Location and Employment Choices of New Firms: An Environmental Model with Discrete and Continuous Variables," *The Review of Economics and Statistics*, Vol. 65 No. 3, 1983; and Roger Schmener, Huber and Cook, "Geographic Differences and the Location of New Manufacturing Facilities", *Journal of Urban Economics*, 21, 1989. Assessments of the net effects of local development initiatives include John Levy, *Urban and Metropolitan Economics* (New York: McGraw

Hill, 1985), Chapter 4; and Norman Glickman and Douglas Woodward, *The New Competitors* (New York: Basic Books, 1989), Chapter 7.

2. Konrad Stahl, "Theories of Urban Business Location," in *Handbook of Regional and Urban Economics*, edited by Edwin Mills, Vol. 2 (Amsterdam: North Holland, 1987), Chapter 19, pp. 759–820.

3. In contrast to the shift-share model, which is primarily an accounting-type and static framework, factor price equalization theory is an equilibrium theory.

4. Steven Kale, "Theoretical Contributions to the Understanding of U.S. Nonmetropolitan Economic Change," *Economic Development Quarterly*, Vol. 3 No. 1 February 1989, p. 59.

5. Raymond L. Fales and Leon N. Moses, "Thunen, Weber and the Spatial Structure of the 19th Century City" in *Models of Employment and Residential Location*, edited by Franklin J. James (New Jersey, Center for Urban Policy Research, 1974), pp. 43–74.

6. John R. Meyer, "Regional Economics: A Survey," *American Economic Review*, Vol. 53 No. 1, March 1963.

7. Seev Hirsch, *Location and International Competitiveness* (Oxford: Clarendon, 1967); Raymond Vernon, "International Investment and International Trade in the Product Life Cycle," *Quarterly Journal of Economics*, 80 (1966); T. Levitt, "Exploit the Product Life Cycle," *Harvard Business Review*, Vol. 43 No. 6, November/December 1965; G. Krumme and R. Hayter, "Implications of Corporate Strategies and Product Cycle Adjustments For Regional Employment Changes," in *Locational Dynamics of Manufacturing Activities*, edited by L. Collings and D.F. Walker (New York: John Wiley & Sons, 1975); and R.D. Norton and J. Rees, "The Product Life Cycle and the Spatial Decentralization of American Manufacturing," Regional Studies, Vol. 13 No. 2, August 1979.

8. Single industries or firms may manufacture several products at different life cycle stages.

9. R.H. Hayes and S.C. Wheelwright, "The Dynamics of Process-Product Life Cycles," *Harvard Business Review*, Vol. 57 No. 2, March/April 1979.

10. M.D. Thomas, "Regional Economic Development and the Role of Innovation and Technological Change," in *The Regional Economic Impacts of Technological Change*, edited by A. T. Thwaites and R. P. Oakley (New York: St. Martin's Press, 1985).

11. R.D. Norton, "Industrial Policy and American Renewal," *Journal of Economic Literature*, Vol. 24, March 1986, p. 31.

12. The emergence of mini-mills helped U.S. manufacturers capture market share from the Japanese, German, and South Korean basic oxygen mills and hastened the decline of open hearth steel mills in the United States, including those in the Mon Valley. See Chapter 7 for more discussion.

13. Paul Peterson, *City Limits* (University of Chicago Press, 1981).

14. Peterson's conception of a common city interest in economic development is similar to the assignment of an overarching interest in profit maximization to firms in microeconomic theory.

15. Jeffrey Henig, "Defining City Limits," *American Political Science Association Meetings*, September 1990, p. 7.

16. Paul Kantor, "The Dependent City," *Urban Affairs Quarterly*, June 1987.

17. Paul Kantor with Stephen David, *The Dependent City* (Glenview Ill.: Scott, Foresman, 1988), p. 168.

18. Paul Kantor with Stephen David, *The Dependent City* (Glenview Ill.: Scott, Foresman, 1988), p. 170.

19. John Logan and Harvey Molotch, *Urban Fortunes: The Political Economy of Place* (Berkeley: University of California Press, 1987). Susan Clarke and Anne Moss, "Economic Growth, Environmental Quality, and Growth Services: Mapping the Potential for Local Positive-Sum Strategies," *Journal of Urban Affairs*, Vol. 12 No. 1, 1990.

20. Judith Garber, "Law and the Possibilities for a Just Urban Political Economy," Journal of Urban Affairs, Vol. 12 No. 1, 1990.

21. While Peterson's and Kantor's theories explaining the political and economic dynamic of cities have been formulated largely deductively, Stone's theories are derived more inductively from the experience in Atlanta. Mollenkopf and Long (see latter below) use both inductive and deductive reasoning in formulating their theories.

22. Clarence Stone, *Regime Politics* (Kansas: University Press of Kansas, 1989), p. 164.

23. John Mollenkopf, *The Contested City* (Princeton: Princeton University Press, 1983).

24. John Mollenkopf, *The Contested City*, p. 210.

25. Contributing to the changing relationship between community groups and local officials was the introduction of federal General Revenue Sharing and Community Development Block Grants (CDBGs) in 1974, which provided significant new sources of revenue that city and county government could distribute more or less at their discretion. See Marilyn Gittell, *Limits to Citizen Participation* (Beverly Hills: Sage Publications, 1980); Ira Katznelson, *City Trenches: Urban Politics and the Patterning of Class in the United States* (New York: Pantheon Books, 1981), p. 179; and Frances Piven and Richard Cloward, Poor People's Movements: Why they Succeed, How they Fail (New York: Vintage Books, 1979), pp. 274–277; for elaboration of the view that locally implemented federal programs tended to quiet discontent and co-opt citizen group mobilization.

26. John Mollenkopf, *The Contested City*, p. 292.

27. Rufus Browning, Dale Marshall and David Tabb (BMT), *Protest is Not Enough* (Berkeley: University of California Press, 1984), p. 44.

28. BMT describe "Berkeley's international image as a city at the cutting edge of local policy" (p. 48). Perhaps a more appropriate description of Berkeley politics is at the far outer edge of liberal politics.

29. See Paul Peterson with Margaret Weir "Is New York City a Deviant Case?" in *City Limits*, edited by Paul Peterson, chapter 10.

30. Ira Katznelson, *City Trenches: Urban Politics and the Patterning of Class in the United States* (New York: Pantheon Books, 1981).

31. Todd Swanstrom, *The Crisis of Growth Politics* (Philadelphia: Temple University Press, 1985), p. 197.

32. Ibid., p. 236.

33. Ibid., p. 237.

34. Norton Long, "Have Cities a Future?" *Public Administration Review*, 1973, p. 547.

35. Ibid., p. 545.

36. Clarence Stone, *Regime Politics*, p. 8.

37. BMT, *Protest is Not Enough*, p. 140.

38. Paul Peterson, *City Limits*, pp. 20–21.

39. In the classical version of the prisoners' dilemma, a district attorney offers, individually, each of two prisoners release from jail if they give evidence that will convict the other. If one remains silent but the other gives evidence, the prisoner who kept silent will receive a heavy jail term but his compatriot will be released. If both remain silent they will both get only a short term in jail. If both give evidence they both will get moderate terms. For each individual, the best strategy is to give evidence on the other; however, if both give evidence, they will each be worse off than if they had kept quiet.

40. Mancur Olson, The Logic of Collective Action (Cambridge: Harvard University Press, 1965).

41. Olson's work is rooted in public choice theory. Beginning in 1957, with Anthony Downs's *Economic Theories of Democracy* (New York: Harper and Row) and culminating in 1986, when James Buchanan won the Nobel Prize in economics for applying to politics a rational choice model based on self-interest, public choice models of political behavior have become increasingly influential. Like economic models, they assume self-interest as the primary motivation for individual and collection action.

42. Mancur Olson, *The Logic of Collective Action*, p. 15.

43. Collective efforts will produce benefits, with different degrees of excludability. Peterson identifies local development as similar to a local public good in which benefits are nonexcludable. Kantor rejects Peterson's view and suggests that development projects primarily benefit local economic elites. In contrast to Peterson and Kantor, Long contends that there is nothing inherent about the excludability and distribution of development benefits and that local politics shape development policies and the distribution of development benefits and costs.

44. John Mollenkopf, *The Contested City*, p. 4.

45. Mancur Olson, *The Logic of Collective Action*, p. 177.

46. Mancur Olson, *The Logic of Collective Action*, p. 53. While small groups might promote intragroup cooperation, they have the potential drawback of representing only a limited number of interests in local development coalitions.

47. Robert Axelrod, *The Evolution of Cooperation* (New York: Basic Books, 1984).

48. Most representations of local development as a cooperative or non-cooperative game have highlighted the "play" between cities and potential

new employers/industries, not the "game" among local actors. See Michael Wolkoff, "Is Economic Development Decision Making Rational?" Association for Public Policy Analysis and Management, Annual Meeting, San Francisco, October 1990.

49. See Jane Mansbridge (editor), *Beyond Self-Interest* (Chicago: University of Chicago Press, 1990), particularly her own contributions, "The Rise and Fall of Self-Interest in the Explanation of Political Life" and "On the Relation of Altruism and Self-Interest," for further elaboration of motivations beyond self-interest in political and social actions.

50. James Q. Wilson and Peter B. Clark, "Incentive Systems: A Theory of Organization," *Administrative Science Quarterly*, 1961, 6:129–66.

51. Wilson's "solidary" incentive can be expanded to include a transformative component. Individuals often gain a sense of solidarity as they discover common interests and transform self-interested preferences in group activities and discourse. This transformative view of collective action is distinct from Peterson's, which assumes that individual parties will act collectively only after they have identified a common interest.

52. Richard Fenno, *Congressmen in Committees* (Boston: Little, Brown, 1973).

Chapter Three
Growth and Decline in Four Cities

1. U.S. Census Bureau, *Population and Housing*, 1880, 1890, 1900, 1910, 1920.

2. U.S. Census Bureau, *Census of Manufacturing*, 1914, 1975.

3. See William Frey and Alden Speare, *Regional and Metropolitan Growth and Decline in the U.S.* (Russell Sage Foundation, 1988) and Weinstein, Gross and Rees, *Regional Growth and Decline in the United States* (New York: Praeger, 1985) for more detailed discussion of regional movement of employment during the post–World War II period.

4. Unless otherwise noted, single and two digit Standard Industrial Code (SIC) employment data from the U.S. Census Bureau, *Population and Housing* are used in the shift-share analysis. There are arguments for using more detailed industrial categories, e.g., three and four digit; however, data availability is restricted because of disclosure problems, especially in smaller cities with fewer companies in detailed industrial segments. In general, if more detailed industrial categories were used in the shift-share analysis, we would expect smaller (in absolute terms) differential shifts. However, in the four cities studied, there is little reason to suspect that the sign or relative scale of the differential shifts would be dramatically affected by using more detailed industrial categories in the shift-share analysis.

5. The "totals" in the differential shift tables represent the sum for single digit industries. Since the tables also have rows of data for relevant two digit industries, e.g., machinery and equipment and textiles and apparel manufacturing, the sum of the figures down the columns do not add up to the totals.

6. It appears that New Bedford performed well in agriculture and textiles and apparel (as measured by positive differential shifts), not because of large increases in employment (see Table 3.2), but because these industries experienced significant declines nationally and in the state.

7. Massachusetts was one of the earliest "victims" of the shift of manufacturing activity within the United States. Much of the manufacturing employment decline in the Commonwealth was concentrated during the 1960s. From 1960 to 1970, manufacturing employment in Massachusetts declined by nearly 10 percent. The decline in manufacturing employment was concentrated in nondurable manufacturing employment, including textiles and apparel.

8. The annual data presented here and used in shift-share analysis is from the Massachusetts Department of Employment and Training (DET). The state employment data is used in much the same manner as the U.S. Census data—to track trends and compare and contrast the most recent economic development experiences of Lowell and New Bedford. The state publishes annual employment data for the Lowell and New Bedford Labor Market Areas (LMAs) and the state. The LMAs encompass the cities themselves plus the surrounding area. In the analysis, we are most interested in comparing trends, year-to-year changes in New Bedford and Lowell, rather than absolute employment levels.

9. The Massachusetts Department of Employment and Training categorization of high technology industries includes segments of electrical and nonelectrical machinery and equipment manufacturing and transportation equipment manufacturing.

10. See Chapter 4 for more detailed discussion of the impact of Wang's decision to locate in Lowell and how local factors effected Wang's decision.

11. Regional Urban Design Assistance Team, "Remaking the Monongahela Valley," *American Institute of Architects*, March, 1988.

12. John Hoerr, *And the Wolf Finally Came* (Pittsburgh: University of Pittsburgh Press, 1988), p. 178.

13. U.S. Census Bureau, *Census of Manufacturing*, 1914, 1954.

14. U.S. Census Bureau, *Census of Manufacturing*, 1954, 1958.

15. Because of disclosure problems concerning a large percentage of employment with one employer, the *Census of Manufacturing* has not published manufacturing employment statistics for McKeesport since 1972. The 1980 employment data is from a survey of households in McKeesport in the U.S. Census Bureau, *Population and Housing*.

16. John Hoerr, *And the Wolf Finally Came*, p. 166.

17. See Benjamin Chinitz, "Contrasts in Agglomeration: New York and Pittsburgh," *American Economic Review*, 51, May 1961, p. 167–178, for more discussion of regional diseconomies associated with metals industry production.

18. Between 1950 and 1980, U.S. furniture and related products manufacturing employment declined by 1 percent and metals manufacturing employment increased by only 35 percent, while total United States employment grew by 73 percent (see Table 3.3).

19. New York State is dominated by New York City (especially with regard to economic and demographic statistics). This suggests that using New York (instead of Pennsylvania) might not have been appropriate.

Chapter Four
Lowell: Successful Revitalization

1. Doeringer, Peter, David Terkla and Gregory Topakian, *Invisible Factors in Local Economic Development* (New York: Oxford University Press, 1987).

2. For more discussion of the use of comparative case studies, see Alexander George, "Case Studies and Theory Development: The Method of Structured Focused Comparison," in *Diplomacy: New Approaches in History, Theory and Policy*, edited by Paul Lauren (New York: The Free Press, 1979), pp. 43–65; and Harry Dickstein, "Case Study and Theory in Political Sciences," in *Handbook of Political Science*, edited by F.T. Greenstein and N.W. Polsby (Reading, Mass.: Addison-Wesley, 1975) Vol. 7, pp. 79–138; and Christine Meisner Rosen, *The Limits of Power* (Cambridge: Cambridge University Press, 1986), pp. 89–91.

3. Geraldine Brooks, "The Road Back: Old New England City Heals Itself; Can One in Midwest Do So Too?," *Wall Street Journal*, February 1, 1985. Fox Butterfield, "In Technology, Lowell, Mass., Finds New Life," *New York Times*, August 10, 1982. "High Tech Ends a Long Slump in an Old Mill Town," *U.S. News and World Report*, April 6, 1981. Jane M. Adams, "High-Tech Credited with Revitalizing Old Mill City Lowell," *New England Business*, November 7, 1983. Suzanne Spring, "Dying 'City of the Future' Reborn in Effort by Townspeople, Business," *The Miami Herald*, February 10, 1985.

4. U.S. Census Bureau, *County and City Data Book*, 1988.

5. The city profile (Table 4.1) and employment (Table 4.2) tables presented in this chapter and the subsequent three "city development analysis" chapters are reproduced from Chapter 3. Those tables were placed in Chapter 3 to facilitate comparative data analysis and to give common reference for the subsequent discussion. While some (old and new) data is presented in Chapters 4 through 7, readers might find it useful to refer back to Chapter 3 for more detailed data presentation and analysis.

6. U.S. Census Bureau, *U.S. Census of Manufacturing*, 1958, 1968.

7. Paul Tsongas served on the Lowell City Council from 1969 to 1972. He was a Middlesex County Commissioner from 1973 to 1974, Congressman from 1975 to 1978, and U.S. Senator from 1979 to 1985, when he retired due to poor health. After recovering his health, he was a candidate for the Democratic presidential nomination in 1992.

8. See John Gaventa, *Power and Powerlessness: Quiescence and Rebellion in an Appalchian Valley* (Urbana: University of Illinois Press, 1980), for one of the best descriptions of community acquiescence in the face of economic decline. Gaventa argues that collective pessimism has had a significant negative effect on the Appalacia economy. In the Mon Valley, see Chapter 7, we

also observe the tendency of local residents—identified by Stephen Elkin in *City and Regime in the American Republic* (Chicago: University of Chicago Press, 1987) p.135—to approve of those who flourish under the existing rules, most notably the U.S. Steel company and local public officials, even when local conditions are depressed. For further discussion of the role of collective optimism and pessimism on local economic performance, see Chapter 9 (in particular, the sections on vision and leadership).

9. Community Revitalization Project (CRP) interview, Paul Tsongas, Summer 1986.

10. CRP interview Pat Mogan, Summer 1986.

11. CRP interview, Frank Keefe, Summer 1986.

12. CRP, *Case Study: Community Revitalization in Lowell*, Center For Business and Government, Harvard University, Summer 1988, p. 3.

13. Ibid. p. 6

14. See Charles Haar, "The Joint Venture Approach to Urban Renewal: From Model Cities to Urban Renewal" and Harvey Brooks, Lance Liebman and Corinne Schelling (editors), *Public Private Partnership* (Cambridge: Ballinger Books, 1984) for critical discussion of the Model Cities program.

15. Address by Pat Mogan, delivered at Harvard University Conference, "Paths to Revitalization: The Experience of Four Industrial Communities," John F. Kennedy School of Government, Center for Business and Government, December 6, 1987.

16. Lowell Historical Preservation Commission, *Information Document*, 1985.

17. U.S. Congress, *PL 95-290*, sections 101(a)(1), 103(a).

18. Ibid., section 1(b).

19. Ibid., section 9.

20. Central City Committee, *Statement of Goals*, 1972.

21. CRP Interview, William Lipchitz, Summer 1986.

22. Central City Committee, "First Quarterly Report of the Lowell Center Cities Development Project," October 10, 1972.

23. Memorandum from Center City Advisory Committee (written by Robert B. Kennedy, Chairman) to Lowell city manager and members of the city council, September 29, 1972.

24. Lowell Center City Advisory Committee, "Statement of Strategy," November 30, 1972.

25. CRP Interview, William Lipchitz, Summer 1986.

26. Ibid.

27. CRP Interview, Paul Tsongas, Summer 1986.

28. Ibid.

29. The LDFC was established in 1975 by special act of the state legislature.

30. 1975 Massachusetts Acts, Chapter 844, section 8.

31. Ibid., section 5(h).

32. The Urban Development Action Grant (UDAG) Program awarded $4.6 billion to assist approximately 3,000 economic development projects in

more than 1,200 cities during its twelve years of operation (1978–1989). To be eligible for an action grant, a city or county had to meet minimum standards of physical, economic, or fiscal distress. See Michael Rich, "UDAG, Economic Development and the Death and Life of American Cities," *Economic Development Quarterly*, Spring 1992. See also Charles Haar, "The Joint Venture Approach to Urban Renewal: From Model Cities to Urban Renewal", in *Public Private Partnership*, for more background information on the UDAG program.

33. CRP Interview, William Taupier, Summer 1986.

34. Michael Rich, "UDAG, Economic Development and the Death and Life of American Cities," *Economic Development Quarterly*, Spring 1992.

35. CRP, *Community Revitalization in Lowell*, footnote 9.

36. CRP Interview, Paul Sheehy, Summer 1986.

37. Ibid.

38. U.S. Census Bureau, *Census of Services*, 1977 and 1987.

39. The corporate executives on the board of the Lowell Plan are from firms headquartered in Lowell, including Wang Laboratories, Joan Fabrics, Courier Corporation, Muro Pharmaceutical, the Lowell Sun, Colonial Gas, and Union National Bank.

40. CRP Interview, Paul Tsongas, Summer 1986.

41. Ibid.

42. CRP Interview, City Manger Joseph Tully, Summer 1985.

43. CRP Interview, Paul Tsongas, Summer 1986.

44. Ibid.

45. Virginia Biggy, Mario D. Fantini, and Robert I. Sperber, *The Lowell Model for Education Excellence*, January 1984.

46. CRP, *Community Revitalization in Lowell*, p.10.

47. Ibid.

48. CRP Interview, Paul Tsongas, Summer 1986.

49. Ibid.

50. Charles Gargiulo, "A Study of Rental Housing Costs in Lowell," unpublished report for Community Teamwork, Inc., March 1986.

51. Letter to Lowell Mayor Robert B. Kennedy from Joseph P. Hannon, Executive Director of the Center City Committee, Northern Middlesex Area Commission, April 17, 1986.

52. Coalition for a Better Acre (CBA), "Coalition for a Better Acre History," unpublished paper, 1988.

53. CRP Interview, Charles Gargiulo, Summer 1985.

54. Ibid.

55. Ibid.

56. The federal Community Reinvestment Act (Title VIII of the Housing and Community Reinvestment Act of 1977) required that financial institutions (including insurance companies) take action to invest funds in neighborhoods in which there had previously been underinvestment. The Act's purposes were "to encourage banks to meet the credit needs of their local community . . . the FDIC will assess the records of banks in satisfying their continuing obligations to help meet the credit needs of local communities,

including low and moderate income neighborhoods." *Federal Register*, Vol. 43 No. 190, October 12, 1978.

57. CRP Interview, Jerry Altman, Summer 1986.

58. Altman put the CBA in contact with the Parker Foundation in Boston and Raytheon, with headquarters on the Route 128 corridor, which later made contributions to the CBA.

59. Data taken from CBA literature on the Home Ownership Project. Twenty-two of the thirty-six homes were single family homes.

Chapter Five
New Bedford: Extended Decline

1. U.S. Census Bureau, *County and City Data Book*, 1988.

2. U.S. Census Bureau, *Population and Housing*, 1980.

3. In New England the earliest mills were located in Lowell and other cities northwest of New Bedford. The first mills in New Bedford, the Wamsutta and the New Bedford Steam Company mills, were started in 1846.

4. New Bedford has historically had above average labor force participation rates, with high rates of female labor force participation. Many families in the city had several members in the labor force, including husband and wife and older children.

5. New Bedford's retention of textile and apparel employment is documented in economic base and shift-share analysis in Chapter 3.

6. Derived from U.S. Census Bureau, *Population and Housing* data combining employment in fishing and food and kindred products and making adjustment for the tendency to undercount in calculating employment in industries with high levels of self and unreported employment, such as fishing. (The U.S. Census estimates of fishing industry employment were adjusted upwards by 50 percent in the derivation of an employment series for the fishing and related industries in New Bedford.) The peak years in New Bedford's fishing industry followed the enactment of the Magnunson-Studds Act in 1977, co-sponsored by New Bedford Congressman Gerry Studds. The act reserved a 200–mile coastal area for "local" (United States) fishing. The boom of the early 1980s was followed by a period of near crisis, as a fish workers' strike in 1985 compounded the problems of overfishing, overcapacity and increasing foreign competition.

7. U.S. Census Bureau, *County and City Data Book*, 1988.

8. The figure in 1950 and 1980 for percent foreign born in the state of Massachusetts was 9 percent.

9. Many inner city ethnic neighborhoods developed near the mills in downtown New Bedford. In contrast, many wealthier families, mostly the owners and managers of businesses, lived outside the city lines in suburban waterside communities.

10. In 1980, according to the U.S. Census Bureau, *Population and Housing*, the median years of education for New Bedford residents was 9.5, compared to 12.6 in Massachusetts and 12.5 in the United States.

11. It is very difficult to determine exactly how much federal money New

Bedford received as a result of Model Cities designation, aside from the $12 million it received in supplemental Model Cities funds from HUD. In addition to the supplemental monies, model cities received priority treatment from HUD and other federal agencies.

12. Would conditions have been even worse without the infusion of federal Urban Renewal program funds? This is a difficult question, but New Bedford in the mid–1980s, as depicted by the Massachusetts' DET employment statistics documented in Chapter 3, does not appear to be any worse off than it was in the early 1970s when significant levels of federal money was injected into the local economy.

13. Herbert Gans, "The Failure of Urban Renewal," in *Urban Renewal: The Record and the Controversy*, edited by James Q. Wilson (Cambridge: The M.I.T. Press, 1966), p. 541.

14. See Bernard Frieden and Lynn Sagalyn, *Downtown, Inc.* (Cambridge: MIT Press, 1989) for discussion of how Urban Renewal worked in many cities as a "Robin Hood in reverse."

15. The New Bedford Redevelopment Authority employed eighty-three at its peak in 1968. Several of the administrators in New Bedford abused the system for their own personal benefit. Howard Bapitista, the first director of the New Bedford Redevelopment Authority, was indicted for taking kickbacks from a Philadelphia, Pennsylvania construction company that was awarded several urban renewal contracts in New Bedford. (Note: Background information and employment figures on New Bedford Redevelopment Authority were collected from *New Bedford Standard Times* articles published during the period of intensive urban renewal activity in New Bedford.)

16. Most of the information regarding the Model Cities program in New Bedford is drawn from *New Bedford Standard Times* articles from 1968 to 1974. Unlike the Urban Renewal program, Model Cities was targeted to the most distressed urban areas. For further discussion of how the Model Cities program was designed to correct for the "sins" of urban renewal, see Nicholas Lemann, *The Promised Land* (New York: Alfred A Knopf, 1991), p. 187.

17. The initial Model Cities target area in New Bedford was the heavily Portuguese South End neighborhood. However, unrest during the summer of 1970 in the predominantly Afro American West End area prompted a move to include the forty-five block and 3,000-resident neighborhood in the target area.

18. New Bedford continued to receive Model Cities aid until 1974, when the Nixon administration phased out the program.

19. Community Revitalization Project (CRP) interviews with local residents from June 1985 to August 1986. An example of local opinion of Urban Renewal and Model Cities Program was reflected in comments by former City Planner Ben Baker in an interview in the summer of 1986. He noted that, in order to receive federal money for the downtown access road to the fishing pier and the public auction the new road had to be a four-lane highway.

20. Richard Boyer and David Savageau, *Places Rated Almanac* (Chicago: Rand McNally, 1985).

21. Various CRP interviews, Summer 1985.

22. CRP interview, Mayor Brian Lawler, Summer 1985.

23. The Zeitarian Theater was successfully completed and then sold to a private group in 1986.

24. The material for this section was gathered during Community Revitalization Project interviews from June 1985 to August 1986 and newspaper stories in *The Boston Globe*, *The New York Times*, and the *New Bedford Standard Times*.

25. Company demands at Morse in March 1982 included reduced vacation time, the elimination of three paid holidays, a reduction in wages and fringe benefits by $4.40 an hour and the right for G&W to regrade all jobs.

26. By 1980 employment in machine manufacturing (combining electrical and nonelectrical) in New Bedford had declined below 3,000, down over 30 percent from its peak of over 4,300 in 1950 (see Table 5.2). At the same time the New Bedford economy was still suffering from high unemployment, with unemployment in the early 1980s hovering above 9 percent. Source: *Massachusetts Department of Employment and Training*.

27. The ICA is a labor research organization based in Sommerville, Massachusetts.

28. *The New York Times* and *Washington Post* published articles on the union battle at Morse in 1983.

29. William Serrin, "In New Bedford, Union Efforts Keep a Plant Alive," *New York Times*, June 15, 1985.

30. Ibid.

31. This was an improvement over the previous two years at Morse, when (under G&W management) the company lost $3.6 million and $1.6 million respectively.

32. Michael Kranish, "A New Twist in New Bedford," *The Boston Globe*, May 19, 1987, p. 65.

33. The majority of material for this section was gathered during CRP field work, including attendance at economic task force meetings.

34. The other task forces included tourism, the environment, the waterfront, and municipal organization.

35. The Economic Development Corporation (EDC) was a private nonprofit agency. It was established in 1983 during the Lawler administration with Community Development Block Grant (CDBG) funds. The EDC replaced the Industrial Development Commission (mentioned previously). The EDC had been unsuccessful in stimulating the development of the local economy during its short life. The EDC from 1983 to 1985 had attracted no new businesses to New Bedford. The lack of activity at the EDC, especially in comparison to similar organizations in neighboring communities, including Jobs For Fall River in neighboring Fall River, disturbed many in New Bedford and, according to Mayor Bullard, limited the agency's potential to be effective in the future.

36. From 1985 to 1986, the unemployment rate in New Bedford was still the highest among cities of its size in the state. Source: *Massachusetts Department of Employment and Training.*

Chapter Six
Jamestown: Attempted Preservation

1. U.S. Census Bureau, *County and City Data Book*, 1988.

2. Jamestown Department of Development, *Information Guide: Jamestown, New York*, 1983, p. 1.

3. Chautauqua Region Community Foundation Inc., *Jamestown the Next 100 Years*, 1986.

4. The Art Metal plant was the largest factory built in New York State between World War II and 1972.

5. Michael McManus, "Western New York Shows the Way to Productivity," *Mid-American Outlook*, Fall 1979.

6. Other factors reportedly contributing to Jamestown's industrial decline included obsolescent factories and high taxes in New York State.

7. Seran Lundstedt and William Calgazier, *Managing Innovation: The Social Dimension of Creativity, Invention and Technology* (New York: Pergamon Press, 1978), p. 216.

8. U.S. Department of Commerce, "Improving the Quality of Worklife," *Jobs Through Economic Development*, January 1979.

9. Charlene Costanzo and Joel Gershenfeld, *A Decade of Change: Ten Year Report of Jamestown Area Labor Management Committee*, 1983, p.8.

10. The National Center for Productivity and Quality of Working Life in Washington, D.C. is the primary source of labor and management committee background information presented here.

11. "Jamestown, New York," *Nation's Cities*, April 1978, p. 18.

12. Ibid., p. 18.

13. U.S. Department of Commerce, "Improving the Quality of Work Life," January 1979, p. 1.

14. Seran Lundstedt and William Calgazier, *Managing Innovation: The Social Dimension of Creativity, Invention and Technology*, p. 218.

15. "Jamestown Pulls Itself Together," *The Economist*, June 21, 1980.

16. CRP interview with Joseph Penagoff, Jamestown Cummins Engine plant manager, Summer 1987.

17. *Nation's Cities*, p. 20.

18. CRP interview with Joseph Penagoff, Jamestown Cummins Engine plant manager, Summer 1987.

19. *Nation's Cities*, p. 20.

20. New York State, Department of Labor Employment Statistics, 1974–78.

21. Seran Lundstedt and William Calgazier, *Managing Innovation: The Social Dimension of Creativity, Invention and Technology*, p. 225.

22. "Jamestown Pulls Itself Together," *The Economist*, June 21, 1980.

23. Charlene Costanzo and Joel Gershenfeld, *A Decade of Change: Ten Year Report of Jamestown Area Labor Management Committee*, 1983, p.14.

24. Statistical sources are a combination of U.S. Census Bureau, *Population and Housing* data and data collected by the The Jamestown Foundation Steering Committee in 1987.

25. U.S. Census Bureau, *Population and Housing* (1980) and *Census of Manufacturing* (1977 and 1982).

26. The corporate survey was undertaken by Ross J. Gittell and Winthrop Knowlton during the summer of 1987 as part of the Community Revitalization Project.

27. CRP interview with a Jamestown-area industrial-plant general manager (off-the-record), summer, 1987.

28. The Chautauqua County Industrial Development Authority (IDA) is a private nonprofit agency serving all of Chautauqua County, which includes the greater Jamestown area. Its purpose is to promote industrial development with public (state, federal, and local) and private funds.

29. Various Jamestown Community Revitalization Project interviews in 1986 and 1987.

30. CRP Interview, Paul Benke, summer, 1986.

31. The community foundation was created with contributions from eight local foundations. Its purpose was to fund selective local projects.

32. Jamestown, for a city of its size, had a significant number of local foundations. This emanated from Jamestown's historical development. Many of the immigrants to the city established profitable medium-sized industrial establishments. In many cases, when the founders of these establishments passed away, their children and grandchildren sold the establishments to larger companies from outside the city. Some of the proceeds from the sale of the businesses were used to establish local foundations.

33. Report on Jamestown Foundation grants prepared by Francis Grow, director of the Jamestown Community Foundation, 1987.

34. CRP interview, Murray Bob, March 1986.

35. CRP Interview, John Hamiltion, executive director of the Gebbie Foundation, Summer 1987.

36. CRP Interview with Hal Bolton, December, 1987.

37. Much of this section is drawn from the steering committee's report to the community foundation of January, 1988.

Chapter Seven
McKeesport: Decline and Struggle

1. There were large steel mills owned and operated by other steel companies in the Mon Valley, including LTV, Weirton, and Wheeling-Pittsburgh Steel; however, the U.S. Steel corporation was the dominant steel producer in the Valley.

2. The assembly line analogy is not exact—each plant specialized in one or more specialized products. For example, the McKeesport plants special-

ized in pipe, speciality tube, ordinance, and iron sheet products; the Clariton Works produced specialized coke; the Donora Works manufactured wire rods and nails; and the Irvin Works at West Mifflin produced sheet steel for cars and appliances.

3. John P. Hoerr, *And the Wolf Finally Came* (Pittsburgh: University of Pittsburgh Press, 1988), p. 169.

4. Ibid., p. 171.

5. Efforts to organize Mon Valley steel workers were started in the 1890s. Industry resistance, together with worker fear of company reprisals, frustrated unionization efforts until after the Depression. In 1936, under protection of the Wagner Act, the precursor to the United Steel Workers union was established under the leadership of John L. Lewis.

6. John P. Hoerr, *And the Wolf Finally Came*, p. 250.

7. The first railroad lines in the Valley were owned and operated by the Baltimore and Ohio (B&O) Railroad.

8. J.P. Morgan and Andrew Carnegie put together the steel trust, which was incorporated February 1, 1901 as the U.S. Steel Corporation. It was initially a holding company of subsidiaries bringing approximately 65 percent of the national steel industry together under a single corporate umbrella.

9. U.S. Census Bureau, *County and City Data Book*, 1988.

10. John P. Hoerr, *And the Wolf Finally Came*, p. 291.

11. Donald Dalena, "Programs in Steel," *United Steel Workers Report*, 1984, pp. 38–39.

12. The national contract did not specify whether the in-plant steel committees should deal with matters other than productivity issues.

13. John P. Hoerr, *And the Wolf Finally Came*, p. 294.

14. Ibid., p. 295.

15. The Mon Valley crosses four Pennsylvania counties—Allegheny, Fayette, Westmoreland, and Washington. Allegheny County is the most urbanized and the largest county in the region. In 1980 Allegheny County had a population of 1.45 million. The city of Pittsburgh was by far the largest city in Allegheny County, with 29 percent of the County's population.

16. Paul Dommel, *Decentralizing Urban Policy* (Washington D.C.: The Brookings Institution, 1982).

17. Mon Valley Commission, *Report to the Allegheny County Board of Commissioners for the Economic Revitalization of the Monongahela, Youghiogheny and Turtle Creek Valleys* (Pittsburgh: Allegheny County Departments of Development and Planning, 1987).

18. Allegheny County is administered by three county commissioners who are elected in countywide elections.

19. In all, the task forces involved more than 200 people and held over 50 meetings.

20. Linda Wilson, "County to buy Idled Mills," *Pittsburgh Post-Gazette*, March 26, 1987, p. 1.

21. Mon Valley Commission, *Report to the Allegheny County Board of Commissioners for the Economic Revitalization of the Monongahela, Youghiogheny and*

Turtle Creek Valleys (Pittsburgh: Allegheny County Departments of Development and Planning, 1987).

22. Governor Robert P. Casey, Speech at Penn State University, McKeesport, Penn., March 25, 1987.

23. Allegheny County Department of Planning, Monroeville Municipal Profile, 1989.

24. David K. Levadansky (Pennsylvania state representative), letter to PA Department of Community Affairs, July 7, 1988.

25. Regional Urban Design Assistance Team (RUDAT), *Remaking the Monongahela Valley* (Pittsburgh: American Institute of Architects, 1988).

26. Ibid.

27. Ibid.

28. Linda Wilson, "Hope for Steel Rebirth Still Flickers," *Pittsburgh Post-Gazette*, March 1, 1988.

29. Ibid.

30. William Mausteller, "Prince Backs the Common Man," *Pittsburgh Press*, March 6, 1988, p. 1.

31. The Allegheny Conference is a private nonprofit citizen's organization founded in the early 1940s in response to Pittsburgh's deteriorating social and economic conditions. It has been credited with being a major contributor to the city of Pittsburgh's much heralded Renaissance. Its executive committee is comprised of twenty-five chairmen of major Pittsburgh corporations, as well as the president of the University of Pittsburgh.

32. Michael Eichler, Letter to LISC President Paul Grogan summarizing his efforts in the Mon Valley, July 1988.

33. LISC is a national nonprofit community development intermediary, begun in 1979. Local corporate and foundation donations for CDC projects are matched with funds raised nationally. By 1987 LISC had provided funds for over 400 community development corporations (CDCs) in 23 areas of concentration (including the Mon Valley), with loans and grants totaling $60 million. Source: *Local Initiative Support Corporation* (LISC), Annual Report, 1989.

34. In 1991, Michael Eichler and LISC started a national demonstration program, introducing the "development team" approach piloted in the Mon Valley in three sites—Palm Beach County, Florida, New Orleans, and Little Rock, Arkansas.

35. Mon Valley Commission, *Report to the Allegheny County Board of Commissioners for the Economic Revitalization of the Monongahela, Youghiogheny and Turtle Creek Valleys* (Pittsburgh: Allegheny County Departments of Development and Planning, 1987).

36. Foundation officials did not want to be put into a position of "picking and choosing" among CDC projects in the Valley. They wanted to encourage cooperation, not competition, between the cities in the Valley.

37. Eichler had the support of Alfred Wishart, the executive director of the Pittsburgh Foundation, and Robert Peace, the executive director of the Allegheny Conference on Community Development. He included Peace and Wishart in meetings with bank executives.

Chapter Eight
Critical Factors in City Revitalization

1. Average wage data is for 1989. Source: Massachusetts Department of Employment and Training, *Employment and Wages in Massachusetts' Cities and Towns*, 1990.

2. Michael E. Porter, *The Competitive Advantage of Massachusetts* (Cambridge: The Monitor Company Inc., 1991), p. 100.

3. Lowell suffered from the bankruptcy of ComFed and the takeover of the Bank of New England by the larger Fleet National based in Rhode Island.

4. The number of Asians in Lowell, according to the U.S. Census Bureau, *Population and Housing*, grew from 600 in 1980 to 11,500 in 1990, increasing from less than 1 percent to over 11 percent of the city's population. Most of the Asians in the city were recent immigrants from Southeast Asia. While the official reports indicated dramatic growth, unofficially city planners reported the city's Asian population as greater than 20,000 in 1990. Jules Crittenden, "Census Shows Downtown Grew Most in Lowell," *The Lowell Sun*, August 4, 1991.

5. Compounding the city's fiscal difficulties, the state's intergovernmental transfers to Lowell and other cities declined with the downturn in the state economy.

6. Michael E. Porter, *The Competitive Advantage of Massachusetts* (Cambridge: The Monitor Company Inc., 1991), p. 100.

7. Michael O'Connell, "Miller: More Wang Cuts Ahead," *The Lowell Sun*, June 19, 1991.

8. The estimate of Wang employment in Lowell in 1991 is from Moody's *Lowell, Massachusetts: Municipal Credit Report*, June 24, 1991. It was not possible to get an exact employment figure, but an estimate of Wang's employment peak in Lowell is 8,000 in 1986. This suggests that Wang employment in the city declined by approximately 43 percent between 1986 and 1991.

9. Lisa Adams, "Wang Layoffs May Hit 2,000 in Bay State," *The Lowell Sun*, June 29, 1991. Michael O'Connell, "Miller: More Wang Cuts Ahead," *The Lowell Sun*, June 19, 1991.

10. As Wall Street analyst Case Stern of Starr Securities Inc. commented about Wang's reorganization, "It is a very very sound business strategy and I think it will help Wang." Lisa Adams, "Wang Layoffs May Hit 2,000 in Bay State", *The Lowell Sun*, June 29, 1991.

11. Lowell Development and Financial Corporation, *1989 Annual Report*.

12. The hotel's employment throughout the late 1980s was approximately 175. There was no change in employment when Coast foreclosed on the property.

13. Kathleen Reilly, "Hilton Manager Optimistic About Name Change," *The Lowell Sun*, July 12, 1991. Michael O'Connell, "Lowell Hilton Switches to Sheraton," *The Lowell Sun*, July 11, 1991.

14. Dana Francis, "MCC Seeking to Expand Lowell Campus," *The Lowell Sun*, June 29, 1991.

15. Unlike the Hilton owners, Wang has not missed a payment on its

UDAG loan and its loan repayments continue to be recycled into the local economy through the LDFC.

16. The Hilton LDFC loan default was more than ten times larger than the three other LDFC loan defaults combined. The next largest loan default was Jordan Marsh for $180,000.

17. Interview, Jim Cook, director of the LDFC and the Lowell Plan, July 1991. What could be questioned is whether the UDAG would have been forthcoming without the promise of "recycling" the original grant.

18. Interview, Jim Cook, director of the LDFC and the Lowell Plan, and Robert Malavich, the director of Planning and Development for the city of Lowell, July 1991.

19. The Lowell Plan, *Annual Report*, 1990.

20. John Collinge, "Lowell Business Center Moving," *The Lowell Sun*, August 23, 1991.

21. Reflective, in part, of the efforts of community groups and the city, the population in the downtown nearly doubled in the 1980s, giving that section the largest percentage growth of all the city's neighborhoods. In addition, in the Acre neighborhood, where the efforts of the Coalition for a Better Acre were concentrated, the population increased by 18 percent, to over 12,500. Jules Crittenden, "Census Shows Downtown Grew Most in Lowell," *The Lowell Sun*, August 4, 1991.

22. In addition to the loans provided through the FMLPP, equity financing for both projects totalling $6.6 million was provided by Fannie Mae and the Bank of New England NA. As part of the rehabilitation project at the North Canal Apartments, the exteriors of the buildings were completely renovated to hide precast concrete facades. This was particularly pleasing to local public and private sector officials, who were embarrassed by the appearance of the housing units in the newly renovated downtown district.

23. The owners, according to several community leaders, were only involved in the project to make quick profits with the assistance of public subsidies—they never intended to hold the property as a long term investment.

24. Coalition for a Better Acre, "The Campaign to Save North Canal," 1989, p. 8.

25. Neal Newman, Executive Director of the Coalition For a Better Acre, interview, July 1991.

26. It could also be argued that, without the CBA in Lowell, local banks would have had difficulty meeting their CRA obligations. Through its extensive political lobbying and careful project planning, the CBA provided local banks with "bankable" projects in areas in which local banks had not invested to the levels required.

27. A significant portion of the LDFC's capital base, apart from the $15 million FMLPP, is represented by two UDAG loans (Wang and Wannalancit Office and Technology Center), with 1990 combined capital of $5.5 million, which are being recycled back into the local economy.

28. An example of a firm in a high growth industry that the city is attempting to attract is FTP Software INC, a 150-employee company. The company produces nonproprietary networking software for IBM and IBM-compatible personal computers and expects to double its size. In August

1991, FTP put Lowell on its "short list" of potential sites, with North Andover and Wakefield, Massachusetts. FTP seems to be attracted to Lowell for a variety of reasons, including low-cost space in an attractively refurbished mill building in the downtown; financial assistance from the LDFC; and location in the Route 128 corridor near other software companies and a supply of skilled workers. Michael O'Connell, "Growing Software Company May Come to Lowell," *The Lowell Sun*, August 13, 1991.

29. An external (dis)economy occurs when an activity yields (costs) benefits to others in addition to the costs and benefits accruing to the transacting parties. The (costs) benefits generated are typically nonexcludable and thus are often unpriced; that is, they are external to the pricing system. Because the active party is not being (charged) reimbursed for the external (costs) benefits generated, there is no inducement to take the (costs) benefits into consideration when deciding upon the level of activity to undertake. In private market transactions, individual parties choose the level of activity at which private marginal benefits from an activity just equal the private marginal costs of undertaking it, thus ignoring the costs and benefits that can simultaneously "spill over" to other parties. The result can be a misallocation of resources.

30. Ronald Coase, "The Problem of Social Cost," *Journal of Law and Economics*, October 1960.

31. Even if a single investor were guaranteed the right to undertake all local projects and capture the increasing returns to scale associated with future development projects, developers may not be able to recover total project costs at marginal cost pricing. Therefore some subsidy may be required to insure that developers recover their full costs.

32. In certain cases, the economic costs of these types of relationships and arrangements—including potential efficiency costs with reduction in competitive incentives and cost of writing and enforcing contracts—will be prohibitive.

33. This line of reasoning is subject to questioning. It would suggest that U.S. Steel, as a large property owner in the Mon Valley, would have contributed more in efforts to revitalize the area. Perhaps U.S. Steel was not as "benign" as expected in the Valley because its headquarters were located outside the Valley and the significance (in the company's total investment portfolio) of its property holdings in the Valley was declining.

34. Ross J. Gittell and Peter Doeringer, "The Georgia Power Company: Public-Private Partnership for State and Local Development," Harvard University, Center for Business and Government, November 1991.

35. Market failure with uncertainty requires transaction-specific investments (e.g., high economic rents and low alternative use value). This is usually the case with local development projects.

36. See David Lax and James Sebenius, *The Manager as Negotiator* (New York: The Free Press, 1986), p. 11, for discussion regarding the potential mutual benefits from adaptive decision making and from building trust among parties.

37. Information failure is broadly defined here. It represents the failure of active parties in development to collect and share mutually useful data and

analysis. Some of the failure to disseminate information may be intentional, e.g., held by one party to gain advantage over another; however, the information sharing considered here is the kind from which there is potential for mutual gains to be derived.

38. Joseph Stiglitz, "Markets, Market Failures and Development," *American Economic Review*, Vol. 79 No. 2, May 1989, p.200.

39. The nontransferability of property rights in human capital (that is, the prohibition of slavery) inhibits the development of a commercial market for investment in people and often makes it difficult for individuals to invest in the efficient level of human capital. See Albert Rees, *The Economics of Work and Pay* (New York: Harper and Row, 1973), p. 35.

40. Public subsidy to industry can take various forms including tax abatement, subsidy of worker training, issuance of industrial revenue bonds (IRBs), and provision of special public services, including access roads, rail links, and utility lines. Public subsidy to relocating industry has been criticized for being inefficient and resulting in unproductive transfers of economic activity between cities. See Glickman, Norman and Douglas Woodward. *The New Competitors* (New York: Basic Books, 1989) and Kotlowitz, Alex and Dale Buss, "Localities' Giveaways to Lure Corporations Cause Growing Outcry," *Wall Street Journal*, September 24, 1986.

41. Charles Wolf Jr., *Markets or Governments: Choosing Between Imperfect Alternatives* (Cambridge: The MIT Press, 1988).

Chapter Nine
The Renewal Process

1. The importance of dynamic economic factors in local area revitalization is highlighted in the discussion of product, process, and factor price cycles in Chapter 2.

2. The objectivity of the only study of the machine tool industry in New Bedford could be questioned. It was sponsored by the local union (277) that had the most at stake in saving the Morse machine tool plant in the city.

3. See John Gavanta, *Power and Powerlessness* (Urbana, Ill.: University of Illinois Press, 1980) for discussion of the psychology of urban and rural development and the tendency for residents to resist change when confronted with depressed conditions.

4. The committee of labor and political leaders organized to save the Morse plant in New Bedford was in direct confrontation with the private sector. It did not intend to find a consensus solution to a common problem, as had some of the collective efforts discussed in the other city development analyses.

5. This section is not intended to provide a theory, or comprehensive discussion, of political leadership in local development. Its focus is on how local leadership can serve as a motivating and organizing agent in city revitalization efforts. For more detailed discussion of the attitudes and strategies of local political leaders in development policy making, see Bernard Frieden and Lynne B. Sagalyn, *Downtown, Inc.* (Cambridge: M.I.T. Press, 1989).

6. The Lowell Plan, *The Plan 1980–1990*, 1986.

7. Regional Urban Design Assistance Team (RUDAT), *Remaking the Monongahela Valley* (Pittsburgh: American Institute of Architects, 1988).

8. Jamestown Economic Development Steering Committee (JEDSC), *Report to Chautauqua Region Community Foundation* (Jamestown, New York: Jamestown Region Foundation Inc., January 1988).

9. Mayor Bullard, in 1986, counted thirty-one agencies involved in economic development in New Bedford, of which twenty-one had no connection whatsoever with city government.

10. Kenneth Arrow, "The Economic Implications of Learning By Doing," *Review of Economic Studies*, 29, June 1962, pp. 155–73.

Bibliography

Adams, Lisa. "Wang Layoffs May Hit 2,000 in Bay State." *The Lowell Sun*. June 29, 1991.

Altshuler, Alan. *The City Planning Process: A Political Analysis*. Ithaca: Cornell University Press, 1965.

Anderson, Martin. *The Federal Bulldozer: A Critical Analysis of Urban Renewal*. Cambridge: MIT Press, 1964.

Arrow, Kenneth. "The Economic Implications of Learning by Doing." *Review of Economic Studies*, June 1962.

Axelrod, Robert. *The Evolution of Cooperation*. New York: Basic Books, 1984.

Bennis, Warren, and Bert Nanus. *Leaders*. New York: Harper and Row, 1985.

Berger, Renee A., and Scott Fosler (editors). *Public-Private Partnerships in American Cities: Seven Case Studies*. Lexington, Mass.: Lexington Press, 1982.

Bergman, Edward (editor). *Local Economies in Transition*. Durham, North Carolina: Duke University Press, 1986.

Biggy, Virginia, Mario D. Fantini, and Robert I. Sperber *The Lowell Model for Education Excellence*. Lowell, Mass.: Report to the City of Lowell, January 1984.

Blair, John, and Robert Premus. "Major Factors in Industrial Location: A Review." *Economic Development Quarterly*. Vol. 1 No. 1, 1987.

Bluestone, Barry, and Bennett Harrison. *The Deindustrialization of America*. New York: Basic Books. 1982.

Boyer, Boyer, and David Savageau. *Places Rated Almanac*. Chicago: Rand McNally, 1985.

Brown, Lawrence D., James Fossett, and Kenneth Palmer. *The Changing Politics of Federal Grants*. Washington, D.C.: The Brookings Institution, 1984.

Browning, Rufus, Dale Marshall, and David Tabb. *Protest is Not Enough*. Berkeley: University of California Press, 1984.

Carlton, Dennis. "The Location and Employment Choices of New Firms: An Econometric Model with Discrete and Continuous Endogenous Variables." *The Review of Economics and Statistics*. Vol. 65 No. 3, August 1983.

Chautauqua Region Community Foundation Inc. *Jamestown the Next 100 Years*. Jamestown, New York: Chautauqua Region Foundation Inc., 1986.

Chinitz, Benjamin. "Contrasts in Agglomeration: New York and Pittsburgh." *American Economic Review*. Vol. 51, May 1961.

Clarke, Susan, and Anne Moss. "Economic Growth, Environmental Quality, and Growth Services: Mapping the Potential for Local Positive-Sum Strategies." *Journal of Urban Affairs*. Vol. 12 No. 1, 1990.

Coase, Ronald. "The Problem of Social Cost." *Journal of Law and Economics*. October 1960.

Collinge, John. "Lowell Business Center Moving." *The Lowell Sun*. August 23, 1991.

Collings, L., and D.F. Walker (editors). *Locational Dynamics of Manufacturing Activities*. New York: John Wiley & Sons, 1975.

Conlan, Timothy. *New Federalism: Intergovernmental Reform From Nixon to Reagan*. Washington D.C.: The Brookings Institution, 1988.

Costanzo, Charlene, and Joel Gershenfeld. *A Decade of Change: Ten Year Report of Jamestown Area Labor Management Committee*. Jamestown, New York: Jamestown Area Labor Management Committee, 1983.

Crittenden, Jules. "Census Shows Downtown Grew Most in Lowell." *The Lowell Sun*. August 4, 1991.

Cummings, Scott (editor). *Business Elites and Urban Development*. Albany: State University of New York Press, 1988.

Cyert, Richard, and James March. *Behavioral Theory of the Firm*. Englewood Cliffs, N.J.: Prentice-Hall, 1963.

Dasgupta, P., and P. Stoneman (editors). *Economic Policy and Technological Performance*. Cambridge: Cambridge University Press, 1987.

Denison, Edward F. *The Sources of Economic Growth in the United States*. New York: Committee for Economic Development, 1962.

Dickstein, Harry. "Case Study and Theory in Political Sciences." In *Handbook of Political Science*. Edited by F.T. Greenstein and N.W. Potsby. Vol. 7. Reading, Mass.: Addison-Wesley, 1975.

Dluhy, Milan, and Kan Chen, (editors). *Interdisciplinary Planning: A Perspective for the Future*. New Brunswick, N.J.: Center For Policy Research, 1986.

Doeringer, Peter B., David Terkla, and Gregory Topakian. *Invisible Factors in Local Economic Development*. New York: Oxford University Press, 1987.

Dommel, Paul R. *Decentralizing Urban Policy*. Washington, D.C.: The Brookings Institution, 1982.

Downs, Anthony. *Economic Theories of Democracy*. New York: Harper and Row, 1957.

The Economist. "Jamestown Pulls Itself Together." June 21, 1980.

Elazar, Daniel. *Cities of the Prairie*. Lincoln, Nebraska: University of Nebraska Press, 1970.

———. *Cities of the Prairie Revisited*. Lincoln, Nebraska: University of Nebraska Press, 1986.

Elkin, Stephen L. *City and Regime in the American Republic*. Chicago: University of Chicago Press, 1987.

Fales, Raymond L., and Leon N. Moses. "Thunen, Weber and the Spatial Structure of the 19th Century City." In *Models of Employment and Residential Location*. Edited by Franklin J. James. New Jersey: Center for Urban Policy Research, 1974.

Fenno, Richard. *Congressmen in Committees*. Boston: Little, Brown, 1973.

Fothergill, S., and G. Gudkin. "In Defense of Shift-Share." *Urban Studies*. Vol. 16 No. 3, October 1979.

Frieden, Bernard, and Lynne B. Sagalyn. *Downtown, Inc*. Cambridge: M.I.T. Press, 1989.

Gans, Herbert. "The Failure of Urban Renewal." In Wilson, James Q. (editor). *Urban Renewal: The Record and the Controversy*. Cambridge, Mass.: MIT Press, 1966.

Garber, Judith. "Law and the Possibilities for a Just Urban Political Economy." *Journal of Urban Affairs*. Vol. 12 No. 1, 1990.

Gargiulo, Charles. "A Study of Rental Housing Costs in Lowell." Lowell, Mass.: Unpublished report for *Community Teamwork, Inc.*, March 1986.

Gavanta, John. *Power and Powerlessness*. Urbana, Ill.: University of Illinois Press, 1980.

Gittell, Marilyn. *Limits to Citizen Participation*. Beverly Hills: Sage Publications, 1980.

Gittell, Ross J., and Peter Doeringer, "Public-Private Partnerships for State and Local Development." *Harvard University, Center for Business and Government*. November 1991.

Glickman, Norman, and Douglas Woodward. *The New Competitors*. New York: Basic Books, 1989.

George, Alexander. "Case Studies and Theory Development: The Method of Structured Focused Comparison." In *Diplomacy: New Approaches in History, Theory and Policy*. Edited by Paul Lauren. New York: The Free Press, 1979.

Gold, Allan. "For Troubled City, All-American Lift." *New York Times*. May 23, 1989.

Greenstein, F.T., and N.W. Polsby (editors). *Handbook of Political Science*, Vol. 7. Reading, Mass.: Addison-Wesley, 1975.

Greer, Scott A. *Urban Renewal and American Cities: The Dilemma of Democratic Intervention*. Indianapolis: Bobbs-Merrill, 1966.

Hayes, R. H., and S. C. Wheelwright. "The Dynamics of Process-Product Life Cycles." *Harvard Business Review*. Vol. 57 No. 2, March/April 1979.

Heilbrun, James. *Urban Economics and Public Policy*. New York: St. Martins Press, 1981.

Henig, Jeffrey. "Defining City Limits." *American Political Science Association Meetings*. 1990.

Hirsch, Seev. *Location and International Competitiveness*. Oxford: Clarendon Press, 1967.

Hirschman, Albert O. *The Strategy of Economic Development*. New Haven: Yale University Press, 1958

Hoerr, John, P. *And the Wolf Finally Came*. Pittsburgh: University of Pittsburgh Press, 1988.

Jamestown Department of Development. *Information Guide, Jamestown, New York*. Jamestown, New York: City of Jamestown, 1983.

Jamestown Economic Development Steering Committee. *Report to Chautauqua Region Community Foundation*. Jamestown, New York: Jamestown Region Foundation Inc., January 1988.

Jacobs, Jane. *Cities and the Wealth of Nations*. New York: Random House, 1984.

Kain, John, and John Meyer (editors). *Essays in Regional Economics*. Cambridge: Harvard University Press, 1971.

Kale, Steven. "Theoretical Contributions to the Understanding of U.S. Nonmetropolitan Economic Change." *Economic Development Quarterly*, Vol. 3 No. 1, February 1989.

Kantor, Paul. "The Dependent City." *Urban Affairs Quarterly*, June 1987.

Kantor, Paul, with Stephen David. *The Dependent City*. Glenview Ill.: Scott, Foresman, 1988.

Kantor, Rosabeth Moss. *The Change Masters*. New York: Simon and Schuster, 1983.

Katznelson, Ira. *City Trenches: Urban Politics and the Patterning of Class in the United States*. New York: Pantheon Books, 1981.

Kidder, Tracy. *The Soul of a New Machine*. New York: Little Brown and Company, 1981.

Kotlowitz, Alex, and Dale Buss. "Localities' Giveaways to Lure Corporations Cause Growing Outcry." *Wall Street Journal*, September 24, 1986.

Kranish, Michael. "A New Twist in New Bedford." *The Boston Globe*, May 19, 1987.

Krumme, G., and R. Hayter. "Implications of Corporate Strategies and Product Cyle Adjustments For Regional Employment Changes." In *Locational Dynamics of Manufacturing Activities*. Edited by L. Collings and D.F. Walker. New York: John Wiley & Sons, 1975.

Ladd, Helen F. "Introduction to Symposium on Managing Local Development." *Journal of Policy Analysis and Management*. Vol. 9 No. 4, Fall 1990.

Lauren, Paul (editor). *Diplomacy: New Approaches in History, Theory and Policy*. New York: The Free Press, 1979.

Lax, David, and James Sebenius. *The Manager as Negotiator*. New York: The Free Press, 1986.

Lemann, Nicholas. *The Promised Land*. New York: Alfred A. Knopf, 1991.

Levitt, T. "Exploit the Product Life Cycle." *Harvard Business Review*, Vol. 43, No. 6, November/December 1965.

Levy, John M. *Urban and Metropolitan Economics*. New York: McGraw Hill, 1985.

Lindblom, Charles E. *The Intelligence of Democracy: Decision Making Through Mutual Adjustment*. New York: The Free Press, 1965.

Logan, John, and Harvey Molotch. *Urban Fortunes: The Political Economy of Place*. Berkeley: University of California Press, 1987.

Long, Norton. *The Polity*. Chicago: Rand McNally, 1962,

———. "Have Cities a Future?" *Public Administration Review*, 1973.

Lowell Central City Committee. *Statement of Strategy*. Lowell, Mass.: Central City Committee, November 30, 1972.

Lowell Development and Financial Corporation. *Annual Report*. 1989.

Lowell Historical Preservation Commission. *Information Document*. Lowell: Mass.: Lowell Historical Preservation Commission, 1985.

Lowell Historic Canal District Commission. *Report to the Ninety-Fifth Congress of the United States of America*. Lowell, Mass.: Lowell Historical Canal District, January 3, 1977.

Lowell Plan. *Annual Report*. 1989, 1990.

Lowell Plan. *The Plan 1980–1990*. 1986.

Lundstedt, Seran, and E. William Calgazier. *Managing Innovation: The Social Dimension of Creativity, Invention and Technology*. New York: Pergamon Press, 1979.

Mansbridge, Jane (editor). *Beyond Self-Interest*. Chicago: University of Chicago Press, 1990.

Markusen, Ann. *Profit Cycles, Oligopoly and Regional Development*. Cambridge, M.I.T. Press, 1985.

———. *Regions: The Economics and Politics of Territory*. Totowa, New Jersey: Rowman & Littlefield Publishers, 1987.

Massachusetts Division of Employment Security. *Employment and Wages in Massachusett's Cities and Towns*. Boston: Massachusetts: Division of Employment Security, 1975–1990.

Mausteller, William. "Prince Backs the Common Man." *The Pittsburgh Press*, March 6, 1988.

Meier, Gerald, and Dudley Seers (editors). *Pioneers of Development*. New York: Oxford University Press, 1984.

Meyer, John R. "Regional Economics: A Survey." *American Economic Review*, Vol. 53 No. 1, March 1963.

Mills, Edwin (editor). *Handbook of Regional and Urban Economics*. Vol. 2. Amsterdam: North Holland, 1987.

Mollenkopf, John. *The Contested City*. Princeton: Princeton University Press, 1983.

Mon Valley Commission. *Report to the Allegheny County Board of Commissioners for the Economic Revitalization of the Monongahela, Youghiogheny and Turtle Creek Valleys*. Pittsburgh: Allegheny County Departments of Development and Planning, Feb. 1987.

Morial, Ernest, and Marion Barry. *Rebuilding American Cities*. Cambridge, Massachusetts: Ballinger Publishing Company, 1986.

McManus, Michael. "Western New York Shows the Way to Productivity." *Mid-American Outlook*, Fall 1979.

Nation's Cities. "Jamestown, New York." April 1978.

Norton, R. D. "Industrial Policy and American Renewal." *Journal of Economic Literature*, Vol. 24, March 1986.

Norton, R. D., and J. Rees, "The Product Life Cycle and the Spatial Decentralization of American Manufacturing." *Regional Studies*, Vol. 13, No. 2, August 1979.

Olson, Mancur. *The Logic of Collective Action*. Cambridge: Harvard University Press, 1965.

Ouchi, William. *The M-Form Society*. Reading, Mass.: Addison-Wesley Publishing, 1984.

O'Connell, Michael. "Miller: More Wang Cuts Ahead." *The Lowell Sun*, June 19, 1991.

———. "Growing Software Company May Come to Lowell." *The Lowell Sun*, August 13, 1991.

Perloff, Harvey. *Regional Resources and Economic Growth*. Baltimore: Johns Hopkins Press, 1960.

Peters, Tom, and Nancy Austin. *A Passion for Excellence*. New York: Warner Books, 1985.

Peters, Tom, and Robert Waterman. *In Search of Excellence*. New York: Harper and Row, 1982.

Peterson, George E., and Carol W. Lewis (editors). *Reagan and the Cities.* Washington, D.C.: The Urban Institute Press, 1986.

Peterson, Paul E. *City Limits.* Chicago: University of Chicago Press, 1981.

———— (editor). *The New Urban Reality.* Washington, D.C.: The Brookings Institution, 1985.

————. "Technology, Race and Urban Policy." In *The New Urban Reality.* Edited by Paul Peterson. Washington D.C.: The Brookings Institution, 1985.

Piven, Frances, and Richard Cloward. *Poor People's Movements: Why they Succeed, How they Fail.* New York: Vintage Books, 1979.

Porter, Michael E. *The Competitive Advantage of Massachusetts.* Cambridge: The Monitor Company Inc., 1991.

Reilly, Kathleen. "Hilton Manager Optimistic About Name Change." *The Lowell Sun,* July 12, 1991.

Rees, Albert. *The Economics of Work and Pay.* New York: Harper and Row, 1973.

Regional Urban Design Assistance Team (RUDAT). *Remaking the Monongahela Valley.* Pittsburgh: American Institute of Architects, March 1988.

Reich, Robert. *The Next American Frontier.* New York: Times Books, 1983.

The Rice Center, Economic Development Administration Report. *Private Sector Initiatives in Economic Development.* Houston: Rice University, October 1987.

Rogel, Stuart. "Utility Powers Community Development." *Urban Land,* January 1984.

Rose-Ackerman, Susan. *The Economics of Non-Profit Institutions.* New York: Oxford University Press, 1986.

Rosen, Christine Meisner. *The Limits of Power.* Cambridge: Cambridge University Press, 1986.

Rothman, Jack, and Margrit Hugentobler. "Planning Theory and Planning Practice: Roles and Attitudes of Planners." In *Interdisciplinary Planning: A Perspective for the Future.* Edited by Milan Dluhy and Kan Chen. New Brunswick, N.J.: Center For Policy Research, 1986.

Sawers, Larry. "New Perspectives on the Urban Political Economy." In *Marxism and the Metropolis.* Edited by William Tabb and Larry Sawers. New York: Oxford University Press, 1984.

Schmener, Roger, Huber and Cook. "Geographic Differences and the Location of New Manufacturing Facilities." *Journal of Urban Economics,* 21, 1989.

Serrin, William. "In New Bedford, Union Efforts Keep a Plant Alive." *New York Times,* June 15, 1985.

Stahl, Konrad. "Theories of Urban Business Location." In *Handbook of Regional and Urban Economics.* Edited by Edwin Mills. Vol. 2. Amsterdam: North Holland, 1987.

Stiglitz, Joseph. "Learning to Learn, Localized Learning and Technological Progress." In *Economic Policy and Technological Performance.* Edited by P. Dasgupta and P. Stoneman. Cambridge: Cambridge University Press, 1987.

————. "Markets, Market Failures and Development." *American Economic Review,* Vol. 79 No. 2, May 1989.

Stone, Clarence. *Regime Politics*. Kansas: University Press of Kansas, 1989.

Stone, Clarence, and Heywood Sanders (editors). *The Politics of Urban Development*. Lawrence, Kansas: University Press of Kansas, 1987.

Swanstrom, Todd. *The Crisis of Growth Politics*. Philadelphia: Temple University Press, 1985.

Thomas, M.D. "Regional Economic Development and the Role of Innovation and Technological Change." In *The Regional Economic Impacts of Technological Change*. Edited by A. T. Thwaites and R. P. Oakey. New York: St. Martin's Press, 1985.

Thompson, Wilbur R. *A Preface to Urban Economics*. Baltimore: Johns Hopkins University Press, 1965.

Thurow, Lester. *Zero-Sum Society*. New York: Basic Books, 1980.

Thwaites, A.T., and R.P. Oakey (editors). *The Regional Economic Impacts of Technological Change*. New York: St. Martin's Press, 1985.

U.S. Bureau of Labor Statistics. *Employment and Unemployment in State and Local Areas*. Washington D.C.: U.S. Government Printing Office, 1982.

U.S. Census Bureau. *Census of Manufacturing*. Washington D.C.: U.S. Government Printing Office, 1914, 1925, 1938, 1948, 1954, 1958, 1964, 1968, 1972, 1977, 1982.

U.S. Census Bureau. *Census of Population and Housing*. Washington D.C.: U.S. Government Printing Office, 1860, 1870, 1880, 1890, 1900, 1910, 1920, 1930, 1940, 1950, 1960, 1970, 1980, (preliminary) 1990.

U.S. Census Bureau. *Census of Retail Trade*. Washington D.C.: U.S. Government Printing Office, 1948, 1954, 1958, 1964, 1968, 1972, 1977, 1982.

U.S. Census Bureau. *Census of Services*. Washington D.C.: U.S. Government Printing Office, 1948, 1954, 1958, 1964, 1968, 1972, 1977, 1982.

U.S. Census Bureau. *Census of Wholesale Trade*. Washington D.C.: U.S. Government Printing Office, 1948, 1954, 1958, 1964, 1968, 1972, 1977, 1982.

U.S. Census Bureau. *County and City Data Book*. Washington, D.C.: U.S. Government Printing Office, 1988.

U.S. Census Bureau. *Statistical Abstract of the United States*. Washington D.C.: U.S. Government Printing Office, 1984.

U.S. Department of Commerce. "Improving the Quality of Worklife." In U.S. Department of Commerce. *Jobs Through Economic Development*. Washington D.C.: U.S. Printing Office, January 1979.

Vernon, Raymond. "International Investment and International Trade in the Product Life Cycle." *Quarterly Journal of Economics*, Vol. 80, 1966.

Vidal, Avis. *Community Economic Development Assessment*, Community Development Research Center. New York, N.Y.: New School for Social Research, 1991.

Wheaton, William, "Metropolitan Growth, Unemployment and Interregional Facto Mobility." In *Interregional Movements and Regional Growth*. Edited by W.C. Wheaton. Washington, D.C.: The Urban Institute, 1979.

———. (editor). *Interregional Movements and Regional Growth*. Washington, D.C.: The Urban Institute, 1979.

Weinstein, Bernard, Harold Gross and John Rees. *Regional Growth and Decline in the United States*. New York: Prager, 1985.

Williamson, Oliver. *Markets and Hierarchies: Analysis and Antitrust Implications*. New York: Free Press, 1975.

———. "Transaction-Cost Economics: The Governance of Contractual Arrangements." *The Journal of Law and Economics*, Spring 1978.

Wilson, James Q. (editor). *Urban Renewal: The Record and the Controversy.* Cambridge, Mass.: MIT Press, 1966.

Wilson, James Q., and Peter B. Clark. "Incentive Systems: A Theory of Organization." *Administrative Science Quarterly*, 6, 1961.

Wilson, Linda S. "County to Buy Idled Mills." *Pittsburgh Post-Gazette*, March 26, 1987.

Wolf, Charles, Jr. *Markets or Governments: Choosing Between Imperfect Alternatives*. Cambridge: MIT Press, 1988.

Index